GLOBAL HISTORY

Cultural Encounters from Antiquity to the Present

Editorial Board and Contributors

325.00
set

Gift
Reference

GLOBAL HISTORY

Cultural Encounters from Antiquity to the Present

Volume One

EDITED BY

David W. Del Testa

Florence Lemoine and John Strickland

SHARPE REFERENCE
an imprint of M.E. Sharpe, Inc.

OCT 2 9 2004

SHARPE REFERENCE

Sharpe Reference is an imprint of M.E. Sharpe, Inc.

M.E. Sharpe, Inc.
80 Business Park Drive
Armonk, New York 10504

© 2004 by The Moschovitis Group, Inc.

Produced by The Moschovitis Group, Inc.
339 Fifth Avenue
New York, New York 10018
www.mosgroup.com

Publisher	Valerie Tomaselli
Executive Editor	Hilary W. Poole
Senior Editor	Stephanie Schreiber
Associate Editor	Sonja Matanovic
Editorial Coordinator	Nicole Cohen Solomon
Editorial Assistant	Jessica Rosin
Design and Layout	Annemarie Redmond
Illustrator and Cartographer	Richard Garratt
Production Coordinator	K. Nura Abdul-Karim
Photo Research	Gillian Speeth
Fact Checking	Blake Stone-Banks, Peter Tomaselli
Copyediting	Carole Campbell, Kathy Wisch
Proofreading	Robin Surratt
Index	Cynthia Crippen

Library of Congress Cataloging-in-Publication Data

Global history : cultural encounters from antiquity to the present.
    p. cm.
Includes bibliographical references and index.
ISBN 0-7656-8043-2 (set: alk. paper)
    1. World history. 2. Civilization, Ancient. 3. Civilization, Modern. 4. Civilization–History.
    5. Globalization. 6. East and West.
D20.G57 2003
909—dc21

2003041560

Printed and bound in Brazil

⊗ The paper used in this publication meets the minimum requirements of the
American National Standard for Information Sciences—Permanence of
Paper for Printed Library Materials,
ANSIZ 39.48-1984.

RRD (c) 10 9 8 7 6 5 4 3 2 1

Table of Contents

Volume Four: The Contemporary World

(1900s to the Present)

List of Primary Documents

Volume Four: The Contemporary World
(1900s TO THE PRESENT)

Preface

Giraffes stimulated this project. As graduate students in the Department of History at the University of California at Davis in the mid-1990s, editor Florence Lemoine and I developed an interest in world history. World history as a discipline refers not just to a study of the histories of the world's peoples, but also to a way of looking at how human civilizations or economies interacted with one another at a macro (large-scale) level. As we learned more about the theory of world history in our graduate classes and began our dissertation research, we noticed how often giraffes served as vehicles of cross-cultural encounters. For example, in 804, the Caliph Harun al-Rashid (r. 786–809) of the Islamic Abbasid Dynasty (750–1258) sent a giraffe from Constantinople (present-day Istanbul in Turkey) to the Roman emperor Charlemagne (r. 800–814) in Aix-la-Chapelle (present-day Aachen in Germany); in 1415, the Chinese navigator Zheng He (1371–1435) received a giraffe from his African hosts in Malindi (in present-day Kenya) as a gift for the Chinese emperor; and in 1826, Muhammad 'Ali (1769–1849) of Egypt sent one to King Charles X (1757–1836) of France. The introduction of these exotic animals must have provoked all kinds of questions and imagining among other cultures. It is through stories like these—African giraffes walking through medieval Germany, early modern China, or postrevolutionary France—that we open the world to students of history and provide them with an avenue to understand the impact of cross-cultural encounters.

Stimulated by recent world events and global trends, "global history" has lately received a great deal more attention as a topic of instruction and as a field of research. Major universities have developed graduate programs in world history. Likewise, the realization that many young Americans lack adequate knowledge of the surrounding world has caused some educators to encourage the United States to emphasize the study of world history in its educational system; a parallel, perhaps, to the investment made by the United States in science education in the late 1950s after the Soviet Union launched the first Earth-orbiting satellite. Important government agencies and private foundations have made significant amounts of money available to promote the study of world history in high schools and colleges. As a result of these changes, scholars and teachers at every level have begun a vigorous reexamination of world history itself and the teaching of world history in the United States.

Some scholars made efforts to demonstrate the significance of cross-cultural encounters. There are two particularly noteworthy sources. First, James Burke's British Broadcasting Corporation series *Connections* (1979) illustrates in a visually stimulating and interesting fashion the historical genealogy of certain technologies and cultural practices. The series was an early effort to show the public the interconnectivity of the world and the speed at which ideas have spread around the globe. Second, the first edition of Jeremy Bentley and Herbert Ziegler's world history textbook, *Traditions and Encounters* (2000), provides a valuable tool for college-level instructors to teach world history as a series of cross-cultural encounters. It differs from many earlier world history texts, which had often emphasized the parallel development of civilizations without acknowledging or accounting for the influence of other cultures on their growth.

Despite the growing interest in world history and the early contributions of a handful of scholars, the authors of this series quickly noticed something missing in the world history materials available to instructors and students. Although some textbooks present brief examples of cross-cultural exchanges, no reference provides in-depth discussions of cross-cultural exchanges that determine the course of history. A text that focuses on such exchanges would demonstrate to readers the importance of cross-cultural exchange as a catalyst for historical change and illustrate the relationship of cross-cultural exchanges to the development of civilizations. The four volumes of *Global History: Cultural Encounters from Antiquity to the Present* appear in response to this gap in contemporary scholarship and reflect the need to reexamine history with a particular emphasis on global trends and dynamics. The series will aid instructors and students: Students can use the text to research and improve their understanding of world history and cross-cultural encounters, while instructors may use the series as a basis for their own presentations.

Rationale for the Selection of Topics

A number of factors influenced the difficult process of selecting the topics included in *Global History*. The main criterion for choosing a subject was its primary focus—which we determined had to be on cross-cultural encounters that produced meaningful, appreciable historical change on a global scale. Beyond the need for cross-cultural exchange, the authors used essentially three criteria to evaluate whether or not to include a particular encounter.

- We focused first on events of obvious global and historical importance that are essential to any analysis of world history. Some examples include the consequences of Christopher Columbus's (1451–1506) voyages from Spain to the Americas after 1492 and the role of the Silk Roads, which connected East Asia with the Mediterranean after the second century B.C.E.

- We then considered cross-cultural interactions known to scholars but not to the general public that would provoke readers to think about exchange in new ways. We searched among these encounters for those that produced profound and counterintuitive changes, such as war encouraging the spread of crafts from one culture to another and the spread of an easy-to-use alphabet around the Mediterranean as a result of extensive trade. Likewise, few students of history may realize that the Battle of Talas (751; in present-day Kyrgyzstan) resulted in the spread of papermaking from China to the Middle East and Europe.

- Finally, we found stories that have global and historical importance but have not received the attention they deserve, including the Vietnamese Nam Tien (March South) or the influence of French-Canadian fur traders in the history of colonial North America. Our discussions include these less familiar encounters and even quirky events that we feel offer readers a new and interesting way to approach world history or expose them to aspects of cross-cultural encounters not addressed elsewhere.

Ideas for the topics of articles originated from three main areas:

- We focused on events of intercultural contact and exchange that appear frequently in classic world history scholarship or in contemporary world history textbooks. In these cases, we tried to augment the story traditionally told with the latest scholarship.

- We located ideas from news features or recent scholarship outside of world history (such as the idea of a unified Eurasian trading zone at the dawn of human history or the impact of the Internet on global culture).

- We investigated our own work. Each author has expertise in a particular aspect of history, and all have noticed particular historical developments with global importance that originated from cross-cultural exchanges.

Although the volumes of *Global History* may not cover every instance of cultural exchange throughout history, the articles in the series cover all regions of the world and suggest how specific moments of cross-cultural exchange may have affected surrounding cultures and civilizations and the world as a whole. Although all areas of the world receive attention, some areas, such as Australia, the islands of the Pacific, and Siberia, remain on the periphery of discussions because the people who inhabited them had much less opportunity throughout history to engage in cross-cultural exchanges with other peoples.

Scope of the Series

In brief, *Global History* contains 80 articles that represent many of the important instances of cross-cultural contact in human history. The four volumes cover specific time periods that correspond to major themes and historical breaks recognized by scholars. The volumes are, respectively, *Antiquity (5000 B.C.E. to 400s C.E.); The Spread of Religions and Empires (400s to 1400s); The Age of Discovery and Colonial Expansion (1400s to 1900s);* and *The Contemporary World (1900s to the Present).*

Each article is organized similarly and contains the same basic elements. The first page includes a date span that indicates the main period of cultural exchange discussed. The text of each article is divided into four major sections: the first section discusses a key moment of exchange and introduces the major themes addressed in the article; the second section provides historical background on the civilizations or societies involved in the exchange or the events leading up to the exchange; the third section describes the actual exchange, while the final section analyzes the ramifications and significance of the exchange or other developments related to the exchange.

Important reference features accompany each article, including a timeline that highlights key events; a bulleted list of the significant cross-cultural exchanges addressed in each article; a section of cross-references (titled "See Also") that point to related articles; and a bibliography of works used by the authors. Important visual elements also complement each article. A photograph opens the article, highlighting a theme of cross-cultural exchange. A dynamic map illustrates a particular process or moment of cross-cultural exchange: the migration of a group or groups; the spread of a cultural product, such as writing, religion, or film; the development of trade networks; the unification of lands under an empire; or the transmission of political ideologies or artistic trends across regions. Finally, a primary document (written or visual, depending on the availability of sources from the period) offers greater insight into various interpretations and outcomes of cross-cultural exchange during the historical period covered. Whenever possible, the authors have selected primary documents from the era discussed in the article, although this was not always possible, in which case a primary source from a later time is used.

Each volume also includes additional reference materials following the articles. A timeline of important events places developments discussed in the articles in a broader historical and global framework. A glossary defines terms and concepts that may be new or difficult for readers. A bibliography identifies key works that will provide readers with additional information. In addition to these three reference features, volume four also includes a cumulative glossary and an extensive bibliography organized by geographical region and theme. A comprehensive name, place, and concept index, covering articles from the entire series, concludes each volume. With the index, readers can investigate the significance of particular people (e.g., the Muslim prophet Muhammad), terms (e.g., monotheism), events (e.g., migration), material goods (e.g., silk), or places (e.g., Mesoamerica) across various eras and areas of the world.

Although the articles have been written in an accessible manner for a broad audience, they do introduce some vocabulary and concepts with which the average reader may not be familiar. For example, a term often used for the spread of cultural values to many peoples or a broad area is *globalization*. This term originated in 1944 to describe the rise of hostilities around the globe during World War II. During the early 1960s, oil companies adapted the term to describe the process through which their operations became multinational. During this period, multinational oil companies became heavily invested in the political stability of the countries in which they operated and, with the complicity of powerful nations, often supported brutal governments in an effort to retain their position and maintain order in oil-producing nations. Therefore, while the term *globalization* refers to the spread of trends to other cultures, it also describes a process that has limited people's choices, as some would say has happened with the spread of English as the world's *lingua franca* (common language).

Other terms and concepts are less complicated. *Cross-cultural exchange* or *cross-cultural interaction* indicate those instances when people of different cultural backgrounds interact and attempt to communicate with one another, either intentionally or accidentally. Such exchanges or interactions sometimes produce a new culture, which can be called hybrid, or syncretic, to reflect its diverse origins and mixture of influences. The volumes' glossaries define other terms and concepts, and the articles often include definitions of specialized words or ideas within the text (either in the context of the article or in parenthesis).

The authors have used some particular terms concerning geography. Throughout these volumes, the authors use the terms *Old World* and *New World*. These expressions have their origin in the voyages of Christopher Columbus to the Americas between 1492 and 1504. *Old World* refers to the continents and peoples of Africa, Asia, and Europe in their entirety (the Eastern Hemisphere). *New World* refers to the Americas (the Western Hemisphere). Scholars still debate where they should include Australia and the Pacific Islands because they were not regularly connected with the Old World or the New World until the eighteenth century. Although these terms are based on a European perspective of the world, the authors believe that they are still valuable in describing the geography of world history. The authors also use the term *Eurasia*, which typically refers to a region of grassland interspersed with mountains that extends some 5,000 miles from present-day Hungary in the west through Ukraine and central Asia to Manchuria in the east. Until the end of the seventeenth century (and in the context of this series), Eurasia served as a vast region of cultural exchange, first among Indo-European (Caucasian) steppe dwellers, and then involving travelers from various origins for whom the area bridged the markets and cultures of Europe, the Middle East, and East Asia.

These volumes use the dating system of B.C.E. (before the common era) and C.E. (of the common era) rather than the traditional system of B.C. (before Christ) and A.D. (anno Domini, Latin for "in the year of our Lord"). There is debate among scholars as to which dating system is preferable, as some critics claim that the B.C.E.–C.E. system tries to conceal the biased nature of this division (which, similar to the B.C.–A.D. system bases the beginning of the common era on the birth of Jesus, an event that is not significant in all the world's civilizations). However, the editors of the series have decided to adopt the B.C.E.–C.E. dating system because it has more universal appeal and has been accepted as the standard style in many academic disciplines.

Acknowledgments

In achieving the goal of the clear communication of world history, I must thank fellow editors Florence Lemoine and John Strickland for their intellectual curiosity, professionalism, and perseverance. In addition, I must thank the writers who contributed individual articles to *Global History*, including John Patrick Farrell, Amy Patterson, Erika Quinn, and Michaela Crawford Reaves.

Next, I must thank our editors at The Moschovitis Group and our publishers at M. E. Sharpe. For coordinating the project, the greatest thanks should go to Stephanie Schreiber, senior editor at Moschovitis, who, with exquisite patience, kindness, and attention to detail, helped the writers tame the vast, awkward drafts they had prepared. Without her tireless dedication, this project would have gone nowhere. Thanks as well to Nicole Cohen Solomon, Sew Jordan, and Sonja Matanovic of The Moschovitis Group for their help on the coordination of this project.

The authors would like to thank Leonard Blusse, Beverly Bossler, Huaiyu Chen, Eric Crystal, Sally Church, Ross E. Dunn, Gunder Frank, Gerald Jackson, Adela C. Y. Lee, Jonathan Lipton, Krystyna von Henneberg, Ann B. Waltner, Jonathan Walz, Charles Wheeler, Luo Xin, and Hafiz B. Zakariya for their advice on various articles and their encouragement. I would like to thank my colleagues at California Lutheran University who supported me in this project, including Michael Brint, R. Guy Erwin, and Paul Hanson. My special thanks to my stepfather Charles "M. G. Charlie" Paradise, who helped me start to see the world.

Finally, I would like to thank my wife, Melissa Pashigian, for her patient understanding as I spent endless hours hunting down references and writing articles. Her anthropological vision of the globalizing world helped me broaden the perspective of many of these articles, and her moral support helped keep me calm and focused as deadlines loomed.

The authors encourage readers to contact them about the content of the articles or the subjects covered so that subsequent editions might include additional examples of cross-cultural exchange or correct any errors or misinterpretations. In any case, all errors in fact or interpretation are entirely the fault of the authors.

—*David W. Del Testa*
Bryn Mawr, Pennsylvania
August 2003

Introduction

The Emergence of Global History as an Area of Study

The concept of global history—the attempt to trace the significance of human interactions throughout history—emerges from a discrete branch of scholarly inquiry and the historical profession known as world history. World history, which focuses on cross-cultural interactions rather than national events, developed in the twentieth century. Not until the 1930s did institutes of higher learning prepare scholars to teach and research these topics. However, in a sense, world history has always existed as a discipline. The early foundation myths and epics of civilizations, such as the Mesopotamians' *Epic of Gilgamesh* (drawn from prehistoric sources) and the Mayans' *Popuh Vol* are, in a sense, world histories, but the scope of these "histories" was limited as these societies did not seem to function within a very wide world. Their worlds had vague frontiers, and they often knew little about the experiences or existence of other peoples and cultures. In addition, these societies did not record events in the way that historians do today. Anthropologists, archeologists, and historians must study the limited stories and artifacts that these societies left behind to interpret the prevailing social and cultural conditions. The Mesopotamians, for instance, left innumerable records of commercial transactions, but little in the way of histories. The Assyrian king Ashurbanipal (668–627 B.C.E.) left an extensive record of his accomplishments, but its boastful and exaggerated style places the historical information in doubt. Societies that recorded and interpreted verifiable facts and kept accurate chronologies of events (such as the Greek, Roman, and Han Chinese civilizations) did not appear until after the sixth century B.C.E.

In his *Histories*, the Greek historian Herodotus (c. 480–425 B.C.E.) presents an account of the history of the world—at that time, the "world" included the Mediterranean and Black Sea basins, as well as the Sudan, Red Sea, and India—that focuses on the cultural relationships that the Greeks had with other civilizations. The surviving fragments of the *Indica* of the Greek historian Megasthenes (c. 350–290 B.C.E.) record the Greeks' contact with the surrounding peoples. The Romans approached history in the humanistic tradition of the Greeks, but used their history to moralize rather than merely distinguish themselves from other peoples. The *Gallic Wars* of Julius Caesar (100–44 B.C.E.) and *Germania* by Tacitus (c. 56–c. 120 C.E.) present fine discussions of the Roman encounter with, respectively, the Gauls (Celtic people living in present-day France at the time of the Romans) and the Germanic tribes. The Roman-era text *Periplus Maris Erythraei* (c. 100 C.E.) is one of the rare examples of a written discussion of Indian Ocean trade networks, and the text *Against Apion* by the Jewish general and historian Flavius Josephus (c. 37–c. 100 C.E.) provides insight into the world of Roman-era Jews. Only a few texts have survived that offer insight into China's relationship with the non-Chinese world, and most of these originated among Buddhist monks who traveled outside China around the fourth and fifth centuries C.E. The *Record of Buddhist Kingdoms* by the Chinese monk Faxian (c. 337–422 C.E.), for instance, offers an account of his travels between 399 and 414 C.E to India and Sri Lanka. In Europe, the humanistic tradition of Herodotus did not survive the fall of the Roman Empire in 476 C.E., but became fused with an apocalyptic view of the world espoused by some religious philosophers, such as Saint Augustine (354–430). Augustine saw cross-cultural interactions as indicative of God's plan for humans and as a sign for Christians to strengthen their faith. Few other direct discussions of cross-cultural encounters exist. Scholars must rely instead on interpretations of stories, legends, images, and commercial records to examine interactions between ancient societies and the cultural influence of these encounters.

As an academic subject, world history originated with the European Enlightenment of the seventeenth and eighteenth centuries. Building on the idea that humans possess free will, an idea that gained wide currency in the fifteenth century with historians Niccolò Machiavelli (1469–1527) and Francesco Guicciardini (1483–1540), Enlightenment thinkers Giambattista Vico (1668–1744), Voltaire (1694–1778), and Edward Gibbon (1737–1794) began to examine human history through stages or cycles. The German political philosopher Karl Marx (1818–83) linked these Enlightenment theories to human history, particularly the transnational importance of economics. In the context of European colonialism, when Europeans self-consciously suppressed the history and culture of non-Europeans and exploited them economically, Marxist history, which emphasized the common economic conditions of humans, remained one of the few efforts until World War I (1914–18) to include all humans in a single historical framework. Because of this inclusiveness and the observable importance of economics to contemporary life, a Marxist interpretation of history continues to be a popular lens through which to view the past.

The devastation of World War I caused many European and American scholars and philosophers to reflect on how the Europeans, considered a civilized and advanced people, could have waged such a destructive war. These scholars posed similar questions about civilizations in general, considering the factors contributing to the collapse and disappearance of entire civilizations throughout history. The *Decline of the West* (1918–22), by the German historian Oswald Spengler (1880–1936), is one example of this concern with the rise and fall of civilizations. *Decline of the West* does not elevate European civilization above others—a first in Western historical thought. Instead, it suggests that all civilizations possess a life cycle and that European civilization represents, in his view, just one cycle coming to an end. Although *Decline of the West* was widely read, Spengler's views on the equality of civilizations were not popular with his peers. Rather, in schools around the world, national histories continued to dominate history instruction as, in the aftermath of World War I, many nations reasserted a strong national identity and taught their own history in the best possible light. In addition, until after World War II (1939–45), most of Africa (except for Egypt and Liberia) and Asia (except for China, Japan, and Thailand) were held as colonial territories. European colonial school systems taught a version of history that favored European perspectives and denigrated the histories and cultures of the colonized.

Three trends came together to promote the modern study of world history. First, in France during the 1930s, the Annales School of historical thinking, with its emphasis on the study of everyday life and sociological categories (e.g., the peasant and middle classes), allowed for comparisons across cultures that previous forms of history had discouraged. Second, in *The Mediterranean and the Mediterranean World in the Age of Philip II* (1949), French historian Fernand Braudel (1902–85) promotes a cross-cultural approach to examining history by studying the interactions between civilizations surrounding the Mediterranean over long periods (what he called the *longue durée*). Third, the growing importance of Marxism and its political expression through communism,

which emerged as a popular ideology after the Russian Revolution of 1917, created an interest in Marxist history in the world's universities. By the end of World War II, world history as a discrete academic pursuit had sufficient theoretical structure to sustain itself.

A major change in the world political scene created an additional demand for understanding the world as a whole rather than in distinct national units: After 1945, the nations of Asia and Africa gradually gained their independence from their colonial occupiers, at which time historians discovered that little scholarship had been produced that addressed these liberated peoples. At the same time, as part of a much larger effort to establish political influence over large areas of the world during the Cold War, the United States and the Soviet Union invested heavily in trying to understand the behavior of newly independent countries, such as the endurance of a peasantry in Latin America and Asia. Indigenous scholars, as well as scholars based in Europe and the United States who were sympathetic to the decolonized nations, began to reconstruct the history of local peoples and explore how these societies had influenced one another before European colonization. In Europe and the United States, immigrant and underrepresented peoples began making demands that their stories be included in the national discussion of history. For example, the importance of Africans and African Americans to the construction of an "Atlantic" civilization beginning in the seventeenth century became an important topic of scholarly inquiry.

The Periodization of Global History

The authors and editors have divided *Global History: Cultural Encounters from Antiquity to the Present* into four volumes based on historic breaks recognized by scholars. However, no consensus exists on the precise number of divisions in human history, on which events should mark each division, or on whether divisions existed among all world civilizations at approximately the same time. For instance, in *World History: Ideologies, Structures, and Identities* (1998), American historian William A. Green (b. 1935) notes in "Periodizing World History" that historians have most commonly divided human history into three periods: ancient, which corresponds to human history up to the fall of the Roman Empire, in 476 C.E.; medieval, which spans the time between the Roman Empire's fall and Christopher Columbus's voyages, beginning in 1492; and modern, which covers historical developments after Columbus's voyages. This tripartite division, however, does not necessarily conform to historical change across all cultures and is tied specifically to European history rather than larger, global trends.

Some scholars have searched for pan-global periodizations that are less Eurocentric (revolving around trends of a European origin). In *The Modern World System* (1974), American sociologist Immanuel Wallerstein (b. 1930) proposes an alternative to the tripartite historical division. In his work, Wallerstein introduces the world-systems theory of history, which defines the accumulation of capital rather than the ownership of the means of production as the driving force of historical change and the determinant of historical periods. This kind of capitalist system emerged starting in the fifteenth century and created unequal relations of power by which the West has dominated the global economy. Although of unequal wealth and varying access to resources, all regions of the world are nevertheless intertwined in reciprocal economic, political, and cultural relations that change constantly. Wallerstein identifies the development of a world-system of trade in the Atlantic beginning in the 1460s as an essential divide between earlier and later history.

The Axial Age argument proposed by the German philosopher Karl Jaspers (1883–1969) is another influential approach to periodization, although historians have not developed it much since it was proposed. Jaspers argues that the major philosophical and religious transformations necessary for modern thinking in every culture (except the pre-Columbian Americas, which he does not fully address) emerged during the Axial Age, between 800 and 200 B.C.E. These transformations include the development of monotheism among the early Jews in the Middle East, the formulation of rationalism in Greece, the flourishing of Confucianism and Daoism in East Asia, and the rise of Buddhism, Hinduism, and Jainism in South Asia. The advantage of periodizing history around the Axial Age is that this theory identifies stimuli for similar human developments across many cultures, although it tends to treat civilizations as monolithic.

Other historians have attempted to identify similarities in systems throughout the world, not so much to build on Wallerstein's theories or to discover the origin and spread of capitalism, but to show how cultures have influenced one another. For example, in *Before European Hegemony: The World System, AD 1250–1350* (1989), American scholar Janet Abu-Lughod (b. 1928) identifies the emergence of a world-system in the Muslim world (encompassing the lower Mediterranean

and North Africa, the Middle East, and the perimeter of the Indian Ocean) by the thirteenth century. In a more radical and controversial theory, British scholar Martin Bernal (b. 1937) suggests in *Black Athena: The Afro-Asiatic Roots of Classical Civilization* (1987–1991) that a world system of exchange and influence between Europe and Africa emerged as early as 2700 B.C.E. and that the Greeks found a great deal of inspiration for their culture—and thus Western civilization—in ancient Egypt. The world-systems theory has become the dominant approach to world history in contemporary scholarship.

The authors of *Global History* have used a combination of the tripartite division, the world-systems theory, and the Axial Age argument to determine the division of the volumes. They argue that the structures of the ancient world collapsed around 400 C.E. and that the world began another era of fundamental change beginning with the great maritime voyages of the fifteenth century. The authors also propose that around 1900, at which point Europe had imposed its economic and political ideologies upon most of the world, a new global age began where all of humanity headed toward interdependence and transnationalism. In addition to these specific divisions of world history, the authors acknowledge other factors that have influenced the development of human history. For instance, at various times, large areas of frequent exchanges (usually around the rims of the oceans but sometimes along terrestrial routes such as the Silk Roads between East Asia and the Mediterranean) have developed and withered in importance. At the same time, the authors accept that at certain moments, social, intellectual, and technological developments have occurred simultaneously around the world, often for reasons scholars have only begun to understand. This hybrid system accounts for the interaction of civilizations while also acknowledging that even larger changes may have been driven by shifts in climate or population.

Volume one, *Antiquity (5000 B.C.E.–400s C.E.)*, addresses the period between the formation of the first human civilizations in Mesopotamia (present-day Iraq) after about 5000 B.C.E. and the collapse of the world's first great multiethnic empires, including those of ancient Rome, China, and Persia (present-day Iran) by about 400 C.E. In approximately 5000 B.C.E., most humans—who for the previous 100,000 years had relied on hunting and gathering for subsistence and lived in small, tribal units—began engaging in agriculture (planting crops and domesticating animals for food and textile production) and forming states. Concurrently, many humans began to develop writing systems, practice organized religion, and participate in bureaucratic governments. As a consequence, people began to develop more organized commerce, visualize themselves as belonging to a community that was not limited to family, organize their labor to produce large surpluses of food for consumption and trade, practice organized violence, and record events based on relatively accurate calendars. These developments contributed to the formation of civilizations, discrete cultural and social practices that unified groups of people and distinguished them from other groups.

Following the emergence of the first true civilization in Mesopotamia, other civilizations developed in Egypt (after 4000 B.C.E.), the Indus Valley (in present-day Pakistan, after 2500 B.C.E.), the Yellow River valley (in northern China, after 2500 B.C.E.), Mesoamerica (present-day southern Mexico and Guatemala, after 2000 B.C.E.), and the Andes (in present-day Peru, also after 2000 B.C.E.). Many of these civilizations subsequently developed political entities in the form of empires, which imposed their beliefs and practices on a large number of people across regions. For instance, between 300 and 30 B.C.E., the Romans, Parthians, Mayans, and northern Chinese each developed administrative structures that unified the peoples affected by their respective civilizations. Within or across their borders, these empires offered new opportunities for cross-cultural exchange. Under the unity of the Romans, Jews began to spread westward from Palestine and influence Roman civilization. The Han Dynasty (206 B.C.E.–220 C.E.) unified China and then pushed south in its quest for trade and diplomatic contacts, imposing its culture on its non-Chinese neighbors in present-day Vietnam and other regions in Southeast Asia. The collapse of these great empires, possibly as a result of the influx of nomadic peoples and the growth of personal religions that undermined state-sponsored religions, brought the period of antiquity to an end.

Volume two, *The Spread of Religions and Empires (400s–1400s)*, addresses the expansion of religions and empires from the fifth century to the end of the fifteenth century. In most places in the inhabited Old World (Africa, Asia, and Europe) during this period, new personalized and often monotheistic (single deity) religions transformed the cultures of the ancient empires; in addition, these religions contributed to new civilizations and cultural exchanges. In contrast to the religions of antiquity, the monotheistic Christian and Muslim faiths and the deeply personal Buddhist religion offered their adherents a sense of hope and personal control over their spiritual destinies. By creating transnational identities and encouraging intellectual activity, these religions sparked and supported cross-cultural exchanges that differed profoundly from those of antiquity. Rather than being based primarily on the spread of cultural forms (e.g., writing or language, a kind of artistic expression, or a type of leadership), the early part of this period is marked by the dominance of religion as a motivation for cross-cultural exchange.

Religions served as the basis of new, hybrid civilizations, which incorporated some of the forms and knowledge of the ancient empires but infused them with a great deal of spirituality. These religions also served as the basis for new, religiously oriented empires that struggled with other empires that espoused rival religions. Sometimes, a particular civilization was influenced by multiple sources of authority (that is, cooperating as well as sometimes competing with various religious, military, civil, and local powers); the Holy Roman Empire (800–1806) in northern Europe and the Byzantine Empire (395–1453) in eastern Europe are examples. In other instances, a religion unified a particular people to oppose the status quo and take over an empire, such as the Seljuk Turks' gaining control in 1055 from the Islamic Abbasid Dynasty (750–1258) in the Middle East. Later in the period, new empires formed that thrived on relative religious tolerance but demanded absolute political obedience, including the Mongol's Yuan Dynasty (1279–1368) in China, the Ottoman Empire (1453–1922) in the Middle East, and the Inca Empire (1438–1532) in the Andes.

At first glance, volume three, *The Age of Discovery and Colonial Expansion (1400s–1900s)*, seems to discuss only the rise and triumph of European powers over the rest of the world. Indeed, articles that address the interaction of Europeans with people of other cultures dominate the pages of this volume. However, volume three also discusses how other empires, including the Kingdom of Kongo (c. 1350s–1665; in present-day Angola and the Democratic Republic of Congo), the Ming Dynasty (1368–1644 C.E.) of China, and the Aztec Empire (c. 1325–1521) of Mesoamerica, tried to assert their power over extensive regions but failed, either because the empire succumbed to external pressures or developed a philosophy that rejected expansion.

During this phase of expansionism and cross-cultural interaction, European peoples and many other peoples began to develop a new sensibility about themselves and the world. Beginning with administrative, commercial, and intellectual elites and gradually extending to the general population, many of the world's peoples began to favor science and rationality over religion and tradition and emphasize what was best for the individual rather than for the community. Although this process of "modernization" had begun in many places prior to the dominance of the Europeans, European conquest or influence often accelerated the tendency to become "modern." For example, Japan, which had isolated itself from the rest of the world in the early seventeenth century, was forced to abandon its *sakoku* (closed-country) policy when the United States forced the Japanese government to permit trade in 1853. The Japanese, threatened by the power of the West, completely reformulated their society to incorporate Western learning and methods as a form of defense against further Western encroachment. However, in the face of European expansionism, many societies sought to retain their traditions, such as the caste system in India and Confucianism in China. Meanwhile many isolated societies, such as the indigenous peoples of Mesoamerica and the Khoisan hunter-gatherers in Africa, had not been exposed to European ideas and culture prior to the nineteenth century. Nonetheless, in the context of the rapid modernization brought about by the Europeans, societies that resisted change were eventually transformed or destroyed by Western colonization.

Finally, volume four, *The Contemporary World (1900s to the Present)*, covers the period during which European dominance over the world began to erode and empires, shattered into a large collection of independent states that asserted separate national identities. As a result of the devastation of World War II, leaders around the world became more willing to cooperate and develop international organizations—the United Nations being the most visible—while the rise of independence movements led to the dissolution of the colonial system in Africa and Asia. After the two world wars, the Cold War—a competition between the United States and the Soviet Union and their respective allies around the world—emerged and endured until the late 1980s. During the Cold War, the United States and the Soviet Union offered financial, military, and political aid to independent nations, so long as they demonstrated allegiance to Washington or Moscow, respectively. In the twentieth century and into the twenty-first century, countries and peoples once divided by national borders and defined by distinct ethnic identities were transformed by mass migrations and the development of international political and economic unions.

During the twentieth century, advances in transportation accelerated the movement of peoples and products across great distances, while advances in communications facilitated the development of new technologies, such as satellite telephones and televisions and, toward the end of the century, the Internet. These technologies created a borderless exchange of information that in a single, widely understood language, English, produced a new environment of cross-cultural exchange. Cultural developments, particularly in American music and film, coincided with these technological advances, leading some critics to accuse the United States and other exporters of such mass culture of homogenizing world culture. Scholars estimate that every year the world permanently loses several of its 6,000 distinct languages and dialects as societies become increasingly homogenized and interconnected. With the multitude of national, ethnic, and religious identities being brought together by transportation and communication systems, the process of globalization became dominant. Globalization encourages the spread of ideas, material goods, and cultural products across the entire planet rather than just between countries, heralding a new age in human relations.

During the contemporary era, a number of problems escalated to an international scale, the AIDS pandemic, human rights abuses, and environmental degradation among them. These kinds of problems reveal a growing disparity between those with access to such basic necessities as fresh water, food, education, and health care (usually in industrialized and developed nations) and those without access (usually in developing nations or impoverished groups). The contemporary world almost seems to resemble, on a much larger scale, the beginning of antiquity, when overpopulation and a struggle for resources brought humans together to make a profound change to their world. Only the tenacity and unbounded creativity of humans determined to solve their problems through mutual cooperation across cultures offer the hope of moving humanity forward, collectively, toward its betterment.

—*David W. Del Testa*

GLOBAL HISTORY

Cultural Encounters from Antiquity to the Present

Volume One

ANTIQUITY (5000 B.C.E.–400S C.E.)

Volume One: Introduction

Antiquity (5000 b.c.e.–400s c.e.)

Antiquity addresses the impact of cross-cultural encounters on human history between 5000 b.c.e. and the fifth century c.e. These encounters are based on a series of innovations in the ways humans lived and associated with one another. At this time, human society became increasingly complex, settled, state-centered, and agricultural, culminating with the formation of empires. Although encounters occurred before 5000 b.c.e., archeological evidence and historical sources do not show the appearance of human civilizations until after this point, so it is difficult for scholars to conclusively state how human cultures influenced one another beforehand.

World History during the Era

Many scholars believe a warming of Earth's climate between 14,000 and 11,000 b.c.e. encouraged a boom in human population. This increase sparked several important, inter-related changes in human existence, including the practice of agriculture, the formation of states, the emergence of institutional religions, and, ultimately, the creation of civilizations. With this increase in population, humans had few choices: perish, migrate, or organize into larger groups for collective food production and mutual defense. This early collective organization formed the foundation of civilizations.

One essential precondition to the formation of civilizations was the development of intensive agriculture. Between 9000 and 3000 b.c.e., a revolution in food acquisition occurred in the Middle East, East Africa, East Asia, and Mesoamerica (in present-day Mexico and Guatemala). By 5000 b.c.e., about half of the world's population practiced primitive agriculture, in which individual families or tribes supplemented hunting and gathering with the production of crops and domestication of animals. In many places, however, an insufficient amount of land placed pressure on these early agricultural societies. In the face of a nutritional crisis in the world's most densely populated areas, people began to develop political and social structures that permitted them to engage in full-time, intensive agricultural production. Irrigation, the leveling and demarcation of individual fields, the collective storage of seed, and the circulation of draft animals all characterized the intensification of agriculture.

In conjunction with intensive agriculture, states emerged around 5000 b.c.e. Earlier societies had governed themselves through tribal chiefdoms, in which elders or other respected leaders loosely controlled a small group of individuals. The formation of states probably occurred when one tribe or set of individuals within a tribe assumed leadership over others through force or by monopolizing religious rituals. As states became more complex, early leaders delegated their responsibilities to others, and full-time priests, soldiers, and accountants appeared. These specialists performed their duties more efficiently than could an individual with many responsibilities and therefore could extend their specialized authority over extensive areas. States also organized labor. Such organization typically revolved around those steps necessary for intensive agriculture.

Institutional religion probably emerged at the same time as states. Prior to the agricultural revolution, within tribes individuals called shamans provided people with a spiritual connection to the world around them. With intensive agriculture, the need to coax the environment to provide bountiful harvest probably became more tied to religious and spiritual functions. Priests attempted to change the weather, improve soil fertility, or reduce the population of pests through divine intervention. Beginning in 5000 b.c.e. in Mesopotamia, and continuing in Egypt, East Asia, Mesoamerica, the Andes (in present-day Peru), and perhaps in the Indus Valley (present-day Pakistan), a small priestly bureaucracy responsible for agricultural productivity developed into a relatively large, professional administration responsible for justice, war, and trade.

Through their management of agriculture, states and institutionalized religions encouraged the development of civilizations. As population densities increased, people began to share values, languages, philosophies, and cultural practices over broad areas, even beyond the authority of a single state. Because of being isolated from one another, the original civilizations arose with relatively little cross-cultural exchange. The first civilizations include those that arose in Mesopotamia and Egypt around 5000 b.c.e., in the Indus Valley and along the Yellow River (in present-day northern China) after about

2500 B.C.E., and in Mesoamerica and along the western side of the Andes after about 2000 B.C.E.

A number of other related innovations resulted from and aided in the formation of civilizations in the ancient world. Writing greatly facilitated the advancement of civilizations and their contact with one another. First emerging in Mesopotamia in 3300 B.C.E. (and later appearing in East Asia and Mesoamerica), writing allowed humans to communicate with one another across vast distances and gave rise to a new form of expression. It is through writing that ideas and events were first recorded for posterity and that history emerged as a discipline. (Thus, scholars often refer to the period before writing as "prehistoric.") Other human innovations important to understanding and distinguishing civilizations include complex architecture, seafaring, weaving, fermentation, animal husbandry, and the wheel, among others.

The preconditions of civilization, including agriculture, states, institutional religions, and writing, might seem to exclude much of the ancient world, especially Africa and the Americas. By accepting a broader definition of civilization that encompasses groups sharing a common identity within certain geographical and temporal boundaries, the editors and authors included sophisticated cultures with influence over broad areas. In particular, volume one of *Global History* treats the early Indo-Europeans of Eurasia, the Nok-Bantu culture of sub-Saharan Africa, and Chavín culture of pre-Columbian Peru as civilizations. None of these groups, however, had writing, and scholars debate whether the Chavín possessed cities or merely religious centers. In antiquity, none of these peoples developed unifying states; yet, they all had unifying and influential cultures that were recognizable across a large area and among subsequent civilizations, particularly the Indo-Europeans and Nok-Bantu. For example, many elements of common law practice in the United States and Europe can be traced back to Indo-European norms, and the spread of the Nok-Bantu civilization underwrote many of the languages and cultural values of contemporary Africa.

The culminating moment in antiquity was the development of great empires, the states that have imposed their authority on several other states and peoples. The invaders usually consolidated their empires by imposing a homogenized and uniform version of their civilization throughout it. Empires attempted to accomplish on a much larger scale what states had done locally: regroup people in order to efficiently extract resources from them, provide for a common defense, ensure a uniform system of government, and promote prosperity.

The first empires developed in the Middle East and North Africa. The Middle East, for instance, hosted a succession of empires, including Babylonian (c. 1900–1595 B.C.E.) and Parthian Persia (238 B.C.E.–224 C.E.). In East Asia, the first empires formed under the Qin (221–206 B.C.E.) and Han (206 B.C.E.–220 C.E.) dynasties. The Olmec (1250–800 B.C.E.) and the Moche (100 B.C.E.–700 C.E.) would form the first empires of Central America and South America, respectively. Only sub-Saharan Africa, Southeast Asia, Japan, and Oceania (Australia, New Zealand, and the islands of the Pacific) did not fall under imperial control.

The Global Impact of Cultural Interactions during the Era

The first meaningful, enduring, and measurable cross-cultural encounters occurred where civilizations engaged in trade, migration, warfare, and other activities. With the advent of agriculture, the switch from an economy of subsistence to surplus accumulation greatly encouraged trade. Much of the world remained isolated during antiquity, and trade remained fairly regional or based on lightweight products until late in the period, when consumer demand and cargo ships made long-distance commerce profitable. Early river-based civilizations, such as those in the Indus Valley and the Yellow River valley, had extensive intraregional trade networks, usually connecting uplands (which had valuable mineral products, hides, wood, and wool) with coasts (with ample plant and animal nourishment). Trade within (but not between) Mesoamerica and the western coast of South America was also common.

In particular regions of the world, trade networks intensified during antiquity, creating opportunities for increased cultural contact. Leaps in transportation technology, such as the construction of seagoing vessels, the domestication of horses for transport, and the use of the wheel, contributed to cross-cultural exchange. In the Mediterranean, the kingdoms of Egypt traded grain and crafts for gold and animal products with the peoples of the Sudan via the Nile River and paths alongside the river. By 2000 B.C.E., items such as amber, silver, and hides regularly reached the Mediterranean from northern Europe on permanent roads and were then transported to Egypt and the Middle East by the Minoan civilization (which reached its height on the island of Crete between 1700 and 1450 B.C.E.) and then the Phoenicians (who emerged in about 1500 B.C.E.). The Silk Roads, land routes that crossed central Asia, carried many kinds of products between East Asia and the Mediterranean region after about the second century B.C.E. The Roman Empire (27 B.C.E.–476 C.E.) traded glass, amber, and gold with China in exchange for its silk and medicines. Cultural products accompanied these items, including artistic motifs, such as Greek humanistic sculpture, that influenced Indian and Chinese religious art.

Perhaps just as impressive as the Mediterranean trade networks and the Silk Roads were the maritime trade routes connecting the regions around the Indian Ocean. Between 2500 and 1750 B.C.E., maritime routes across the Indian Ocean connected Mesopotamia and the Indus Valley. By 1000 B.C.E., traders from Southeast Asia had emigrated to the Horn of Africa (present-day Somalia and Djibouti) to facilitate the shipment of spices to the Mediterranean region, and South Asian traders began to work along Africa's eastern coast shortly thereafter. Beginning in about 200 B.C.E., merchants from the Mediterranean and Persia traded silver and wine for spices in India.

Migration and demographic exchanges also facilitated much of the cross-cultural exchange of the ancient world, often unintentionally. For instance, in about 1500 B.C.E., Indo-European nomads from the Eurasian steppe migrated to the Indus Valley and completely transformed the culture of the peoples from the Indian subcontinent. During a period of disunity in China, between about 220 and 589 C.E., nomadic peoples north of China who spoke Turko-Mongol languages began to migrate south for better pastureland and plunder and eventually established mixed Chinese-nomadic kingdoms in northern China. Outside of Eurasia, other great migrations influenced civilizations. For example, the migration of the Nok-Bantu peoples from their homeland in West Africa to East Africa and southern Africa beginning in about 1 C.E. completely altered the existing cultures of sub-Saharan Africa. Usually, the great migrations of early antiquity came about gradually and without the violence and suddenness that would later occur. In every case, though, migrant and host cultures became intertwined.

With the emergence of institutional religions in the ancient world, religion had an increasingly important, even controlling, role in people's lives. Monotheism, the worship of one god, gradually developed among many civilizations and replaced state-sponsored polytheistic (multiple gods) faiths. The Israelites (or Jews), a nomadic people who lived in Palestine in the late second millennium B.C.E., became the world's first civilization to develop monotheism, which in turn would serve as the foundation for Judaism as well as Christianity and Islam. Religion also served as

a vehicle for spreading cultural values as much as spiritual ones. In some cases, a whole worldview, complete with different artistic expressions and administrative methods, accompanied a new religion. For example, in western pre-Columbian Peru after 900 B.C.E., the religion of Chavín culture, including its style of worship, support for peace, and religious motifs, attracted people from the surrounding areas, and they abandoned or modified their old practices to accommodate it. Along the Silk Roads, religious ideas, such as Zororastrianism from Persia and Buddhism from India, spread among traders. As these traders circulated along the Silk Roads, they spread these religions to other traders and into the larger population.

Warfare was another important form of cross-cultural encounter during antiquity. The cultural consequences of violent interactions could be felt across whole continents. For instance, the Indo-Europeans, in addition to spreading their language and religious values to Europe, the Middle East, and South Asia in repeated invasions beginning in about 1500 B.C.E., introduced also a culture of violence to the people they conquered, encouraging individual self-identification over group identification, male-centered military aristocracies, and brutal warfare. In Asia, Chinese military campaigns imposed Chinese culture on Vietnam and Korea between 150 and 30 B.C.E. Roman legions imposed their rule and law across the Mediterranean and Europe between 180 B.C.E. and 410 C.E. In many instances, however, the conquering group often was influenced by the culture of the people over whom they ruled. For example, when Alexander the Great (356–323 B.C.E.) invaded Egypt, the Greeks exported their humanistic vision of life to the newly conquered region, but in turn Alexander and the leaders he appointed in Egypt adopted Egyptian practices, including the belief in the deification of leaders.

Finally, the formation of great empires facilitated exchanges under the umbrella of one administrative entity. Empires often ruled over many different peoples, and the borderlessness of empires—combined with the peaceful trade they permitted—encouraged entrepreneurs of many backgrounds to circulate within imperial boundaries. The creation of the Greek Empire under Alexander the Great permitted many Greeks to become important traders and leaders throughout the Middle East and introduce Greek language and Greek artistic forms to Persia, East Asia, and South Asia. Likewise, China's control of northern Vietnam between 111 B.C.E. and 939 C.E. led to Chinese cultural values influencing traditional Vietnamese culture. Later, the northern Vietnamese conquered what is now southern Vietnam, whose peoples had been transformed by the culture and religious ideas of ancient India.

During antiquity, the earliest civilizations evolved in isolation from one another, but later contact between subsequent civilizations became frequent and of great consequence. By the end of the period, however, cross-cultural contacts had become so prevalent and influential that they began to tear states, empires, and civilizations apart and led to the formation of new civilizations. Roman and barbarian civilization blended in Germany as a harbinger of Europe's Middle Ages, which began in the fifth century C.E. The civilizations of the Chinese and nomadic peoples blended in Mongolia and China and anticipated a hybrid Chinese culture. Although cross-cultural encounters at the end of antiquity contributed to the demise of some civilizations, they also remained the bases of many future cultural exchanges and interactions between civilizations.

Approaches to Examining Cross-Cultural Encounters during the Era

Although historians have paid a great deal of attention to the individual states, peoples, and empires of the ancient world, very little has been accomplished in systemizing the impact of cross-cultural encounters between peoples. Scholars, however, have developed some theories and approaches that have become incorporated into current historiography. For instance, positive historians, who view history as progressing forward toward an inevitable conclusion, have viewed antiquity as a time during which humans abandoned the paradise of equality and equal distribution and created private property, states, and social constraints. In many works, German philosopher Karl Marx (1818–83), discussed how in his view Roman society during antiquity consisted mainly of slaves and masters, but that history changed when the masters began to hire administrators to oversee the slaves in their absence. After the collapse of the Roman Empire and the start of Europe's Middle Ages, the administrators became the new masters, but instead of owning slaves, they ruled over people as serfs, who were free in body but tied to the land. Cyclical historians view antiquity as the repository of the first civilizations that wilted and served as the fertilizer for subsequent civilizations. Cyclical historian Oswald Spengler (1880–1936), for example, discusses in *Decline of the West* (1918–22) how each civilization has an inevitable life cycle and how from each dying civilization a new one emerges.

Since the end of World War I (1914–18), historians have examined the peculiarities of global innovation in antiquity and the consequences of early cross-cultural contacts. Two trends, one intellectual and one economic, have dominated historians' thinking about how cross-cultural encounters functioned on a theoretical level. For instance, in the 1930s, the German philosopher Karl Jaspers (1883–1969) postulated that a unique and global set of philosophical and religious breakthroughs occurred during the Axial Age between 800 and 200 B.C.E., marking the essential moment of transition for human history. Some significant events that occurred during this period include the development of monotheism among the early Jews in the Middle East, the formulation of rational thinking in Greece, the flourishing of Confucianism and Daoism in East Asia, and the rise of Buddhism and Jainism in South Asia. Jaspers classified all other human history as either pre- or post-Axial. The Axial Age periodization of history identifies stimuli for similar human developments across many cultures, although events in the Americas do not fit into Jaspers's schema well. Few historians have developed Jaspers's compelling argument further, but it remains otherwise influential.

In *The Modern World System* (1974), American sociologist Immanuel Wallerstein (b. 1930) proposes what he calls the world-systems theory of history, which emphasizes the movement of goods and people as the motor of historical change and the determinant of historical periods. He identifies the development of a world-system of trade in the Atlantic beginning in the 1460s. Scholars have only just begun to apply this way of seeing the world to antiquity. The most famous extension of world-systems theory to the ancient world is British scholar Martin Bernal's (b. 1937) effort to show the development of a world-system of cultural exchange between Africa and classical Greece. In *Black Athena: The Afroasiatic Roots of Classical Civilization* (1987–1991), Bernal suggests that the exchange between Greece and an African-influenced Egypt greatly affected the development of Western civilization. In response, American scholar Mary Lefkowitz (b. 1935) argues in *Not Out of Africa: How Afrocentrism Became an Excuse to Teach Myth as History* (1996) that Egypt disassociated itself from black Africa. Nonetheless, world-systems theory has become the dominant approach to interpreting world history in contemporary scholarship. As archeologists and historians uncover more evidence from the ancient world, and as scholars make more comparisons of the information available, the intensity of cross-cultural encounters during antiquity will become better understood.

—*David W. Del Testa*

Eurasian Trade and Migration

5000–500 B.C.E.

Around 3000 B.C.E., a red-haired, fair-skinned, tartan-wearing people traveled from their homeland between the Black and Caspian seas (in present-day Kazakhstan) and settled in the Tarim Basin, a large desert area between the Tian Shan and Kunlun mountain ranges in central Asia. They differed in appearance and culture from the brown-skinned Mongoloid peoples they would encounter in their travels to Tarim. They were Caucasians, a subset of a larger group of Eurasian steppe dwellers, whose influence would stretch from the British

Gold plaque (c. fifth–third centuries B.C.E.) from the Scythians, a nomadic group from the Eurasian steppe, depicting a man on horseback attacking a warrior with a spear. (The Art Archive/Hermitage Museum, Saint Petersburg/Dagli Orti)

35,000 B.C.E.	**5000–2500**	**4000**	**3600**	**3000**
Homo sapiens sapiens settle in central Asia	Indo-European-speaking pastoralists inhabit the area between the Black and Caspian seas	Horses are domesticated	Eurasian steppe peoples use horses for transportation	Eurasian steppe peoples begin to migrate to Anatolia and the Tarim Basin

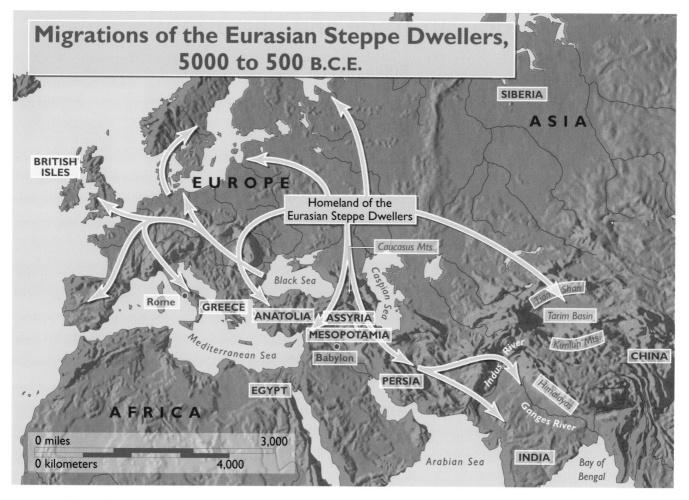

Migrations of the Eurasian Steppe Dwellers, 5000 to 500 B.C.E.

Between 5000 and 500 B.C.E., Eurasian steppe dwellers migrated across Europe and Asia, coming into contact with civilizations on the edges of the steppe.

Source: Adapted from Jerry H. Bentley and Herbert F. Ziegler, *Traditions and Encounters: A Global Perspective on the Past* (Boston: McGraw-Hill, 2000), 65. Reproduced with permission of The McGraw-Hill Companies.

Isles to western China. The Eurasian steppe—a 6,000-mile area covered mostly by grassland and affected by continental weather patterns of hot summers and frigid winters—stretches from Hungary in central Europe to China and is sandwiched north to south between the boreal forests of Siberia and the Caucasus and Himalayan mountains. Scholars imagine a vast area populated by dynamic peoples who spoke related languages and had similar cultures for thousands of years. Although time and the demographic pressure of Mongoloid peoples from East Asia eventually overwhelmed the Caucasian inhabitants of the

Tarim Basin, the peoples of the Eurasian steppe have had a profound impact on the rest of Eurasia.

The evidence in western China of tartans, twills, and mummies with features that originated with Caucasian peoples provides but a few examples of the enormous cultural sphere of the people of the Eurasian steppe. Between 5000 and 500 B.C.E., these peoples also migrated to or invaded other early civilizations on the edges of the Eurasian steppe with some regularity. In terms of its range, impact, and duration, the contact between the Eurasian steppe dwellers and the great early

2000	1500	1400	1200
Eurasian steppe peoples begin to use horse-drawn chariots	Aryans migrate into India	Hittite Empire begins its growth	Hittites, because of their ability to smelt iron, become the most powerful empire in the eastern Mediterranean and Middle East

civilizations might qualify as the first and most important cross-cultural contact of the civilized world (that is, the world of settled agriculturists who lived in or were administered from cities). These exchanges significantly affected the development of Europe, the Middle East, and South and East Asia. The Eurasians not only brought their own culture into the lands they invaded or migrated to, but they also incorporated characteristics of other people's culture into their own and carried these innovations across Eurasia. The members of the influential, relatively homogenous culture inhabiting the Eurasian steppe created, absorbed, and communicated many social, material, and intellectual innovations throughout the civilizations of the Old World (Africa, Asia, and Europe).

A Stimulus for Change in the Old World

Between 100,000 and 10,000 B.C.E., early humans (*Homo sapiens sapiens*) moved out of their African homeland and across Asia, Europe, the Americas, and Oceania, displacing or replacing earlier hominids (*Homo erectus*) and sapiens variants (*Homo sapiens neanderthalis*) as they traveled. The steppe of central Asia was settled by Homo sapiens sapiens via East Asia and Persia by 35,000 B.C.E. These early humans, who were hunters and gatherers, found the steppe of Eurasia particularly fruitful because of its abundant population of herd animals (e.g., mammoth and reindeer). Despite the sometimes harsh climate, these peoples also appreciated the variety of plant nutrition available on the steppe, in its occasional mountain ranges, and along the rivers that cut through the steppe.

Between 5000 and 2500 B.C.E., simple societies of pastoralists (people extracting much of their nutrition from small herds of domesticated animals and engaging in some fishing and farming) developed in an area between the Black and Caspian seas. They spoke related languages with a common origin now collectively called Indo-European. (This term also refers to a member of this language group.) The Eurasians had long ago organized their tribes into bands of patriarchal (male-dominated) warriors. Social organization revolved around small tribes of up to a hundred members led by a headman, linked to

larger tribes headed by a chief, and occasionally confederated across tribes by a king.

One major force that sparked the migration of the Eurasian steppe peoples was their domestication of animals, including sheep and horses, in about 4000 B.C.E. Instead of relying solely on wild animals for meat, they derived nutrition from the milk, milk products (cheese and yogurt), and meat of domesticated animals. They gathered wild plants, traded grain with settled neighbors, and grew their own millet and barley to supplement their meat and milk diet. The changing climate of the steppe also played a role in the movement of the Eurasian steppe peoples across Eurasia. Global desertification and increasingly strong temperature fluctuations in central Asia pushed the nomadic steppe dwellers eastward and westward to where the weather was less harsh during the summer and winter and the supply of game and pasturage was better. Here, they came into contact with the early ancient civilizations.

A development related to the domestication of animals was the use of animals for transportation. Beginning in 3600 B.C.E., the Eurasian steppe dwellers may have become the first of the world's peoples to use horses for transportation, which liberated them from narrowly delimited geographic areas. Around 2000 B.C.E., steppe dwellers began to use horses to pull two-person war chariots (including a driver and an archer). Archeologists remain unsure whether steppe dwellers developed the horse-drawn chariot themselves or adapted it from donkey-drawn carts created in Sumer (present-day Iraq). The essential innovation was not so much the vehicle itself but spoked wheels that could bear punishing travel across the uneven terrain of the steppe. In about 900 B.C.E., Eurasian steppe dwellers began to use the bow and arrow from horseback and abandon the expensive chariots. With this innovation, the steppe dwellers would become the most technologically advanced military in the world.

In about 1000 B.C.E., transhumance pastoralism, whereby large herds are moved from summer grazing in mountain meadows to winter pasturage in the lowland steppe, had replaced simple pastoralism and spread across central Asia, leading to improved nutrition, population

1000	900	500	200
Transhumance pastoralism becomes the dominant agricultural practice on the Eurasian steppe	Eurasian steppe peoples begin riding and using the bow and arrow from horses	End of great migrations by Indo-European speakers	Beginning of Turko-Mongol migrations

increases, and new migrations. Transhumance pastoralism spread and became the dominant way of life of the people of the Eurasian steppe for the next 2,500 years. The various steppe peoples began to move vast herds of animals along much broader circuits that were tied less to specific geography and more to vague ethnic or political boundaries. After the development of transhumance pastoralism, the predominant kingdoms of the Eurasian steppe peoples, such as the Scythians, the Sakas, and the Kushans, developed. The steppe dwellers usually adopted settled agriculture soon after migrating or invading new areas and brought with them agricultural innovations learned elsewhere, such as the iron-tipped plow, that enabled them to improve harvests, nutrition, prosperity, and thus their chances of survival.

Steppe Migrations throughout Eurasia

Beginning around 3000 B.C.E. and continuing through 500 B.C.E., Eurasian steppe peoples used the innovation of horse-powered transportation and intruded on the early civilizations of East Asia, South Asia, and the Mediterranean Basin, often with profound consequences. The invaders spread early Indo-European languages as well as a strong military culture wherever they went, which in turn became permanent cultural features of Europe, Mesopotamia (present-day Iraq), and northern India. Over time, the Eurasian steppe dwellers or their immediate descendants introduced militarized aristocracies to the cultures they conquered. This occurred indirectly in Anatolia (present-day Turkey) around 3000 B.C.E. to the peoples who would eventually become the Hittites and in Greece to the Mycenaeans in about 2000 B.C.E. A militarized culture was introduced directly in India to the Aryans, a subset of the larger steppe-dwelling group, in about 1500 B.C.E. In other cases, they significantly disrupted societies, as with, for example, the "Sea Peoples," groups of nomadic seafarers who originated from an area north of Greece and invaded Egypt in about 1200 B.C.E.

The migrations and invasions between 3000 and 500 B.C.E. had two phases. In the first phase, around 3000 B.C.E., Indo-European languages became established across Eurasia, from the British Isles to western China and as far south as the Middle East. In the second phase, beginning in about 1500 B.C.E., Indo-European Aryans invaded northern India, taking over the abandoned cities of the Harappan civilization on the Indus River and the Dravidian chiefdoms of the Ganges River (the Harappans had established an urban-based agricultural civilization beginning in about 2500 B.C.E.). These invasions greatly affected the society of India, resulting in a distinct and recognizable cultural change, including that of language. The second phase ended between 900 and 500 B.C.E., when descendants of the Eurasian steppe peoples, known as Persians and Medes, invaded and conquered significant portions of the Middle East, including Babylon (present-day central Iraq) and Assyria (a kingdom that included parts of present-day Iraq, Syria, Iran, and Turkey).

In a pattern that became typical during the next two millennia, Eurasian steppe peoples became leaders of the civilizations they conquered while quickly adapting the culture and society of the people they ruled. The great chieftains of the steppe dwellers who remained in or returned to the steppe often built kingdoms whose organization mirrored the structure of the empires they conquered. Thus, by the seventh century B.C.E., the Scythians of the western steppe had a system of kingship and courts vaguely resembling those of the Assyrians they had raided.

Around 500 B.C.E., with the collapse of many early Old World civilizations and the development of their replacements (Rome, Han China, Mauryan India) under way, the pressure that the peoples of the Eurasian steppe posed to the world around them abated. To some degree, the invasions and migrations of Eurasian steppe dwellers temporarily depopulated the western steppe, relieving internal political motivations and demographic pressures in that region. The western steppe emptied so severely after the migrations of the Eurasian steppe peoples that the peoples of the eastern steppe, who spoke Turko-Mongol languages and whose economic development had lagged, began to expand westward. These peoples, known as the Xiongnu (called the Huns in the West), pushed the remaining Indo-European speakers of the steppe, including the Slavs and Goths, into Europe by 500 C.E. Beginning around 200 B.C.E., the Xiongnu formed a large, regional confederation and began raiding China, Persia, and eventually Rome.

Inserting the Steppe into Civilization

When viewed as a whole, the consequences of the Eurasian steppe dwellers' invasions of Europe, Mesopotamia, South

Asia, and China have no equal in the ancient world. Although the invasions and migrations occurred over an almost four-thousand-year period, in the context of rapid change and innovation, the culture and society of the Eurasian steppe dwellers demonstrate a distinct pattern of global historical importance. During every invasion or migration, the steppe peoples amalgamated with local societies, intermixing cultural practices, but often stimulating massive sociocultural changes among the peoples they conquered. The particular pattern of invasion and migration by the steppe dwellers redirected humankind away from the slow, static development of individual civilizations toward a period of rapid political change based on the formation of empires and the initiation of intense intercultural contact.

By creating a large area of common language and shared culture, the Indo-Europeans provided an opportunity for the exchange of innovations across Eurasia between the Indo-European groups, and from them to the peoples on the borders of Eurasia (the Mediterranean, the Middle East, India, and China). For example, the domesticated horse, which offered humans incredible mobility, alone changed the pace of history. Except in sub-Saharan Africa, South Asia, and Southeast Asia, where horses will not thrive, this animal became an essential element in military campaigns and individual transport (oxen remained the favored field animals). After the end of the major expansion of Eurasian steppe dwellers in 500 B.C.E., China fought vigorously to control the Tarim Basin and its supply of high-quality horses.

Likewise, Eurasian cultural norms altered societies that the steppe peoples invaded or entered as migrants. The continuing dominance of Indo-European languages in Europe, parts of the Mediterranean Basin, and India reflects the significant cultural transformation caused by the Eurasian steppe peoples. In addition, as a result of their invasions and migrations, religious practices based around the worship of a pantheon or single god with many manifestations, and social norms such as strong, patriarchal warriors as leaders, became dominant throughout Europe, the Middle East, and South Asia. In India, for instance, the invasion of the Aryan peoples had a very visible and enduring impact. The Eurasian steppe dwellers gradually took over and subsumed the local Dravidian people on the Indian subcontinent. The Aryans used a sacred language (Sanskrit), and spoke a less

> **Cross-Cultural Exchange**
> ↔ Horses become primary mode of military transportation throughout the Old World (except sub-Saharan Africa and South and Southeast Asia)
> ↔ Indo-European languages form the basis of dominant languages in ancient Europe, the Middle East, northern India, and on the Eurasian steppe as far as the Tarim Basin
> ↔ Societies across Europe and the Middle East become more patriarchal and militarized

formal version of it (Prakrit), that has become the basis of many of the modern languages of South Asia.

In addition to introducing new cultural practices, the Eurasian steppe dwellers also refined and communicated innovations they encountered during their migrations and invasions. For example, in about 3000 B.C.E., Eurasian steppe dwellers invaded Anatolia and began to create chiefdoms that would coalesce into the Hittite Empire by 1400 B.C.E. The Hittites developed a technique of iron smelting by 1200 B.C.E., which enabled them to manufacture advanced weapons that made them the most powerful people in Mesopotamia. Iron was much less expensive, more durable, and more plentiful than the bronze that it replaced. Within five hundred years, trade and exchange with the Hittites introduced iron smelting to the steppe peoples of the area around the Black Sea. The steppe peoples used iron-tipped plows, which had sharp blades that could easily break up topsoil, to speed their expansion into India. The linguistic commonalities and horse-based transportation of the Eurasian steppe dwellers probably enabled innovations to spread within their cultural sphere more quickly than between other peoples, although the many subgroups of Eurasians developed different dialects and societies within and around the Eurasian steppe.

The Eurasian steppe dwellers initiated significant historical processes and developments in the Old World. For example, between 1400 and 1000 B.C.E., a migration of Eurasian steppe peoples may have directly or indirectly caused a complete disruption of the cultures and societies of the eastern Mediterranean. During this period, the Indo-European Sea Peoples destroyed Mycenae in Greece, the Hittite Empire in Anatolia, Babylon in Mesopotamia, and seriously challenged

Egyptian hegemony in the Middle East and North Africa. The absence of an imperial authority on the Greek peninsula allowed Greece, the basis of Western civilization, to develop independently.

The movement of the Eurasian steppe dwellers into the civilized world established a pattern of invasion that endured well after the end of this phase in 500 B.C.E. The Mongol Empire of the thirteenth and fourteenth centuries C.E. continued the process of the westward migration of Turkic and Mongol peoples from Manchuria (present-day northeastern China), and like other similar invaders, encouraged a period of cross-cultural exchange, such as contact with the Venetian merchant Marco Polo (1254–1324) in China. This pattern continued until the Qing Manchurians conquered Ming China in 1644 and the Austrians halted the advance of the Ottoman Turks at Vienna in 1683. In this light, the cross-cultural contact by Eurasian steppe dwellers with surrounding peoples impacted the ancient world for an astonishing 6,000 years, ultimately helping to transform the static civilizations of the ancient world into vibrant multinational empires.

See Also

VOLUME ONE: Indo-European Migration to the Indus Valley; The Silk Roads; Barbarians in China; Barbarians in the Roman Empire

VOLUME TWO: The Seljuk Turks and Islamic Civilization; The Mongols and the Civilizations of Eurasia

Bibliography

Davis-Kimball, J., V. A. Bashilov, and L. T. Yablonsky, eds. *Nomads of the Eurasian Steppes in the Early Iron Age.* Berkeley: Zinat Press, 1995.

Grousset, René. *The Empire of the Steppes: A History of Central Asia.* New Brunswick: Rutgers University Press, 1970.

Mallory, J. P. *In Search of the Indo-Europeans: Language, Archeology and Myth.* New York: Thames & Hudson, 1989.

Mallory, J. P., and Victor H. Mair. *The Tarim Mummies: Ancient China and the Mystery of the Earliest Peoples from the West.* London: Thames & Hudson, 2000.

Renfrew, Colin. *Archeology and Language: The Puzzle of Indo-European Origins.* Cambridge: Cambridge University Press, 1987.

—*David W. Del Testa*

Primary Document
Blacksmith's Tools and Iron Objects

Iron ingot, blacksmith's tools, and objects (sixth–fifth centuries B.C.E.) from Moravia (present-day Czech Republic). The network of trade and cultural exchange in Eurasia between 5000 and 500 B.C.E. encouraged the spread of a variety of important technological innovations and cultural advances, including iron smelting. The Hittites had developed iron smelting by 1200 B.C.E., and through their contact with the peoples of the Eurasian steppe, this technology had spread to Europe and East Asia by 600 B.C.E. Iron was less expensive and more widely available than the materials that constitute bronze (tin and copper) and thus "democratized" metal tools, making them more widely available.

Source: © Erich Lessing/Art Resource, NY.

The Phoenician Trading Empire and the Spread of the Alphabet

2500–800 B.C.E.

Plutarch, a Greek writer and historian of the first century C.E., wrote an unflattering portrayal of the Phoenicians: "They are a people full of bitterness and surly, submissive to rulers, tyrannical to those they rule, abject in fear, fierce when provoked, unshakable in resolve, and so strict as to dislike all humor and kindness" (Harden 1971). Yet Plutarch wrote these mostly derogatory words using the Greek alphabet, which the Greeks had adopted from the Phoenician alphabet centuries earlier. Although treated with suspicion by many ancient sources besides Plutarch, the Phoenicians (who were part of a group called the Canaanites) made an important contribution to language in the form of a more flexible method of writing than the pictographic and syllabic systems that preceded the advent of the alphabet. This alphabet, much easier to learn than earlier forms, helped spread literacy to other Mediterranean peoples, among them the Greeks and later the Romans.

In an ironic and unfortunate accident of history, virtually all Phoenician literature has been lost, leaving only a few fragments inscribed on stone tablets, mainly dedications to the gods of the Phoenicians. It has been the task of archeologists to uncover the Phoenician civilization and its role in the development of trade and settlement around the Mediterranean Sea. Their excavations have revealed the substantial role that the Phoenician city-states played in establishing trade networks and in founding colonies around the Mediterranean Sea. This expansion of the original Phoenician homeland helped to spread the alphabet to other Mediterranean civilizations.

The Origin of the Phoenician Alphabet

Writing first emerged in Mesopotamia (in the Tigris-Euphrates Valley in present-day Iraq) around 3300 B.C.E. Egyptian hieroglyphic writing developed independently approximately two centuries later. Writing began first as a tool of commerce, a form of accountancy, but was also adopted by rulers to display law codes and for propaganda, usually on large stone tablets called *stele*. The earliest writing was in the form of pictograms, pictorial representations of everyday objects, mainly commonly traded items. A purely

A small stone marker (c. seventh–sixth centuries B.C.E.) from Malta with a bilingual inscription in the Phoenician and Greek alphabets. The Greeks would adopt the Phoenician alphabet in approximately 800 B.C.E. (© Erich Lessing/Art Resource, NY)

3300 B.C.E.	2500	1500	1200	1200–700
Writing systems emerge in Mesopotamia	Semitic-speaking peoples migrate into the Levant	Phoenicians emerge as a distinct ethnic group	Invasions by Hebrews, Philistines, and Aramaeans limits the Phoenician territory	Height of Phoenician prosperity

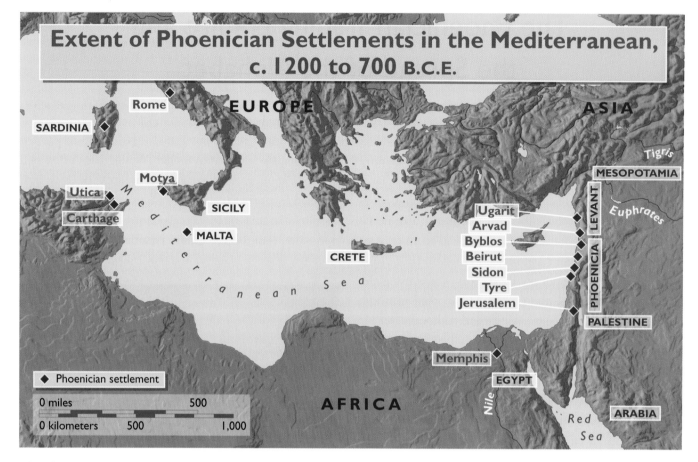

Extent of Phoenician Settlements in the Mediterranean, c. 1200 to 700 B.C.E.

The Phoenicians established extensive trade networks throughout the Mediterranean region, creating settlements that would help spread the alphabet to other civilizations.

Source: Some data compiled from María Eugenia Aubet, *The Phoenicians and the West: Politics, Colonies and Trade*, 2nd ed., translated from Spanish by Mary Turton (New York: Cambridge University Press, 2001), fig. 2 and fig. 22.

pictographic system, however, could not express more than simple concepts, and soon these pictograms came to represent specific phonetic values (that is, they represented either a vowel, a consonant, or syllabic sound). Both Sumerian (Mesopotamian) cuneiform (meaning "wedge shaped," named after the style of writing) and Egyptian hieroglyphics contained a combination of pictograms and phonetic symbols.

The earliest solid evidence of the use of an alphabet occurs in Ugarit (in present-day Syria), a Phoenician city-state, around 1400 B.C.E. However, this alphabet—written using a set of simplified cuneiform signs—was not adopted by the Phoenicians and did not spread

beyond its birthplace. At first, the Phoenicians used cuneiform, but then they developed a wholly new alphabetic writing system that was easier to learn and whose relative simplicity facilitated the recording of merchant transactions. Early versions of the Phoenician alphabet, dating from about the eleventh century B.C.E., combined a pictographic with an alphabetic script and may have been inspired by Egyptian hieroglyphic symbols. Initially, the letters were written both vertically and horizontally and interchangeably from left to right and right to left. By the close of the second millennium B.C.E., however, the Phoenicians had settled on the horizontal orientation from right to left and had further simplified

1000s	800	c. 800	750	701
Emergence of early Phoenician alphabet	Trade networks and colonies are established by Phoenicians in the western Mediterranean	Greeks adopt the Phoenician alphabet	Etruscans adopt the Euboean alphabet, a variation of the Greek alphabet	Phoenicia is conquered by the Assyrian Empire

the characters, reducing pictographic elements until each letter had become an abstract representation of a distinct consonantal or vowel sound.

The Development of the Phoenicians' Trade Networks

The Phoenicians belonged to the linguistic group known as the Semitic-speaking peoples, who included Hebrews, Arabs, and many other ethnic groups in the Middle East. Around 2500 B.C.E., they migrated to the eastern Mediterranean shores (also known as the Levant) to present-day Syria, Lebanon, and Israel. The Phoenicians did not split into a distinct group until about 1500 B.C.E., when they became vassals of the Egyptian Empire for the next three hundred years. They paid tribute to Egypt but were allowed to continue trading with relative independence.

As a result of invasions by the Hebrews into Palestine, the Philistines onto the coast of Palestine, and the Aramaeans into Syria, the Phoenicians' territory was limited to present-day Lebanon by about 1200 B.C.E. The geography of this smaller area influenced the development of Phoenician civilization. The mountains of present-day Lebanon formed the eastern boundary of Phoenician territory and protected it from incursions by the Assyrians from the east. Narrow river valleys provided some fertile lands for cultivation, but not enough to sustain a dense urban population. The coastal region offered several protected natural areas where the Phoenicians settled their principle cities: Tyre and Sidon in the south, Beirut in the center, and Byblos and Arvad in the north. These cities, each ruled by independent monarchies and never unified under a single ruler, became important centers of trade, not only for the immediate region but also for the entire Mediterranean Basin.

Trade routes established links with Egypt as early as around 2700 B.C.E., when there was great demand for the cedars, pines, firs, and other timber that grew in the mountains of Lebanon. The Phoenicians also manufactured a type of purple or red dye extracted from the murex, a mollusk native to the region. The Phoenicians became so famous for their purple dye and cloth that,

according to one theory, the Greeks called them Phoenicians because the name means "purple dye" in ancient Greek. The Phoenicians established trading posts in southern Palestine and in the Nile Delta and Memphis in Egypt and they acted as the commercial intermediary between Egypt and the inland states to the east in what is now Syria, Iraq, and Iran.

Free of Egyptian rule and not yet threatened by the Babylonian Empire in the east that would rise around 600 B.C.E., the Phoenicians enjoyed the height of their prosperity from 1200 to 700 B.C.E. In the tenth century B.C.E., the Phoenician city of Tyre, under King Hiram (r. 969–936 B.C.E.), took the lead in establishing important diplomatic and trade relations with King David of Israel (r. c. 1000–965 B.C.E.) and then expanded these contacts under the reign of King Solomon (r. 965–928 B.C.E.). In exchange for building materials and technical assistance (for example, in the building of the Temple to house the Ark of the Covenant in Jerusalem), the Tyrian Phoenicians gained access to interior trade routes to Syria, Mesopotamia, and Arabia. The Phoenicians also began to launch expeditions into the Mediterranean Sea, venturing beyond the Strait of Gibraltar, between Spain and North Africa, and into the Atlantic Ocean, eventually making contact with the British Isles.

By about 800 B.C.E., some Phoenician city-states had established permanent trade networks in western Europe for the purpose of trading for certain metals, such as tin and silver, as well as pottery, wine, olive oil, and slaves. Perhaps in response to overpopulation in the Phoenicians' homeland, and the need to expand agricultural production, the Phoenicians founded colonies along the coast of the Mediterranean: the island of Malta; Carthage and Utica in present-day Tunisia; Motya on the island of Sicily; Cádiz in southern Spain; and smaller settlements in southern Sardinia and the Balearic Islands. Eventually, these colonies gained their independence from the Phoenician city-states. In the third and second centuries B.C.E., Carthage had become wealthy and powerful enough to challenge the Roman Republic (509–27 B.C.E.) for dominance of the Mediterranean, but was defeated after

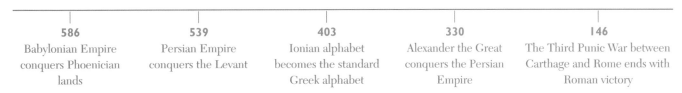

586	539	403	330	146
Babylonian Empire conquers Phoenician lands	Persian Empire conquers the Levant	Ionian alphabet becomes the standard Greek alphabet	Alexander the Great conquers the Persian Empire	The Third Punic War between Carthage and Rome ends with Roman victory

decades of hostility and warfare known as the Punic Wars. At the conclusion of the Third Punic War in 146 B.C.E., Carthage was destroyed, and the surrounding lands became a colony of Rome's growing empire.

The Phoenician homeland was invaded from the east. In 701 B.C.E., most of Phoenicia was conquered by Assyria, which at its height ruled over parts of present-day Iraq, Iran, Syria, and Turkey. In 586 B.C.E., the Babylonian Empire replaced the Assyrians, followed by the Persian Empire in 539 B.C.E. Alexander the Great (356–323 B.C.E.; king of Macedonia, 336–323 B.C.E.) took the chief Phoenician city of Tyre in 332 B.C.E. for the expanding Greek Empire and, in 330 B.C.E., conquered the Persian Empire. In turn, the Roman Empire (27 B.C.E.–476 C.E.) administered the Phoenician cities as part of the province of Syria. The Phoenician language was displaced by Aramaic, another Semitic language spoken by many peoples of the Levant. Although the Phoenicians had lost their independence to greater imperial powers, their legacy to Western civilization—their alphabet—had long been adopted by most of these same conquerors.

The Spread of the Alphabet and Its Contributions to Western Civilization

The Phoenicians, and the many other peoples who later adopted the alphabet as a way to transcribe their languages into written form, undoubtedly recognized its multiple advantages. The alphabet was a less ambiguous writing system than hieroglyphics or cuneiform, both of which were highly complex and often unclear. For example, an individual sign could represent dozens of words or syllables, and the reader had to know the context to understand the meaning of the sign. Not surprisingly, it required years of intensive study to learn hieroglyphs or cuneiform. Only a few students undertook this arduous training in order to become scribes, an honored profession in Egypt and Mesopotamia. Consequently, only a small percentage of the population in the eastern Mediterranean was literate. By contrast, the Phoenician alphabet, with its limited number of characters, simplified this ambiguity. Adults and children could learn the alphabet in only a few months. The alphabet was quicker to write, making it a valuable tool for merchants and traders. The relative simplicity of the alphabet spread literacy.

Record keeping was facilitated, as was interstate trade, the lifeblood of the Phoenician people.

The Phoenician alphabet was soon adopted and altered to fit the needs of other peoples of the Levant, who spoke the related Semitic languages of Aramaic, Hebrew, Ammonite, and Arabic. The principles of the alphabet continued to be spread east to India by those speaking Aramaic. The Aramaic alphabet displaced cuneiform, becoming the official script of the Babylonian, Assyrian, and Persian empires in the first millennium B.C.E.

The Greeks adopted the alphabet in approximately 800 B.C.E., the earliest evidence being found on potsherds (pieces of broken pottery) recovered on the Italian island of Sardinia. There was no single encounter in which the Phoenician alphabet was transmitted to Greek civilization. The Greeks themselves claimed that the mythological Cadmus, son of the king of Phoenicia, had taught them the alphabet. (According to Greek mythology, Cadmus had founded the Greek city of Thebes while searching for his sister Europa, who had been abducted by the god Zeus.) In reality, this transfer of technology took place over centuries, as the Phoenicians extended their trading network across the Mediterranean. It seems likely that Greek traders living in the Phoenician cities brought the alphabet back home to Greece, where it was eventually adopted by the local population. It is also likely that the Greeks hired Phoenicians to teach them the alphabet, sounding out the letters until the Greek students had learned which letters worked for their language and which did not. The Phoenician alphabet consisted exclusively of consonants (22 in all). The Greeks used "leftover" letters representing sounds not used in their language and applied them to vowels. Surprisingly, the earliest examples of the use of the Greek alphabet involve noneconomic concerns, private matters, and literature. Indeed, some scholars argue that the Greeks adopted the alphabet in order to transcribe Homer's epics, which had originally been related orally.

The Greeks then spread the alphabet to western Europe through trade and colonization. The Etruscan civilization, located in the present-day region of Tuscany in central Italy (and whose people often interacted with the Romans to the south), adopted a variation of the Greek alphabet called the Euboean around 750 B.C.E., and passed it on to the Romans, who developed today's Latin alphabet. Another variation, the Ionian alphabet, became the standard Greek alphabet in 403 B.C.E. (In the ninth century C.E., the Cyrillic alphabet would be adapted from the Greek alphabet by Greek Christian Orthodox missionaries and would become the script for about 60 mostly Slavic languages.)

The alphabet was adopted by the speakers of many different languages, thus having a great impact on Western civilization. Evidence suggests that the alphabet affected thought patterns and changed the way people perceived the world. The alphabet developed into a standardized set of arbitrary signs from which all the words of a language could be composed. Breaking up the written language into discrete phonemes seemed to encourage the fragmentation, specialization, and classification of knowledge, all hallmarks of Western science and intellectual thought. In the same way that the alphabet is arranged to create words, ideas could be linked to form arguments in a type of deductive logic, which derives universal principles from the study of specific evidence. For example, laws could be more easily classified and codified, weights and measures more easily standardized. Whereas ideographic writing systems (such as Egyptian hieroglyphics or Chinese characters) encouraged concrete thought, the use of the alphabet encouraged abstract thinking, a precursor to the search for the basic principles that underlie Western science.

The potential of the alphabet to expand intellectual thought in these directions was first evidenced in Greek civilization. When the Greeks added vowels and certain consonants to duplicate all the sounds in the Greek language, they could then transliterate the spoken word into a visual sign. This innovation made it easier to transmit more information and culture to the next generation in the form of the written record. The Greeks were able to build on previous scientific inquiries and develop the first examples of the rational philosophy, formal logic, and abstract science that would characterize Western civilization for millennia.

The introduction of the alphabet also had a profound impact on religious thinking, especially in the Middle East. The Modern Hebrew script evolved from the Aramaic in the third century B.C.E., enabling a blossoming of literary culture to take place among the Hebrews. By the seventh century B.C.E., Hebrews were

Cross-Cultural Exchange

↔ The alphabet is invented and introduced to other civilizations in the Mediterranean region and parts of Asia, such as India

↔ A Mediterranean trade network develops involving Phoenicians, Egyptians, Greeks, Etruscans, and Romans

↔ The alphabet spreads literacy among the various civilizations that adopt it

↔ The alphabet encourages abstract thought and rational inquiry, which become the hallmarks of Western civilization

defining Judaism through the medium of the Bible and thus became known as "People of the Book." This transition to the written word helped to transform Judaism into a strictly monotheistic religion based on universal guiding principles handed down by one God. The sense of the abstract that the alphabet encouraged in the minds of its readers facilitated generally the development of monotheism. Judaism, Christianity, and Islam, whose scriptures were all written in alphabets derived from the Phoenicians, have at their core this concept of a supreme deity.

The alphabet was also well suited to the printing press, which greatly enhanced its impact. The Chinese invented the printing press in the eleventh century C.E., and Europeans independently invented a printing press, on the same rough model in the fifteenth century C.E. In the 1450s, Johannes Gutenberg (d. c. 1468) and others invented a printing press that used a movable metal type with each letter of the alphabet cast in molds.

Like the alphabet, the printing press spread literacy, and therefore sparked movements that spread the ideas that came to define the early modern world: the Renaissance, starting in the fourteenth century, revived interest in ancient Greece and Rome and in the cultivation of knowledge; the Protestant Reformation, a widespread sixteenth-century rebellion against the authority of the Catholic Church founded many new Christian churches and encouraged the translation of the Christian Bible into common, everyday language instead of Latin; and the Scientific Revolution, which from the sixteenth century began to promote rational investigation of natural forces. While the alphabet was not the primary cause of these changes, it played a vital role in transmitting new ideas that became the foundation of the modern world.

See Also

VOLUME ONE: Jerusalem and the Rise of the World's Monotheistic Civilizations; The Greek Empire: The Creation of the Hellenistic World; The Roman Empire and the Mediterranean World

VOLUME TWO: The Establishment and Spread of Islam

Bibliography

Aubet, María Eugenia. *The Phoenicians and the West: Politics, Colonies and Trade.* 2nd ed. Translated by Mary Turton. New York: Cambridge University Press, 2001.

Diringer, David. *A History of the Alphabet.* Old Woking, U.K.: Unwin Brothers, 1977.

Harden, Donald. *The Phoenicians.* Middlesex, U.K.: Penguin Books, 1971.

Logan, Robert K. *The Alphabet Effect: The Impact of the Phonetic Alphabet on the Development of Western Civilization.* New York: William Morrow, 1986.

Markoe, Glenn E. *Phoenicians.* Berkeley: University of California Press, 2000.

Moscati, Sabatino. *The World of the Phoenicians.* 1968. Reprint, London: Phoenix Giant, 1999.

Robinson, Andrew. *The Story of Writing.* New York: Thames & Hudson, 1995.

—*Florence Lemoine*

Primary Document
Herodotus's *The Histories*

Herodotus (c. 480–425 B.C.E.) is considered one of the first Greek historians. His work The Histories *combines analysis of real historical events with stories that today would be considered inaccurate or even fanciful. In this excerpt, Herodotus's account of the introduction of the alphabet fits into both these categories. He correctly credits the Phoenicians with introducing the alphabet to the Greeks, but he also claims that the mythological Cadmus, son of the king of the Phoenicians, played a role in this cross-cultural exchange.*

The Phoenicians who came with Cadmus—amongst whom were the Gephyraei—introduced into Greece, after their settlement in the country, a number of accomplishments, of which the most important was writing, an art till then, I think, unknown to the Greeks. At first they used the same characters as all the other Phoenicians, but as time went on, and they changed their language, they also changed the shape of their letters. At that period most of the Greeks in the neighbourhood were Ionians; they were taught these letters by the Phoenicians and adopted them, with a few alterations, for their own use, continuing to refer to them as the Phoenician characters—as was only right, as the Phoenicians had introduced them. The Ionians also call paper "skins"—a survival from antiquity when paper was hard to get, and they did actually use goat and sheep skins to write on. Indeed, even to-day many foreign peoples use this material. In the temple of Ismenian Apollo at Thebes in Boeotia I have myself seen cauldrons with inscriptions cut on them in Cadmean characters—most of them not very different from the Ionian. There were three of these cauldrons; one was inscribed: "Amphityron dedicated me from the spoils of the Teleboae," and would

date from about the time of Laius, son of Labdacus, grandson of Polydorus and great-grandson of Cadmus. Another had an inscription of two hexameter verses:

> *Scaeus the boxer, victorious in the contest,*
> *Gave me to Apollo, the archer God, a lovely offering.*

This might be Scaeus the son of Hippocoön; and the bowl, if it was dedicated by him and not by someone else of the same name, would be contemporary with Laius' son Oedipus. The third was also inscribed in hexameters:

> *Laodamas, while he reigned, dedicated this cauldron*
> *To the good archer Apollo—a lovely offering.*

It was during the reign of this Laodamas, the son of Eteocles, that the Cadmeans were expelled by the Argives and took refuge with the Encheles. The Gephyraei remained in the country, but were later forced by the Boeotians to withdraw to Athens, where they have certain temples set apart for their own special use, which the other Athenians are forbidden to enter; one of them is the temple of Demeter Achaeia, in which secret rites are performed.

Source: Excerpted from Herodotus, *The Histories*, translated by Aubrey de Sélincourt (Harmondsworth, U.K.: Penguin Books, 1972), 361–362.

The Greek Bronze Age:
Minoan and Mycenaean Influence and Exchange

1700–1200 B.C.E.

In 1900, Sir Arthur Evans (1851–1941), an amateur archeologist, began excavations at Knossos, a site on the island of Crete located southeast of the Greek mainland. He unearthed a vast palace complex, which he believed was the home of the mythical King Minos. Drawing on Greek mythology, Evans named his discovery the Minoan civilization, after Minos, the son of the god Zeus who ruled the island of Crete. Among the ruins Evans also uncovered clay tablets that had been hardened in a fire and so preserved. On these tablets were two different but interrelated scripts, which he named Linear A and Linear B. Linear A has yet to be deciphered; most scholars believe that it does not express Greek, but a still unknown language in the script of the Minoan civilization. Linear B, on the other hand, was fully deciphered in 1953 by a British architect named Michael Ventris (1922–56) after another Linear B tablet was found at ancient Pylos. Ventris and others decided that Linear B was an early form of Greek now identified with the Mycenaean civilization, which replaced the Minoan in approximately 1450 B.C.E. The Linear B tablets feature the oldest Greek dialect to have been deciphered.

Evans's discoveries occurred on the heels of those made by Heinrich Schliemann (1822–90), who excavated the main centers of the Mycenaean civilization starting in 1870. Schliemann was convinced that Homer's works of Greek poetry, the *Iliad* and the *Odyssey* (written around the ninth century B.C.E.) contained accounts of actual historical events. He excavated sites in present-day Turkey (in search of Troy, the city besieged by the Greeks in Homer's epics) and Greece, discovering evidence linking the epic stories of Homer to the Mycenaean civilization. The discoveries of these amateur archeologists, and of the professionals who followed them, have elevated our understanding of the Greek Bronze Age (c. 2000–1000 B.C.E.) out of myth and into historical reality. The island of Crete, serving as a central point of contact between the Middle East and the European borderlands, played a key role in the development of the Minoan and Mycenaean civilizations. These civilizations served as transmitters of cultural influence from western Asia and Egypt to the emerging Greek civilization.

The throne room of the palace complex at Knossos, on the island of Crete. (© Erich Lessing/Art Resource, NY)

6000 B.C.E.	2000	1700–1450	c. 1450
Evidence of human habitation on Crete	Migration of Indo-Europeans (Mycenaeans) from the Balkans to the Greek mainland	Height of Minoan civilization on Crete	Mycenaean civilization takes control of Crete

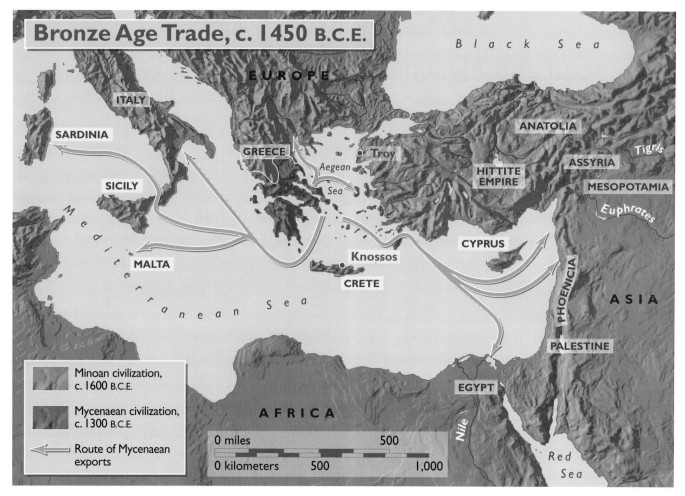

Between about 1700 and 1450 B.C.E., Minoan civilization developed on the island of Crete, eventually forming an extensive trade network throughout the Mediterranean. Around 1450 B.C.E., Mycenaean Greeks gained control of Crete and would soon dominate trade and commerce throughout the region, exporting products, like pottery, to Egypt, Syria, and Phoenicia.
Sources: Some data compiled from María Eugenia Aubet, *The Phoenicians and the West: Politics, Colonies and Trade*, 2nd ed., translated by Mary Turton (New York: Cambridge University Press, 2001); and John Haywood, *Historical Atlas of the Ancient World: 4,000,000–500 B.C.* (New York: MetroBooks, 2001), 1:22.

Crete and the Development of Minoan Civilization

Crete occupies a key position in the southern part of the Aegean Sea. It is accessible from the Middle East and mainland Greece, but is isolated enough to be sheltered from threatening attacks by outside invaders. Nonetheless, its proximity to the eastern Mediterranean provided the motivation to expand trading opportunities with the Middle East, the Greek mainland, and beyond. Evidence of human

habitation from at least 6000 B.C.E. has been found on Crete, and these early inhabitants cultivated olive trees and grapevines, both of which flourish in the Mediterranean. As the Minoan civilization reached its peak between about 1700 to 1450 B.C.E., during a period in the ancient Middle East called either the "first international age" or the age of the "nascent world system," trading contacts were established with Mesopotamia, Egypt, and the coastal cities of Assyria. At this time, the Egyptian and Hittite empires

1200	1200–800	800–323	334
Mycenaean civilization declines	Dark Age of Greek history	Greek Renaissance and the Classical Age	Alexander the Great invades the Persian Empire

competed with each other for control of Assyria and Palestine to the east. The demand for commodities by both of these powerful empires led to increased contact with the Minoans of Crete, who produced valuable agricultural products and textiles. Partly as a result of this extensive trade, a sophisticated civilization developed on the island whose influence subsequently spread to other islands in the Aegean and to the mainland of Greece.

From about the third millennium B.C.E., Crete could sustain several urban settlements dominated by a palace civilization. These palaces most likely controlled many of the political, cultural, and economic activities of the surrounding territory on Crete. The palace economy apparently functioned as a kind of redistribution center, taking in raw materials from the countryside, supervising the manufacturing of certain goods, and conducting trade. There were also smaller palaces, lavish townhouses, and country estates where the wealthy Minoan elite resided and maintained their control of the local economy. The chief settlement of Crete was located at Knossos, where an elaborate and sophisticated palace complex was built that included royal apartments, altars for religious ceremonies, and storage rooms containing agricultural produce such as wine and olive oil, and other manufactured products. The excavation of the palace at Knossos and other Cretan sites also revealed excellent examples of fresco wall paintings in which artistic themes featured formal landscapes, dolphins and other sea creatures, and depictions of people involved in religious ceremonies.

It is not completely clear how the Minoan civilization structured its political life, but evidence suggests that political and religious leadership were fused into one, with the rulers portraying themselves as divine—a practice similar to neighboring states in the Middle East—but without a central ruler, such as a pharaoh (as in Egypt) or a king (as in Mesopotamia). Trade might have been conducted between Crete and the states in the Middle East as forms of "tribute" between rulers or as part of diplomatic negotiations.

Although trade constituted Crete's chief method of contact with the outside world, agriculture formed the foundation of its economy, as was true in most of the ancient world. Olives, figs, grapes, and other produce of the orchard, along with wheat, constituted the largest part of Cretan agriculture. Animal husbandry was also well developed, concentrating on sheep, goats, pigs, and occasionally horse, cattle, and a variety of other commonly domesticated animals.

In the sixteenth and early fifteenth centuries B.C.E., Minoan influence grew throughout the eastern Mediterranean and spread onto the Greek mainland. The Cretans mainly exported agricultural items, but increasingly specialized in a number of crafts, such as textiles, painted pottery, faience (glazed earthenware), and metalworking (in silver, copper, lead, and bronze). These items were manufactured by skilled craftsmen, who enjoyed an elevated status in the community, and possibly by palace slaves. Because of their high artistic quality, Cretan pottery, stone vases, metalwork, and alloys such as bronze were traded widely in the Aegean and imitated in parts of Greece. The Cretans developed an extensive merchant marine to ply this increasing trade and a navy to defend it. Their sea power was so great that their palace complexes did not require the large walled fortifications for protection typical in the Middle East. They built large ships to transport not only their own trade items, but also such goods as gold, silver, obsidian, and other precious stones, ebony, ivory, ornaments, perfumed oils, and other luxury items they obtained from southwest Asia, northern Africa, the Aegean, and as far away as Afghanistan and central Europe. It was at this time that the Linear A script was developed and inscribed on clay tablets in order to keep track of an increasingly complex trading system.

The Minoan civilization underwent a period of crisis around 1750 B.C.E., when the palaces at Knossos and other sites were destroyed, possibly by an earthquake. Most were rebuilt, however, and Crete experienced a resurgence characterized by rich artwork and increased trade with the Middle East. Its prosperity lasted another three hundred years, until about 1450 B.C.E., when the Mycenaean Greeks gained control of the island, demolished the palace complex at Knossos, and took control of Cretan trade in the Mediterranean.

The "Minoanization" of the Mycenaean Civilization

The Mycenaean Greeks, who were named by Heinrich Schliemann after one of the settlements he had excavated on the Peloponnesian peninsula in southern Greece, had arrived on the Greek mainland around 2000 B.C.E. They were an Indo-European-speaking people who originally lived north of the Black Sea. The Mycenaeans migrated down the Balkan Peninsula into Greece and from there out toward the islands. More warlike and less sophisticated in some ways than the Minoans, the Mycenaean Greeks spread throughout the eastern Mediterranean. Eventually they arrived on Crete and began to adopt Minoan cultural and artistic practices.

The Minoan influence on the Mycenaean Greeks is apparent in their arts and crafts, such as frescoes and pottery, as well as in their architecture. Yet the Mycenaean civilization did not adopt Minoan art to the extent that they adopted the Minoans' economic structure. Beginning in the fifteenth century B.C.E., the Mycenaean Greeks built palace complexes similar to those constructed during the Minoan era, but which included massive fortified walls, reflecting the military orientation of the Mycenaean civilization. The Mycenaean Greeks also adapted Linear A to their language, an early form of Greek, creating a new script, Linear B.

Just as the Minoan economy had required more advanced record keeping, so did the Mycenaean economy. Like the Minoans before them, the Mycenaeans controlled a good deal of trade and commerce throughout the Mediterranean during the fifteenth century B.C.E. Mycenaean merchants established communities within the trading ports of the region. Their pottery was traded in Egypt, Assyria, and Phoenicia in the east and the island of Sicily and southern Italy in the west. Their continued development of trade networks increased the wealth of Mycenaean Greece, which was reflected in the numerous luxury items discovered in the graves of rulers that archeologists uncovered in the nineteenth and twentieth centuries. The meager records they found indicate that monarchical rulers, the *wanax*, fused political and religious authority to wield power over their populations. The wanax were assisted by military commanders and border patrol troops.

Mycenaean dominance came to an end in about 1200 B.C.E. According to the writings of Greeks of the Classical Age (c. fifth century B.C.E.), the decline of the Mycenaean civilization followed the sack of Troy, after which the Mycenaeans returned to find their homeland in turmoil. The collapse was probably precipitated by a crisis in their domestic economy, coupled with invasions of the so-called Sea Peoples (probably from Anatolia, or present-day Turkey), who devastated much of the eastern Mediterranean at that time, causing massive disruptions that temporarily diminished trade in the region.

Crete as a Nexus of Exchange for Greek Civilization

The geographical location of Crete and the Greek mainland put them at the nexus of the civilizations throughout the Mediterranean and beyond, making this region perfectly situated for commercial and cultural interchange. Because of this advantageous geographical position, cultural influences from the societies of the Middle East resulted from trade, not conquest. The Minoans and Mycenaeans selected those aspects of the Middle Eastern cultures that best suited them.

The Middle Eastern civilizations based their societies on the temple/palace complex, in which religious and civil life intermingled, and the Minoan civilization adopted this model and worshipped similar gods. The Minoan political leadership emulated other administrative techniques from the Middle East as well, such as the use of seals to monitor the storage and transportation of goods. Influenced perhaps by the practices of the larger states in the Middle East, trade was almost certainly controlled by political rulers. As in the Middle East, the patronage of the palace encouraged manufacturing and superior craftsmanship in order to have a supply of everyday and luxury items for personal consumption and for trade. Each of these adaptations was shaped to fit the particular circumstances of the emerging Greek world.

While the design of a system of writing was another idea that originated in the Middle East and spread to Greek settlements on the Aegean Sea, Linear A was a totally local invention. As in the Middle East, the Minoan script was inscribed on clay tablets. Rather than being baked, however, these tablets were sun-dried, making them more vulnerable to disintegration over the centuries. The only tablets to survive were inadvertently baked when a fire broke out at the Knossos palace. Evidence suggests that these tablets were used mainly for record keeping, not for recording myths or other literature.

Art and techniques of craftsmanship were also imported and modified by Cretan creativity. The technology for metalworking may have arrived from the

Anatolian Peninsula. Faience and an adhesive made with lead and used to attach knife handles were of Middle Eastern origin. Imports such as ivory and precious stones and metals from around the eastern Mediterranean were essential to the creation of many Cretan works of art. Themes in Minoan and Mycenaean artwork, such as images of winged sphinxes and griffins, were imported from the Middle East and mixed with indigenous themes, such as female figurines and snake, lion, and bull motifs. Works of art incorporating these themes may have served a religious function, but the evidence is inconclusive. A painstakingly detailed figurine of a man leaping over a bull, as well as a wall painting depicting a similar scene, may have celebrated youth and athleticism, which became essential ideals of later Greek culture. A stone vase depicting a procession of men chanting and dancing on their way to the harvest reflects an exuberant and three-dimensional quality that is a departure from the single-file orderliness of Middle Eastern art.

Certain architectural forms were also influenced by Middle Eastern models, but the design of the Minoan palace was in many ways a purely Cretan invention. Whereas the palaces of the ancient Middle East were massive and fortresslike, the Minoan palaces employed a more open design, which allowed air and light to penetrate the interior. Palace architects used wooden columns to provide flexibility in case of earthquakes, which were common in the region. These artistic forms and techniques were perfected on Crete and spread to the Greek mainland in the fifteenth century B.C.E.

Just as the Minoan civilization adapted certain Middle Eastern influences to fashion a unique Mediterranean culture, so too did the Mycenaeans through the medium of the Minoan civilization. Yet it was the increasingly intensified commercial interaction with the Middle East that may have strained the Mycenaean economy to the breaking point. It is possible that the Mycenaeans became overcentralized and specialized too narrowly in raising agricultural crops that were necessary to maintain trade. Thus, when the Middle East underwent a period of disorder, it precipitated the collapse of the nexus of exchange and the decline of the Mycenaean civilization.

After 1200 B.C.E., trade was reduced, life became more local for the Greeks, and some of the specialized

Cross-Cultural Exchange

↔ Minoans and Mycenaeans adopt political and religious institutions from the Middle East
↔ Idea for written script from the Middle East is adopted by Minoans and copied by Mycenaeans
↔ Art and architecture are adopted from the Middle East and shaped to fit the Minoan and Mycenaean civilizations
↔ Classical Greek civilization spreads to Middle East

crafts were lost when the palace economy collapsed. At the same time, many fortified cities were destroyed, heralding the so-called Dark Age (1200–800 B.C.E.) of ancient Greek history, characterized by political fragmentation, a decline in trade, and decreased innovation in Greek art. Yet, although trade diminished, it did not cease completely; contact between Greece and the Middle East was maintained, but on a lesser scale.

By the ninth century B.C.E., political stability started to return to the Middle East, and trade with Greece resumed, expanding contacts into the Greek Classical Age, which reached its high point in the fifth century B.C.E. Few specific elements of the Minoan and Mycenaean Bronze Age civilizations remained to influence classical Greece. What did survive consisted mainly of the stories in Homer's epic poems, the *Iliad* and the *Odyssey*, which told of the exploits of a Greek warrior class that was probably based on the Mycenaeans. The heroic warrior ethos that formed the core of Homer's narrative provided a model of sorts to classical Greeks. The emphasis on such values as *arête* (excellence, especially on the battlefield) was shaped to fit the social and cultural needs of the city-states that dominated classical Greek civilization. The heroic ideal was subsequently embraced by Alexander the Great (356–323 B.C.E.; king of Macedonia, 336–323 B.C.E.), who launched an invasion of the Middle Eastern empire of Persia in 334 B.C.E., scoring spectacular victories that destroyed the Persian state. Greek and Macedonian colonists spread Greek culture when they settled in the Middle East after Alexander's conquests. The ancient civilizations of the Middle East that had once provided models for the early civilizations of Greece had now, themselves, become the targets of Greek invasion and colonization.

See Also

VOLUME ONE: The Phoenician Trading Empire and the Spread of the Alphabet; The Greek Empire: The Creation of the Hellenistic World

Bibliography

Dickinson, Oliver. *The Aegean Bronze Age.* Cambridge: Cambridge University Press, 1994.

Fitton, J. Lesley. *The Discovery of the Greek Bronze Age.* Cambridge: Harvard University Press, 1996.

Hood, M. S. F. *The Minoans.* London: Thames & Hudson, 1971.

Hooker, J. T. *Mycenaean Greece.* Boston: Routledge/Kegan Paul, 1976.

Robinson, Andrew. *The Story of Writing.* New York: Thames & Hudson, 1995.

—*Florence Lemoine*

Primary Document

Pylos Tablet with Linear B Characters

The few surviving written sources from the Minoan and Mycenaean civilizations consist of clay tablets. These tablets provide mundane information on items to be traded or stored. This Pylos tablet, using Linear B characters, lists various types of containers used for storage. The lack of written sources that could shed light on social, political, or cultural conditions has severely limited a more complete understanding of the Minoan and Mycenaean civilizations.

Source: © Gianni Dagli Orti/Corbis.

Indo-European Migration to the Indus Valley

1500–500 B.C.E.

A small clay figurine from about 2000 B.C.E. reveals traces of a South Asian cross-cultural encounter between the Indo-European peoples from the steppe north of the Hindu Kush mountains in central Asia and the South Asian peoples of the Harappan civilization (named after Harappa in present-day northwest Pakistan, the place where archeologists first found evidence of this culture). The figure, clad in a simple tunic, gazes onto the world through half-closed eyes, as if in a trance or waking dream. One shoulder is bared. Archeologists and historians believe the drooping eyelids indicate that the figurine represents a priest of some sort who has ingested *soma*, a powerful hallucinogenic substance made from an unknown plant or possibly a mushroom. Soma figured prominently in the cultures of the Indo-European peoples, suggesting that the migration of the Indo-Europeans southward encouraged the adoption of the substance among the peoples of South Asia. The cultural influences engendered by the Indo-European migrations had an enduring religious impact in South Asia as well. For example, the bared shoulder became a profound symbol of respect in Buddhism, a religion that emerged over a millennium after artisans crafted this statue.

Before the Indo-European migrations into South Asia, the Indo-European and Harappan societies lived far apart in distinct societies that only occasionally came into contact with one another. Indo-European speakers traveled across the Hindu Kush mountains to occupy northern South Asia in about 1500 B.C.E. By that time, the Harappan civilization had collapsed for reasons that still remain shrouded in mystery. The invaders, a group known as the Aryans, were a tribe of Indo-Europeans whose name is derived from the Indo-European word *aryo* (the noble ones) and serves as the basis of the names of Ireland (Eire) and Iran today. The cross-cultural encounter between the Aryans of the Eurasian steppe and the

Harappans of pre-1500 B.C.E. South Asia produced a legacy clearly visible in the society of India and in many other cultures across Asia today.

Indo-European and South Asian Societies Prior to Contact

The Rise of the Harappan Civilization

Between 2500 and 1750 B.C.E., the people of the Harappan civilization inhabited a large area on both sides

A clay figurine (c. 2000 B.C.E.) from Mohenjo-daro in the Indus Valley. The figure seems to be of a man, probably a priest, who has ingested soma, *a hallucinogenic substance that originated among Indo-Europeans. (© Scala/Art Resource, NY)*

5000 B.C.E.	3000	2500	1900	1750
Steppe society of Eurasia begins	Agriculture becomes a feature of the Indus Valley	Cities appear in the Indus Valley; beginning of the Harappan civilization	Calamities of an unknown nature strike the Harappan civilization	Harappan civilization collapses, with remnants remaining on India's northwest coast

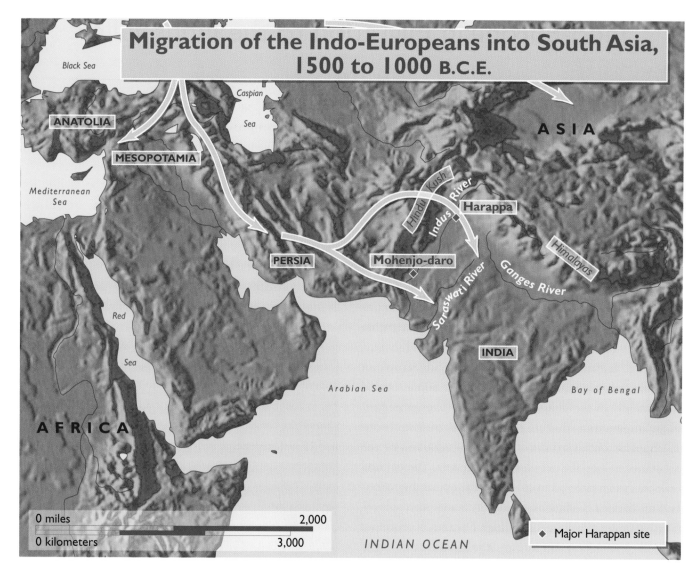

Migration of the Indo-Europeans into South Asia, 1500 to 1000 B.C.E.

Beginning in about 1500 B.C.E., a tribe of Indo-Europeans (known as Aryans) from the Eurasian steppe migrated into South Asia, coming into contact with the peoples of the Harappan civilization. As a result of this contact, the Aryans introduced new religious ideas, social structures, and languages, as well as iron smelting and horses to the Indus Valley.
Source: Some data compiled from Jerry H. Bentley and Herbert F. Ziegler, *Traditions and Encounters: A Global Perspective on the Past* (Boston: McGraw-Hill, 2000), 65.

of the Indus River in present-day India and Pakistan. This civilization extended from the northern region in present-day Pakistan to about 500 miles south, down the coast of the Arabian Sea from the current border of Pakistan and India, stretching from Pakistan's contemporary border with Afghanistan to Delhi, a city centered on the Indus and Saraswati rivers. Sometime around 3000 B.C.E., settled

agriculture (in which land is used continuously for crop or livestock production) became a feature of the fertile Indus River valley. This civilization depended on the annual distribution of alluvial soil (containing materials deposited by running water) from the Indus River from the Hindu Kush and Himalayan mountains to the north. The Indus flooded during the summer, and farmers

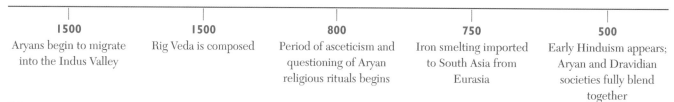

1500	1500	800	750	500
Aryans begin to migrate into the Indus Valley	Rig Veda is composed	Period of asceticism and questioning of Aryan religious rituals begins	Iron smelting imported to South Asia from Eurasia	Early Hinduism appears; Aryan and Dravidian societies fully blend together

planted wheat and barley in the rich mud that the receding waters left behind. Although somewhat unpredictable, the Indus River ensured regular harvests and a sufficient surplus of grain to support cattle, sheep, goats, elephants, and the world's first domesticated chickens.

As food supply increased, so did the population and the need to organize labor to produce the food for the growing society. By 2500 B.C.E., the people of the Indus Valley had begun to build impressive cities at sites where, according to archeologists, some sort of leadership group regulated the material and religious needs of the population and coordinated cooperative labor, especially for irrigation projects. Two great cities—Mohenjo-daro and Harappa—arose quite suddenly and had close ties with about 70 subsidiary and significantly smaller towns. It is believed that Mohenjo-daro and Harappa had populations of 20,000 to 45,000 individuals, quite large for civilizations of that time. They may have served as alternative capitals for a unified empire, as capitals of separate empires, or simply as large commercial and religious centers.

Because of the ravages of time, thousands of years of accumulated silt, and a rising water table, archeologists cannot access the remains of Harappan society from before 2500 B.C.E. However, the picture of Harappan civilization that emerges from its height in 2500 B.C.E. to its collapse in 1750 B.C.E. suggests order and prosperity. At enormous cost in terms of resources, workers had raised the sites of Mohenjo-daro and Harappa above typical flood levels and built high walls, stout citadels, and large granaries for the cities. These features suggest that Mohenjo-daro and Harappa served as centers of tax collection and redistribution and had leaders able to orchestrate massive public works projects. These cities also had large markets, residential areas, temples, and public buildings accessible to one another along broad streets and alleyways built at right angles to one another and aligned on either a north-south or an east-west axis. Smaller cities had similar features. One of the advantages that enabled the Harappans to build such strong and vibrant cities was that they used uniform weights, measures, and brick sizes. Another advantage was that even though archeologists have uncovered different kinds of habitation, indicating distinct differences in wealth, almost every habitation had its own showers and toilets serviced by a municipal water and sewer system. These societies used a script, still indecipherable, consisting of about four hundred symbols representing sounds and ideas and dating back to approximately 3300 B.C.E.

The Harappan civilization evolved around the productive agriculture of the Indus River valley, and it appears to have existed in an environment in which cross-cultural commerce and exchange occurred frequently. Some scholars believe that because of the wealth the Indus Valley cities generated through active maritime trade with Mesopotamia and Egypt, they became larger than they otherwise would have. Harappans are known to have reached Mesopotamia and Egypt by sea through the Persian Gulf—it is not known if traders used the Red Sea—and by land over the Persian plateau (present-day Iran). The Harappans traded Indian copper, silver, ivory, pearls, and semi-precious stones in exchange for Sumerian wool, leather, and olive oil. This trade also extended from the Indus Valley into the rest of South Asia. Archeological evidence shows that workshops in Harappa and Mohenjo-daro produced pottery, tools, and ornamental items for domestic consumption throughout the Indus Valley. At many Harappan sites, archeologists have found imported products, including turquoise from Persia and a jadelike stone from southern India.

The religious beliefs of Harappan society are difficult to determine through the fragmentary evidence available to scholars. It is known that Harappans worshipped gods and goddesses strongly associated with fertility and creation and that they considered trees and animals to be sacred. There are examples of a mother-goddess and a horned fertility god. The apparent obsession with cleanliness by the people of ancient Harappa seems connected to the existence today of bathing platforms (*ghats*) at the edge of rivers for ritual ablutions by Hindus.

Sometime around 1900 B.C.E., natural or other calamities led the Harappans to abandon their cities and flee to the countryside, a process completed by 1750 B.C.E. This migration is suspected by archeologists because of the absence of new construction and the presence of unburied skeletons in the streets of Mohenjo-daro. Archeologists know that the civilization had already begun to decay, indicated by increasingly crowded and poorly built houses and signs of extensive flooding in Mohenjo-daro. One theory suggests that an expanding population probably led to an ever-increasing consumption of wood, which became scarcer over time. As people harvested even the smallest saplings for firewood, the ground became unstable in the face of the periodic floods of the Indus, washing away soil, permitting cataclysmic inundation, and destroying the surplus food supply that had supported the cities. An alternative thesis suggests that millet and rice farming, imported from Africa and Southeast Asia, respectively, opened huge tracts to land-hungry Harappan settlers in southern India, greatly lessening the organizational purpose of Harappan cities in the north. Massive earthquakes and wild rivers charting new courses may have also damaged the infrastructure of Harappan civilization. The society endured in outlying cities until perhaps 1500 B.C.E. and may have formed the nucleus of a new civilization that appeared in southern India.

The Rise of the Aryans

Whereas the Harappans were a settled society, the peoples of the steppe were nomadic. Between 5000 and 2500 B.C.E., a variety of peoples who spoke Indo-European languages developed complex societies based on pastoralism across the Eurasian steppe. From their homeland around the Black and Caspian seas (in present-day Kazakhstan), the Aryans organized themselves into a series of chiefdoms of several hundred members each, occasionally linked through kinship to larger tribes or even a temporary king. Because of the Eurasian steppe's violence and intertribal competition, the Indo-Europeans developed a patriarchal (male-dominated), militaristic society whose ferocious warriors, fighting in chariots and on horseback, had no peer in the ancient world. Aryan society revolved around horses and cattle, which served as a source of food (meat and milk products) and as a currency for trade.

Aryan religion centered around the worship of male gods, the most prominent of whom was Indra (the god of weather). Indra was a boisterous, boastful, and violent deity on whom the Aryans depended for their agricultural prosperity and military success. The Aryans also worshipped numerous other gods associated with natural occurrences and features (e.g., health, disease, dawn, the sun). While the Aryans' chief deity, Indra, acted with violence, the god Varuna served as a moral judge, punishing evildoers severely with disease, death, and exile to the House of Clay, a terrible underworld of suffering. Varuna rewarded the virtuous with an afterlife in the World of the Fathers. Aryan religious worship consisted of elaborate rituals conducted by a priestly class who cremated massive numbers of domesticated animals as sacrifices to the gods.

Without a system of writing, the Aryans preserved their religious and literary traditions through oral communication. Around 1500 B.C.E., they slowly began to push in increasingly larger groups across the Hindu Kush, possibly in response to overpopulation and climatic change on the steppe or to seek out the wealth of the Indus River valley. The Aryans, who found themselves in a land recently vacated, imposed themselves on the scattered remains of Harappan society.

Migration of Aryans to the Indus Valley

The Aryans appear to have migrated gradually into the Indus Valley, where some of the remaining Harappans welcomed them while others violently opposed their presence. Scholars have derived primary information about the encounter between the Aryans and Harappans from the Vedas (veda means "wisdom"), sacred collections of Indo-European songs, prose, and poems written down between 1500 and 500 B.C.E. For a long time, overly literal interpretations of the Vedas suggested that in about 1500 B.C.E. the Aryans had invaded and conquered the civilization of the Indus and Saraswati river valleys. Now, scholars believe that the Aryans slowly transformed the Harappan civilization through gradual migrations and encounters with surviving Harappans.

The most important of the Vedas, the Rig Veda (Wisdom of Verses) was composed around 1500 B.C.E. The three other Vedas—the Yajurveda (Wisdom of Sacrificial Formulas), the Samaveda (Wisdom of the Chants), and the Atharvaveda (Wisdom of the Atharvan Priests)—were composed after the Rig Veda. They recount, in part, the Aryans' conquest of the Dravidian peoples, called Dasas (subject peoples). The Dravidians were the larger language group to which the Harappans probably belonged, and it was they who inhabited the rest of the Indian subcontinent in complex societies. The perspective of the Vedas is sacred in nature, using the god Indra to represent the actions of the Aryan peoples. The Vedas describe Indra as smashing the citadels, dams, and buildings of the peoples of the Indus Valley. Written from the perspective of the victors, the Vedas reveal how the Aryans defeated Harappan society. They may have, for example, broken the waterworks the Harappans used for agriculture and in their cities. In addition, the Vedas describe fierce internal battles among the Aryans as they slowly advanced from the mountains down into the Indus Valley. The Vedas also indicate that the Aryans learned, through imitation or friendly exchange, a great deal of knowledge from the Dravidians they encountered. For example, they learned about settled agriculture from Harappans.

Although successful in their conquest, the Aryans did not completely abandon their ties to their homelands in the area north of the Hindu Kush. At the time, due to climate and disease, horses did not flourish in India, so the Aryan migrants continued to maintain a steady trade in horses with other steppe peoples. This trade probably also exposed the Aryan invaders to iron smelting, which another group of Indo-European migrants, the Hittites, had developed in Anatolia (present-day Turkey) by 1200 B.C.E. With this knowledge, the Aryans developed iron weapons and plows that enabled them, after 750 B.C.E., to enhance food supplies, increase their population, and further colonize northern and central India.

In addition to maintaining their old trade networks, the Aryans also preserved their social order. Originally, the Aryans had brought with them a simple society of herder/warriors and chiefs, but in order to distinguish themselves from the Dravidians whom they conquered and intermingled with in the Indus Valley, they applied a division of society based on the so-called Varna, or skin "colors." These Varna distinguished the "wheaten-colored" Aryans from the darker Dravidian-speakers of Harappa and other places in South Asia that they conquered. Over time, the Varna placed great limitations on professions, behavior, intermarriage, and contact. In English, these societal divisions became known as "castes," from the Portuguese word for strata, *casta*. The four main Varna consisted of Brahman (priests), Kshatriya (warriors and aristocrats), Vaishya (merchants/craftspeople), and Shudra (landless peasants and serfs, probably mostly Dravidians). After 500

Cross-Cultural Exchange

↔ The fusion of Aryan and Dravidian traditions into Hinduism
↔ The dominance of Indo-European languages and writing systems in South Asia
↔ The unification of northern India under one cultural system
↔ The introduction of the horse and iron into South Asia

B.C.E., a fifth group, known as the untouchables, was added to refer to those who performed ritually impure or dirty tasks, such as tanning leather. Until the Aryans established cities, this fivefold division worked well; but subsequently a more complex social organization expressed itself in subgroups known as *jati*, which acted as castes within castes. The adaptations that the Aryans made to India's social order have endured to the present day, albeit in a greatly modified form.

The Aryans also transferred their strong sense of patriarchy to Dravidian society as they overwhelmed it in northern India. Because of their militaristic and nomadic culture, the Aryans restricted the public role of women, and Aryan men retained all the public functions, such as leadership, religion, and economic production, for themselves. Although women remained influential in their private worlds, they had few legal rights. The Lawbook of Manu—written around 100 B.C.E. after the Vedic Age (1500–500 B.C.E.), when the religion reflected in the Vedas was in practice—reveals the Aryans' perspectives regarding the role of men and women in society. According to the Lawbook, men (fathers, husbands, and sons) controlled all public decision making for women, including matters dealing with property, marriage, and inheritance.

Impact of the Aryan Migrations

The encounter between the Aryans and the Harappans transformed religion in South Asia, although this did not occur immediately. South Asian religion appears to have been influenced by traditions that predated the Aryan invasion. Many of modern-day Hinduism's earliest gods are distinctly non-Aryan gods, such as Ganesh (the elephant god) and Hanuman (the monkey god). Ganesh, for example, may have originated from the totem of a particular family of Dravidian speakers who became important in the syncretic (where two or more traditions blend into a new practice) Aryan-Dravidian religion that developed into Hinduism.

As they did with political leadership, the Aryans initially limited the practice of religious rituals to themselves in the higher castes of the Brahman priests. However, intermarriage quickly merged the differentiation between Aryan and Dravidian beliefs except at the very lowest levels of society. The imported religious practices of the Aryans encountered those traditions of Harappa, blending them over the course of several hundred years into a religion that would form the basis of both Hinduism and Buddhism.

The Aryans were the primary influence on postmigration religious traditions in South Asia, but their own traditions were already syncretic, and the religions that emerged after their migration to the Indus River valley blended local traditions with their own polyglot beliefs. The Indo-Europeans came from an environment in which weather-related gods dominated religious life, such as the sky-god Dyaus (who became Zeus in Greek mythology). Similarly, the resemblance of Ahura Mazda, the fire spirit of Zoroastrianism (an early Persian religion), to the Vedic god Varuna indicates that the Indo-Europeans were influential in southwestern Asia as well.

In about 800 B.C.E., many people, including some Brahman priests, became dissatisfied with the routine animal sacrifice that the Aryans had earlier made the dominant expression of ritual in northern India and retreated into the forests to contemplate the meaning of spiritual truth. The arcane rules of sacrifice and the enormous cost of it no longer satisfied peoples' spiritual needs. For example, during this period, Siddhartha Gautama (c. 563–483 B.C.E.), well known as the "Buddha" (or "enlightened one"), undertook a spiritual quest that would eventually lead to the establishment of Buddhism. From this period of questioning, a whole new religious tradition arose based on a series of writings known as the Upanishads, the most important of which appeared between 800 and 400 B.C.E. (but which continued to emerge until 1500 C.E.). The central feature of the conclusions reached in the early Upanishads—the importance of reincarnation in peoples' spiritual lives—would gradually be brought into practice by the Brahman and become the basis of Hinduism. The Upanishads also suggested that the devoted could internalize sacrifice, making it a spiritual process rather than the physical one that the Vedic priests practiced. This made religion more personal and more accessible to the poor, who often had difficulty supporting the costs of Vedic Age ceremonies.

During this period of questioning, reincarnation became a central feature of religion. The Brahman essentially adopted (or revived) a Dravidian tradition. Prior to the Aryan invasion, the Dravidians had often worshipped spirits of nature and fertility and believed that sometimes peoples' spirits could depart one body and become associated with another. The endless cycle of death and reincarnation called *samsara*, which became central to canonical Hinduism, blended Dravidian elements (such as the possibility of reappearing in another form and "reassignment" to different kinds of life based on behavior in a previous life) with Aryan notions of an afterlife, such as their belief in the god Varuna, who judged the demised. Similarly, Buddhists adopted reincarnation into their doctrine.

The Dravidian notion of samsara also combined with the Aryans' caste system, the Varna, which ensured that members of the lower castes obeyed social restrictions to avoid accumulating *karma* (influence of an individual's actions on future lives), which might contribute to a difficult time in the next life or lead to their reincarnation as an animal or plant. Virtuous individuals who lived an ascetic life might reappear in a higher Varna upon reincarnation; those who led a perfect life, free of physical desire, might achieve *moksha*, a dreamless sleep associated with oneness with Brahman. Thus, adhering to the caste system introduced by the Aryans became a religious obligation to the people of South Asia.

The Aryan invasion also had a profound influence on language. Sanskrit, the sacred spoken language of the Aryans, became in its written form important to the religions of South Asia and Southeast Asia as it accompanied the spread of Hinduism. It forms the basis of modern written Thai, for example. Likewise, Prakrit, the common language of the Aryans, developed into Hindi, Bengali, and Urdu, the spoken languages of northern India. Hindi and Bengali eventually used the written alphabet developed for Sanskrit to portray their Prakrit-based languages.

By 500 B.C.E., the blended culture of the Aryans had been established across northern and central India, settling the first small cities of South Asia since the collapse of the cities of Harappa more than a thousand years earlier. By this time, Aryan and Dravidian societies had thoroughly combined with one another. The end of the Vedic Age in 500 B.C.E. coincided with the emergence of Hinduism as a religious system and a social structure. As a religious system, it melded Aryan institutional structures and rituals with Dravidian concerns with nature and the spirit. As a social structure, it combined the strict social hierarchy of the Aryans with the religious connotations of progress toward moksha, which Hinduism came to emphasize. Together with the Buddhist-influenced emphasis on personal salvation that emerged in the fourth century B.C.E., Hinduism synthesized South Asian spiritual practices into a single form.

See Also

VOLUME ONE: Eurasian Trade and Migration; The Silk Roads

Bibliography

Allchin, Bridget, and Raymond Allchin. *The Rise of Civilization in India and Pakistan.* Cambridge: Cambridge University Press, 1982.

Bentley, Jerry H. *Old World Encounters: Cross-Cultural Contacts and Exchanges in Pre-Modern Times.* New York: Oxford University Press, 1993.

Bryant, Edwin. *The Quest for the Origins of Vedic Culture: The Indo-Aryan Migration Debate.* New York: Oxford University Press, 2001.

Fairservis, Walter A. *The Roots of Ancient India.* 2nd ed. Chicago: University of Chicago Press, 1975.

Ratnagar, Shereen. *Encounters: The Westerly Trade of the Harappa Civilization.* Delhi: Oxford University Press, 1981.

———. *Understanding Harappa: Civilization in the Greater Indus Valley.* New Delhi: Tulika, 2001.

Roy, S. B. *Early Aryans of India, 3100–1400 B.C.* New Delhi: Navrang, 1989.

—*David W. Del Testa*

Primary Document

"Who Is Indra?" from the Rig Veda

Composed in about 1500 B.C.E., the Rig Veda includes songs, poems, and prose considered sacred to the Aryans. In this selection, the poem "Who Is Indra?" honors Indra, a boisterous and violent god of weather of the Aryans. It probably was passed orally among generations for centuries before appearing in print. Indra represents the Aryan people and their boastful celebration over successfully defeating the Dravidian-speaking people of South Asia.

The god who had insight the moment he was born, the first who protected the gods with his power of thought, before whose hot breath the two world-halves tremble at the greatness of his manly powers—he, my people, is Indra.

He who made fast the tottering earth, who made still the quaking mountains, who measured out and extended the expanse of the air, who propped up the sky—he, my people, is Indra.

He who killed the serpent and loosed the seven rivers, who drove out the cows that had been pent up by Vala, who gave birth to fire between two stones, the winner of booty in combats—he, my people, is Indra.

He by whom all these changes were rung, who drove the race of Dasas down into obscurity, who took away the flourishing wealth of the enemy as a winning gambler takes the stake—he, my people, is Indra.

He about whom they ask, "Where is he?," or they say of him, the terrible one, "He does not exist," he who diminishes the flourishing wealth of the enemy as a gambler does—believe in him! He, my people, is Indra.

He who encourages the weary and the sick, and the poor priest who is in need, who helps the man who harnesses the stones to press Soma, he who has lips fine for drinking—he, my people, is Indra.

He under whose command are horses and cows and villages and all chariots, who gave birth to the sun and the dawn and led out the waters, he, my people, is Indra.

He who is invoked by both of two armies, enemies locked in combat, on this side and that side, he who is even invoked separately by each of two men standing on the very same chariot, he, my people, is Indra.

He without whom people do not conquer, he whom they call on for help when they are fighting, who became the image of everything, who shakes the unshakeable—he, my people, is Indra.

He who killed with his weapon all those who had committed a great sin, even when they did not know it, he who does not pardon the arrogant man for his arrogance, who is the slayer of the Dasyus, he, my people, is Indra.

He who in the fortieth autumn discovered Sambara living in the mountains, who killed the violent serpent, the Danu, as he lay there, he, my people, is Indra.

He, the mighty bull who with his seven reins let loose the seven rivers to flow, who with his thunderbolt in his hand hurled down Rauhina as he was climbing up to the sky, he, my people, is Indra.

Even the sky and the earth bow low before him, and the mountains are terrified of his hot breath; he who is known as the Soma-drinker, with his thunderbolt in his hand, with the thunderbolt in his palm, he, my people, is Indra.

He who helps with his favor the one who presses and the one who cooks, the praiser and the preparer, he for whom prayer is nourishment, for whom Soma is the special gift, he, my people, is Indra.

You who furiously grasp the prize for the one who presses and the one who cooks, you are truly real. Let us be dear to you, Indra, all our days, and let us speak as men of power in the sacrificial gathering.

Source: Alfred J. Andrea and James H. Overfield, *The Human Record: Sources of Global History*, 4th ed. (Boston: Houghton Mifflin, 2001).

Olmec Influence in Mesoamerica

1250 B.C.E.–300 C.E.

Tlachtli (t'latch-lee) is a ritualized ball game that first appeared sometime before 400 B.C.E. among the Olmec peoples at La Venta, a prominent Olmec city, on the southeastern Gulf coast of Mexico. (*Tlachtli* is the Aztec word for the game because scholars do not know what the Olmec called it.) In early Olmec times, the goal of the game was to use elbows, knees, or hips to knock a rubber ball into the opposing team's court. The game had strong religious overtones and was often quite violent. In tlachtli, the I-shaped court represented the universe, the players were the gods, and the ball was either the sun, moon, or stars. Subsequent cultures of the Olmec peoples altered the purpose of the game to knocking the ball through a stone ring. Like other Olmec practices, tlachtli

Monumental Olmec head brought from the ruins of La Venta to Villahermosa, Tabasco, in southeastern Mexico. (© Danny Lehman/Corbis)

9000–7000 B.C.E.	2500	1500–900	c. 1250	900–300
Earliest agriculture is practiced in Mesoamerica	Maize, beans, and squash are farmed in Mesoamerica	Early Formative Period in Mesoamerica	Olmec center at San Lorenzo is established	Middle Formative Period in Mesoamerica

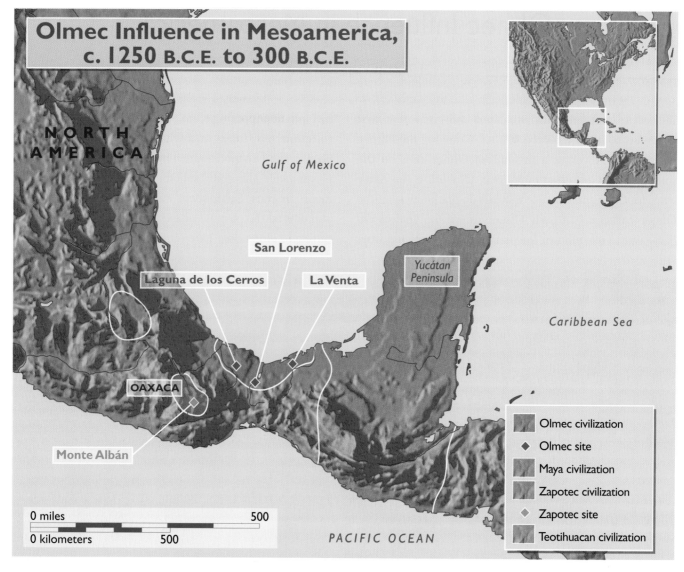

Olmec Influence in Mesoamerica, c. 1250 B.C.E. to 300 B.C.E.

NORTH AMERICA

Gulf of Mexico

San Lorenzo

Laguna de los Cerros

La Venta

Yucátan Peninsula

Caribbean Sea

OAXACA

Monte Albán

0 miles 500

0 kilometers 500

PACIFIC OCEAN

Olmec civilization
◆ Olmec site
Maya civilization
Zapotec civilization
◆ Zapotec site
Teotihuacan civilization

In about 1500 B.C.E., the Olmec became the first civilization to evolve in Mesoamerica, emerging eventually at San Lorenzo, Laguna de los Cerros, and La Venta. The Olmec gained control over the trade and administration of much of Mesoamerica between 900 and 300 B.C.E., but would be challenged by more sophisticated civilizations—including the Zapotec, the Maya, and the Teotihuacan—and disappear as a distinct culture by 300 C.E.

Sources: Some data compiled from Brian M. Fagan, *People of the Earth: An Introduction to World Prehistory*, 10th ed. (Upper Saddle River, N.J.: Prentice Hall, 2001), 534; and John Haywood, *The Complete Atlas of World History* (New York: Michael Friedman Publishing Group, 2000).

became and endured as an essential sign of civilization and community in Mesoamerica (the parts of southern North America that were occupied by advanced civilizations during pre-Columbian times). It is theorized that the Hohokam people of southern Arizona adopted and played tlachtli from about 600 to 700 C.E. The Hohokam continued to play it until their sudden disappearance in the thirteenth century, and the game endured in

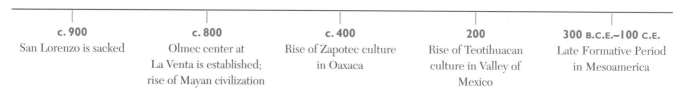

c. 900	c. 800	c. 400	200	300 B.C.E.–100 C.E.
San Lorenzo is sacked	Olmec center at La Venta is established; rise of Mayan civilization	Rise of Zapotec culture in Oaxaca	Rise of Teotihuacan culture in Valley of Mexico	Late Formative Period in Mesoamerica

successive cultures and in the rest of Mesoamerica until the Spanish conquered the region beginning in 1519.

Tlachtli is one of the great markers of the Olmec culture that indicates how, in the context of a highly ritualized event that probably took place at a very specific date on the Olmec calendar, it placed man in a symbolic struggle replicating the cycle of life, death, and rebirth. The spread of tlachtli also indicates that the Olmec inspired cultural practices and a cosmology in a wide variety of peoples who found them flexible enough to adapt to their own needs for almost two thousand years. This exchange proves that cultural contact occurred within Mesoamerica, as well as between Mesoamerica and the cultures of the American Southwest. The peoples of Mesoamerica who adopted Olmec culture were not united politically into one Olmec state, and while the Olmec are addressed here as a monolithic civilization influencing others, they themselves lived in a period of rapid cultural change throughout the region, in which other peoples certainly influenced them. Yet once Olmec culture developed its standard features—monument building, calendars, writing, and ritual practices—it became the foundation on which many subsequent Mesoamerican cultures were built.

The Evolution of Olmec Civilization

Most historical knowledge about the Olmec rests on a great deal of speculation and inference because scholars have relatively little material on which to base their theories. Due to the tropical climate in which the Olmec peoples lived, most material goods deteriorated very quickly unless made of stone or metal or buried in a site that encouraged preservation. Additionally, the age of many of the sites—the early Olmec center at San Lorenzo (on the southeastern Gulf coast of Mexico) dates back to perhaps 1250 B.C.E.—and the ravages of tomb raiders, natural calamities, and various pests have made gathering information about the Olmec even more difficult. Fortunately, modern archeology and date-testing methods as well as continued discoveries of new Olmec sites add credible knowledge to what scholars have already surmised.

In order to understand the Olmec, one must understand the environment and societies from which they evolved. The Olmec appear to have suddenly developed the traits of a civilization, such as cities, administration, and hierarchy, out of a disparate collection of societies not yet necessarily predisposed to such organization. Wild and unsubstantiated theories based on circumstantial evidence have arisen about their abrupt transformation, which might best be described as "radical cross-cultural contact theory." The most popular theories suggest that the Olmec had occasional interactions with the Zapotec, a native group from Oaxaca, because of the Olmec use of glyphs (symbols that convey information nonverbally) for writing and that they had transoceanic contact with the Egyptians because of the Olmec use of step "pyramids." Another theory suggests that, as with many of the early civilizations (Mesopotamia and India in particular), climatic change encouraged various peoples to organize around one or a small group of peoples who showed a predilection for mass social organization and the development of material culture.

Archeologists and anthropologists believe that settled agriculture began in the Americas sometime around 9000 to 7000 B.C.E. with the development of small gardens just outside people's houses that supplemented their take from hunting and gathering activities. Apparently occurring first in Panama or Guatemala, which had temperate climates, this approach to agriculture developed as an innovation rather than as a learned technique. (Elsewhere, knowledge of agriculture, which had originated in Mesopotamia, was transferred through cultural exchanges.) The inducement to grow food may have resulted from living in a natural environment that could no longer support the hunting and gathering that dominated other societies in the Americas. The environment may have become degraded through overpopulation, since Central America's small area could not support a significant hunter-gatherer population. The climate, changing globally at this point in time, may also have left the local peoples with declining food supplies, a situation that demanded urgent innovations. Indeed, it is

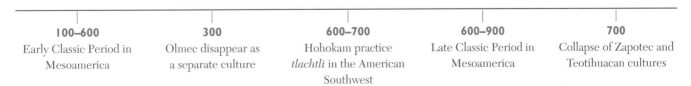

100–600	300	600–700	600–900	700
Early Classic Period in Mesoamerica	Olmec disappear as a separate culture	Hohokam practice *tlachtli* in the American Southwest	Late Classic Period in Mesoamerica	Collapse of Zapotec and Teotihuacan cultures

known that global warming caused thick jungle to overtake the grassland (along with its vast herds of grazing animals) that had dominated Mesoamerica and provided its peoples with much of their food.

Slowly, between 9000 and 1500 B.C.E., crop variety improved and agriculture spread, with the triad of maize, beans, and squash as the staples of the Mesoamerican land by 2500 B.C.E. Early Mesoamericans also cultivated chili peppers, manioc (a plant whose roots were used to make a kind of bread), sunflower seeds, avocados, and nuts, and grew cotton for its fiber. Unlike other societies in the world, those in the Americas did not rely heavily on the domestication of animals; they only raised dogs, turkeys, and bees (for honey). They relied much more heavily on vegetable matter for their protein. Curiously, one foreign crop, a kind of gourd useful for making containers, did wash up on the shores of Central America from Africa and become an important part of early American agriculture. Agricultural innovation and intensification produced three consequences among the population of Mesoamerica. First, population pressures encouraged peoples in the lowland areas of central and southern Mexico to settle the relatively empty highlands. Second, agriculture produced a sufficient surplus to permit lowland peoples to engage in activities other than food production. Third, the growing population created the need for leadership groups to control human resources in exchange for the provision of subsistence.

Scholars can verify that the Olmec were the first civilization to evolve in Mesoamerica and that what they designate as Olmec civilization began approximately around 1500 B.C.E. In what scholars call the Early Formative Period (1500–900 B.C.E.), groups of people in the Yucatán and Tabasco areas of modern Mexico organized themselves into loosely affiliated, occasionally hostile, city-states. These city-states brought territory under direct administration or under a system of vassalage (a condition in which one people swears loyalty and pays tribute to another). City populations remained small throughout the entire Olmec-dominated period—perhaps

2,500 permanent as well as many more transient residents in the cities—with most of the population living in dispersed villages responsible to a central governing body located at a religious center. The Olmec based their strength on a unified culture, superior military technology and organization, and dominance in trade of vital lowland products to the highlands of southern Mexico. Some archeologists and anthropologists postulate that the Olmec of the Early Formative Period may have evolved from clans who had been willing to accept the responsibility of performing rituals. Along with certain agricultural conditions, this monopolization of ritual eventually implied leadership and sparked sufficient creativity for a civilization. Other scholars argue that competition for rich, alluvial lands encouraged the growth of a military class of Olmec landowners who could manipulate excess resources for state and temple building.

In this period of civilization formation among the Olmec, certain essential features of Mesoamerica became standardized throughout the "civilized" areas and differentiated the Olmec civilization from earlier societies:

- a strong leader who was responsible for religious and political leadership and who gained loyalty through the redistribution of tribute (gifts or taxes) he received from his own and other peoples;
- city-centered civilization;
- organized, priest-centered religions and ritual games, such as tlachtli;
- intensification of agricultural production, manifested by the Olmec in complex stone and earth canal and drainage systems and raised fields;
- massive construction projects for defensive or ritual purposes; and
- late in Olmec civilization, a form of writing based on symbolic glyphs.

Sometimes one particular family or clan dominated politics, but at other times, power became quite diffuse among many city-states. These cultural traits and social organization would quickly spread throughout lowland Mesoamerica.

900	1200	c. 1325	1519	1521	1530
Rise of Toltec civilization	Fall of Toltec civilization	Rise of Aztec civilization	Beginning of conquest of Mesoamerica by Spanish	Collapse of Aztec civilization	Collapse of Mayan civilization

Trade and Cultural Exchange in Mesoamerica

The earliest known Olmec site was at San Lorenzo. An agricultural, trade, and religious center, it consisted of a compact plateau rising above fertile coastal lowlands onto which the Olmec built, at great effort, a manmade earthen platform to support altars, ball courts, enormous carvings, and some housing. Some of the carvings weighed up to 44 tons and would have required incredible social organization to transport the raw stone from its quarry some 50 miles to the west. Among these carvings, gigantic sculpted heads are the most remarkable in their size and careful detail, and they may represent, because of the helmets they wear, sacred tlachtli players. Although many kinds of carvings existed, common images include the were-jaguar (half-man, half-jaguar) and a thick-lipped man whose features resemble a baby. These carvings and sculptures often represented leaders, ritual practices, or supernatural half-man/half-animal creatures popular in the Olmec system of deities. The appearance of these monuments, sculptures, and raised farming fields indicates that, in contrast to its neighbors, the leadership of San Lorenzo must have found a way to organize society to produce extensive surpluses, engage in widespread trade, and dedicate many of its citizens to worship and edification.

Around 900 B.C.E., at the beginning of the Middle Formative Period, San Lorenzo and the rest of Olmec civilization weakened temporarily for unknown reasons. There is evidence that outsiders, perhaps angry trading partners, sacked and badly damaged San Lorenzo. The Olmec reoccupied the site three hundred years later, in about 600 B.C.E., but by then the civilization had changed in subtle ways, and power had relocated. Another Early Formative Olmec site, Laguna de los Cerros in present-day Veracruz, Mexico, has a similar history but was probably independent of the leadership of San Lorenzo.

Scholars believe that during the Middle Formative Period (900–300 B.C.E.), because of overpopulation the Olmec cities monopolized certain aspects of life—probably either ritual or food distribution—in order to assert social and political control over subject peoples. At this time, Olmec colonies spread along trade routes into the mountains of Oaxaca and into Guatemala. Archeologists

Cross-Cultural Exchange

↔ Massive exchange of trade goods (jade, iron ore mirrors, feathers, salt, honey) from central Mexico to Guatemala

↔ Development of civilization based on cities, administration, political and social hierarchies, advanced agricultural production, and organized religions across Mesoamerica

↔ Spread of culturally similar rituals in increasingly diverse forms and adaptations across much of the American Southwest, Mexico, and Central America

↔ Common artistic motifs, such as rounded glyphs representing animals, humans, and monsters, influence subsequent Mesoamerican cultures, such as the Maya

believe that for the early Olmec to expand their control beyond the lowlands, they gained power through, and based their surplus-generating economy on, the trade of salt as well as on a less important but almost equally desirable product, honey, produced by domesticated bees. In this way, the early Olmec could receive products important to their rituals (e.g., feathers, certain kinds of stone, such as serpentine and jade, and polished slabs of iron ore that acted as mirrors) as well as surplus food. Where they could not assure trade, or where trade items were too precious or too hotly coveted, the Olmec seem to have engaged in direct conquest and administration.

The Middle Formative Period is characterized by the growing significance of the Olmec over a wider area, the regionalization of their culture, and the increasing cultural complexity of Mesoamerica. The Olmec city of La Venta, which became important after 800 B.C.E., differs from San Lorenzo in that it displayed true urbanization rather than San Lorenzo's mainly sacred and commercial purposes. While La Venta also had elaborate ritual structures, such as massive pyramids, and served as an important center of long-distance trade, the trade that took place there occurred on a far larger scale than at San Lorenzo, as evidenced by the presence of types of jade only available in the farthest reaches of Central America. As a result of this trade and a tendency on the part of the Olmec toward lavish gift giving, Olmec culture spread far beyond its cultural core in the Yucatán, Tabasco, and the southeastern coastal mountains to as far south as El Salvador and as far north as present-day Mexico City. It appears as if the Olmec engaged in active colonization during this period in order to secure supplies of scarce precious resources, especially stone. At this point, the Olmec developed a very early version of the standard Mesoamerican calendars (sacred year, secular year, and Long Count calendars), religious hieroglyphs, and perhaps a few secular glyphs.

Between the Late Formative Period (300 B.C.E.–100 C.E) and the Early and Late Classic periods (100–900 C.E), more sophisticated groups, who based their cultures on the Olmec, overwhelmed and absorbed the Olmec. Beginning in 400 B.C.E. and enduring until 700 C.E., the Zapotec civilization arose at Monte Albán in Oaxaca, using Olmec cultural forms as well as improving the Olmec calendar and glyph-based writing system. Other groups, including the Maya of the Yucatán from 800 B.C.E. to 1530 C.E. and the Teotihuacan of central Mexico from 200 B.C.E. to 700 C.E, developed into separate polities, sometimes in competition with one another and often intensively linked to one another through trade. Although certainly challenged by the presence of culturally sophisticated competitors, Olmec culture and the Olmec polities endured, especially in the Yucatán and in the Valley of Mexico, on the northern fringe of what had been the Olmec culture zone. By 300 C.E, however, the signs of Olmec cultural leadership had completely disappeared. Hereafter, invaders from northern Mexico and the culturally distinct Maya peoples began to dominate Mesoamerican politics while absorbing elements of Olmec culture that were useful to them, such as calendars and ritual games..

The Olmec Provide the Foundation for Mesoamerican Civilization

Although the Olmec probably did not intentionally facilitate any extraordinary cross-cultural contact, they provided the social, cultural, economic, and political language to underwrite two millennia of trade and exchange between the peoples of Mesoamerica and beyond. The structures, symbols, and styles, as well as the beliefs, ideas about cosmic order, and political hierarchy that began with the Olmec and continued after their demise was selectively adapted by and evolved under the subsequent Maya and Toltec

(900–1200 C.E.) and Aztec (c. 1325–1521 C.E.) of central Mexico, as well as groups such as the Hohokam and Anasazi in the American Southwest. In particular, early Olmec efforts at writing blossomed into a rich written tradition among the two great successor states, the Maya and Zapotec.

In an environment in which three larger and several smaller language groups dominated the hundreds of local societies, Olmec cultural forms and social organization provided the elements that united peoples and created the foundation on which many subsequent Mesoamerican civilizations could be built. This included the kinds of gods worshipped (12 or so gods linked to important aspects of the climate, subsistence, and nature) and the motifs through which Mesoamericans represented themselves and their beliefs. Although the Olmec certainly imposed their culture on other peoples, as during the colonization efforts of the Middle Formative Period, Olmec culture probably also attracted many adherents on its own. To aspirant leadership groups, Olmec culture provided a template by which to gain prestige and social and political control of peoples. For potential trading partners, elevating Olmec cultural forms put traders on an equal basis, and gave them a common cultural vocabulary, with Olmec traders eager for local products. For groups concerned with neither trade nor leadership, Olmec culture might have offered inclusion in ritual circles whose power seemed evident in the wealth and influence of the Olmec. With the exception of indigenous groups in the northwest of Mexico who consistently resisted outside influences, all of Mexico had adapted the remnants of Olmec culture by the Classic Period.

The Hohokam peoples of the American Southwest represent one particularly interesting example of Olmec influence, if not direct exchange. Archeologists and anthropologists wonder if the Hohokam *kivas*—round, partially buried assembly halls used for ritual purposes—had precedence in Olmec religious structures, particularly the subterranean portions of these structures. Likewise, the Hohokam adopted tlachtli. Although Hohokam religious practices do not resemble that of the Olmec, and the Hohokam did not adopt writing, they do appear to have borrowed cultural features from the Olmec that suited their belief system and in turn communicated these features throughout the western United States. For instance, the Hohokam heavily influenced two subsequent Native American groups, the Anasazi and Pueblo. Although the Hohokam played tlachtli long after the dissolution of the Olmec civilization into replacement groups, such as the Maya, the game suggests how large the scale of trade in Mesoamerica was at the end of the Late Formative and Early Classic periods. Traders on foot would have had to carry the rubber balls used in the game for more than 1,000 miles of rough terrain to reach the Hohokam in the American Southwest.

Olmec traditions became the basic material that subsequent cultures borrowed for their own needs, but with the arrival of the conquering Spaniards, the Olmec legacy ended as an active cultural force. Unlike such invaders as the Toltec and Aztec or such neighboring cultures as the Maya, who all adapted and modified elements of the ancient Olmec symbols and their derivatives, the Spaniards worked hard to destroy vestiges of the past. The Olmec cultural symbols, however, illustrate a vital road map that reveals the vibrant and developed cultures and peoples that existed in Mesoamerica before the appearance of Europeans.

See Also

VOLUME THREE: Christopher Columbus and the Columbian Exchange; The Spanish Empire and the Civilizations of Mexico

Bibliography

Davies, Nigel. *The Toltec Heritage: From the Fall of the Tula to the Rise of Tenochtitlan.* Norman: University of Oklahoma Press, 1980.

Frazier, Kendrick. *People of Chaco: A Canyon and Its Culture.* New York: W. W. Norton, 1999.

Lekson, Stephen H. *The Chaco Meridian: Centers of Political Power in the Ancient Southwest.* Walnut Creek, Calif.: AltaMira Press, 1999.

Marcus, Joyce, and Kent V. Flannery. *Zapotec Civilization.* New York: Thames & Hudson, 1996.

Molitor, Martha. *The Hohokam-Toltec Connection: A Study in Culture Diffusion.* Occasional Publications in Anthropology, Archeology Series, vol. 10. Greeley: Museum of Anthropology, University of Northern Colorado, 1981.

Scarborough, Vernon L., and David R. Wilcox, eds. *The Mesoamerican Ballgame.* Tucson: University of Arizona Press, 1991.

Soustelle, Jacques. *The Olmecs: The Oldest Civilization in Mexico.* Translated by Helen R. Lane. Garden City, N.Y.: Doubleday, 1984.

—*David W. Del Testa*

Primary Document
Mayan Ball Game Marker

This Mayan ball game marker (590 C.E.) was used for tlachtli, *a ritualized game invented by the Olmec peoples of southeastern Mexico. The Mayan civilization succeeded the Olmec after its collapse in 300 C.E. and would adopt and modify many of the Olmec's cultural practices, such as* tlachtli. *The adoption of the game by other Mesoamerican civilizations, such as the Maya, indicates the extensive trade networks throughout the region.*

Source: © Danny Lehman/Corbis.

Jerusalem and the Rise of
the World's Monotheistic Civilizations

C. 950 B.C.E.–700 C.E.

The queen was weary from her travels. So she felt relief when, from the shaded recesses of a gilded carriage, she glimpsed the rugged, densely populated hill rising from the desert in the distance. Her attendants confirmed that this was indeed Mount Zion, the most prominent landmark of the city called Jerusalem. The long royal caravan at whose head she sat had finally reached its destination. It had journeyed overland from Sheba, a kingdom located on the distant southwestern coast of Arabia (present-day Yemen). Its people, the Sabeans, were some of the wealthiest and most powerful in the ancient Middle East. Recently, however, they had received strange reports of a new people rising in the north. Known as the Israelites (or Jews), this people was described by traveling merchants as equal to the Sabeans in wealth and power. They had conquered the ancient Semitic city of Jerusalem, which dated from around

This nineteenth-century Ethiopian painting shows the Queen of Sheba presenting gifts, including gold, ivory, and a lion, to King Solomon. (The Art Archive/Private Collection/Dagli Orti)

c. 3000 B.C.E.	c. 1000	c. 950	c. 900	c. 722
Jerusalem is settled by Semites	Jerusalem is conquered by King David of Israel	Queen of Sheba travels to Jerusalem	Cult of Baal spreads under the influence of Jezebel	Northern kingdom is conquered by the Assyrians

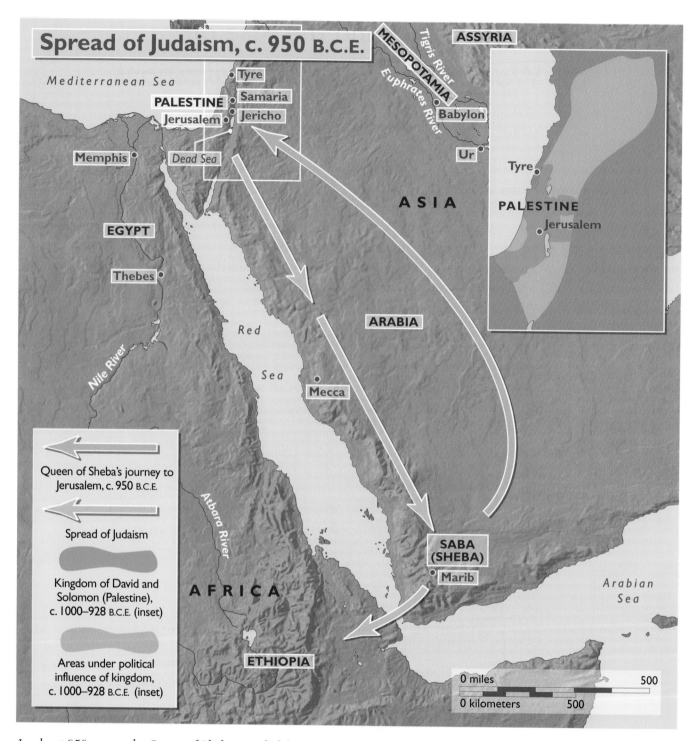

Spread of Judaism, c. 950 B.C.E.

Mediterranean Sea

ASSYRIA

MESOPOTAMIA

Tigris River

Euphrates River

PALESTINE
Tyre
Samaria
Jericho
Jerusalem

Babylon

Ur

Dead Sea

ASIA

Memphis

EGYPT

Thebes

Red

Sea

ARABIA

Mecca

Nile River

Tyre

PALESTINE

Jerusalem

Legend:

Queen of Sheba's journey to Jerusalem, c. 950 B.C.E.

Spread of Judaism

Kingdom of David and Solomon (Palestine), c. 1000–928 B.C.E. (inset)

Areas under political influence of kingdom, c. 1000–928 B.C.E. (inset)

Atbara River

AFRICA

SABA (SHEBA)

Marib

Arabian Sea

ETHIOPIA

0 miles   500

0 kilometers   500

In about 950 B.C.E., the Queen of Sheba traveled from the southwestern coast of Arabia to Jerusalem to meet with King Solomon and the Israelites. This encounter initiated the spread of Judaism across Arabia and then across the Red Sea to Africa.

Source: Some data compiled from John Haywood, Historical Atlas of the Ancient World: 4,000,000–500 B.C. (New York: MetroBooks, 2001), 1:14.

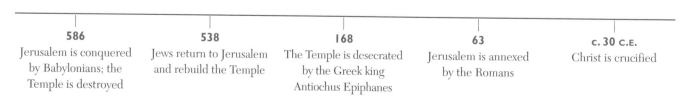

586	538	168	63	c. 30 C.E.
Jerusalem is conquered by Babylonians; the Temple is destroyed	Jews return to Jerusalem and rebuild the Temple	The Temple is desecrated by the Greek king Antiochus Epiphanes	Jerusalem is annexed by the Romans	Christ is crucified

3000 B.C.E., and had made it their capital. What was most astonishing, however, were reports that they worshipped only one god, to whom the magnificent Temple had been built by their king on Mount Zion. The Queen of Sheba had traveled some 1,500 miles to investigate these reports and to meet the famous King Solomon.

This encounter took place in about 950 B.C.E. and was one of the earliest recorded exchanges (appearing in the Bible) between two great civilizations in world history. It appears to have made a deep impression upon them both. For the Queen of Sheba, Jerusalem turned out to be as glorious as its reputation. It was ruled by a king whose extraordinary wisdom was matched only by the immense prosperity of his people. With great interest she examined the Temple's lavish construction and observed the majestic ceremonies that took place within it. The queen asked for and received painstaking instruction about the God of Israel from Solomon. So impressed was she by this experience that before departing she lavished gold, gems, and spices upon the king. The Israelites were also impressed by the encounter. For King Solomon, the queen's largesse helped to confirm the preeminence of his kingdom within the region. Even more significant was the honor she paid to the Jerusalem Temple and to the god to which it was dedicated. Whatever the queen's response to the religion might have been, her interest in it reminded the Israelites of their unique status as the world's only monotheistic (single deity) civilization. This, perhaps, was the most important result of the encounter.

Polytheism and the Rise of Jewish Monotheism

To understand the importance of this encounter, it is necessary to consider the character of Israelite civilization and the civilizations that surrounded it in the early first millennium B.C.E. Throughout the world, people were highly religious, at least by modern standards. As a result, all civilizations manifested a belief in the existence of spiritual powers, and in many cases, the immortality of the soul. Before the rise of Israel, this belief was expressed only by polytheism, the worship of multiple deities. From the

Olmec in Central America to the Bantu in Africa and the Aryans in Asia, people believed that many gods existed, that these gods were responsible for the order of the universe, and that the personal and corporate salvation of humanity was ultimately in their hands. This was true also in the Middle East. The Sabeans of Arabia, for instance, associated some of their gods with celestial objects. One of the most important such deities was a god of the moon, to whom they dedicated a temple at their capital city of Marib. In Mesopotamia, a god of the moon was also venerated at a temple in the city of Ur, while a cult of a god named Marduk flourished at the great ziggurat in the city of Babylon. Closer to the Israelites, a god of the sun known as Baal was the object of numerous cults in Canaanite (Phoenician) cities such as Tyre.

By the time the Israelites arrived in Palestine (present-day Israel, Gaza, and the West Bank) in the late second millennium, however, a unique religion had already begun to take shape among them. One of the earliest episodes in its development centered upon the Hebrew patriarch Abraham, who had been called out of the polytheistic city of Ur by the one God of the Israelites to settle in Palestine. Abraham nearly offered his son Isaac as a sacrifice on Mount Moriah (possibly conflated with Mount Zion) before an angel of this god intervened to stop him. Through this test of faith, Abraham proved his commitment to God, who in return blessed Abraham and his people, the Israelites. Abraham's descendants were later enslaved by the Egyptians, and during their exodus from Egypt, God delivered to the Prophet Moses the written core of Judaism known as the Torah (law). It included an exclusive faith in God; the moral teaching known as the Ten Commandments; and the conviction that they, the Jews, had been chosen by God from among all pagan peoples, known as the Gentiles, to bring salvation to the world. Soon after Moses' death, the Israelites conquered the Canaanite city of Jericho in Palestine, and, in about 1000 B.C.E., they conquered Jerusalem under the leadership of King David. Solomon was David's son, and his construction of the Temple in Jerusalem represented the consolidation of the world's first monotheistic civilization.

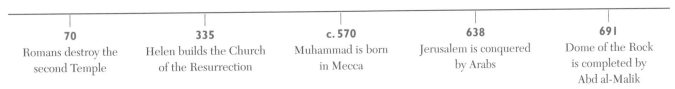

70	335	c. 570	638	691
Romans destroy the second Temple	Helen builds the Church of the Resurrection	Muhammad is born in Mecca	Jerusalem is conquered by Arabs	Dome of the Rock is completed by Abd al-Malik

Exchanges between the Israelites and Their Neighbors

Moses had warned the Israelites against relations with the Gentiles, but soon after their arrival in Palestine several forces produced contacts and exchanges, such as the visit of the Queen of Sheba. The first was political. As a powerful state in the Middle East, Israel soon earned the respect of its neighbors. King Solomon took an Egyptian princess as a wife and formed an alliance with the powerful King Hiram of Tyre (r. 969–936 B.C.E.). Economic relations also brought about exchange. Solomon's vast building projects, which were not limited to the Temple, demanded considerable quantities of lumber and gold. Many of these materials he obtained through Hiram, whose kingdom dominated commerce along the eastern coast of the Mediterranean. Solomon also obtained precious goods from Sheba. The Sabeans were famous throughout the Middle East for their spices and incense, some of which came ultimately from India. They maintained an especially vital trade with the Assyrians, for instance, whose kings left inscriptions praising the wealth of Sheba and the caravans of camels that regularly traveled to Babylon. Finally, religious exchanges grew out of the proximity of Israel to surrounding civilizations. While the Sabeans left behind no written record of their history, their encounters with Jerusalem inevitably resulted in knowledge about the unique religion of the Israelites. Legends later arose claiming that the Queen of Sheba or some other agent had brought Judaism to Arabia, and that from there, it spread across the Red Sea to Africa. By the end of the millennium, there were Jews not only in Arabia, but in Ethiopia as well. For the Israelites of Palestine, however, such political, economic, and religious exchanges were a mixed blessing that would overshadow their history for centuries to come.

Solomon seemed to fulfill Moses' prophecy about the perils of cross-cultural exchange. Having established contacts with surrounding peoples through intermarriage and trade, he soon violated the Torah's commandment against worshipping Gentile gods. He is said to have modeled a temple in Jerusalem on a Canaanite temple built to honor Baal. The division of the Israelite kingdom that followed his death was thus interpreted as an act of chastisement by God. A southern kingdom called Judah (which retained Jerusalem) and a northern kingdom called Israel (centered upon the city of Samaria) arose, and the irrepressible tendency toward religious intermingling continued. It became most extravagant under the influence of a pagan Canaanite princess named Jezebel, who married King Ahab of Israel in around 900 B.C.E. She brought to her marriage a devotion to Baal, and soon the Gentile god was worshipped in much of the northern kingdom. Jezebel's daughter, Athaliah, thereafter seized the throne of the southern kingdom and introduced the pagan cult there. She even seems to have banned the worship of the Jewish God in the Jerusalem Temple. The influence of Jezebel and her daughter finally came to an end around 850 B.C.E., but the cult of Baal continued to challenge the exclusive worship of God. In 722 B.C.E., the northern kingdom was conquered by the Assyrians, leaving the southern kingdom as the last outpost of Judaism. King Josiah of Judah worked to reestablish and strengthen Judaism after acceding to the throne about 640 B.C.E., but in 586 B.C.E., the great city of Jerusalem was conquered by the Babylonians under Nebuchadnezzar II (r. 605–562 B.C.E.). The Temple was destroyed and the Jews were deported to Mesopotamia, to the city of the pagan god Marduk.

The Jews now found themselves living in a land of polytheists and forced, as a contemporary lamented, to amuse their captors with "the songs of Zion" (Psalms 137:3). Yet their adherence to monotheism seems to have been strengthened by this contact. The Babylonian Exile, as the experience came to be known, witnessed a resurgence of Jewish prophecy. The Prophet Isaiah, for instance, reassured the Israelites that they were indeed the chosen people of God. Furthermore, he asserted that this very God would make of them "a light to the Gentiles," from which the Messiah (or Christ in Greek) would come one day, bringing "salvation unto the end of the earth" (Isaiah 49:6). Jewish monotheism thus produced a belief in a universal salvation that would include, notably, "all they from Sheba" (Isaiah 60:6). For the first time in history, cross-cultural contact assumed a messianic importance.

When the Jews were allowed to return to Jerusalem in 538 B.C.E. by Persia's Cyrus the Great (r. 559–530 B.C.E.), who had conquered Babylon, they rebuilt the Temple and restored its worship, yet they continued to live under the shadow of surrounding Gentile kingdoms. In 168 B.C.E., the Greek king Antiochus Epiphanes (r. 175–164) seized the holy city, outraging its inhabitants by abolishing Jewish worship and establishing a cult of the Greek god Zeus in its place. This provoked the famous Maccabean Revolt, which brought the city back into the hands of the Israelites, but their victory was temporary. In 63 B.C.E. the Roman general Pompey (106–48 B.C.E.) annexed the city and the freedom of the Israelites ended. In 70 C.E., the Romans responded to yet another war of independence by once more destroying the Temple. The only section they left intact was a short section of the western wall, known to later generations of Jews as the Wailing Wall. Finally, in 135 C.E., the failure of the Jews to win the Bar Kochba Revolt resulted in their expulsion from Jerusalem altogether.

The Rise of Other Monotheistic Civilizations

Ironically, it was under polytheistic Roman rule that Jerusalem gave birth to a truly universal monotheism, Christianity. Jesus of Nazareth was born a Jew and taught his gospel (good news) in the Jerusalem Temple before he was crucified by the Roman authorities in about 30 C.E. Yet the Gospels, while quoting the Torah and the prophets abundantly, called upon Jews to fulfill their messianic calling as the chosen people of God by practicing love instead of legalism and by gathering all of humanity into a single community called the Church. After Jesus' death and reported resurrection from the dead, many Jews worshipped Jesus as the expected Messiah and began to disseminate the Gospel to "all nations" in the known world (Matthew 28:19). Paul was the most celebrated among these early apostles, replacing the ethnic exclusivity of Judaism with a doctrine that assured converts that "there is neither Jew nor Greek, there is neither bond nor free, there is neither male nor female, for ye all are one in Christ Jesus" (Galatians 3:28). With this message of universal equality before God, Christianity spread far beyond the boundaries of Palestine and became the religion of approximately one-tenth of the predominately polytheistic Roman Empire by the end of the third century. Then, after Emperor Constantine (r. 306–37)—who had inherited the territories of the Roman Empire—converted to Christianity in 312, it grew to become the dominant faith of Europe, from Ireland to Russia. Ruled by a Christian emperor, Jerusalem now became a Christian city. In about 335 Constantine's mother, Helen, traveled there on a pilgrimage, reputedly discovered the cross on which Christ had been crucified, and built a great church over the site. This Church of the Resurrection (also known as the Church of the Holy Sepulcher)

Cross-Cultural Exchange
↔ Gold, timber, incense, and spices traded between Jerusalem and Middle Eastern states, such as Sheba
↔ Dynastic ties formed between Israel and Middle Eastern states
↔ Monotheistic religions spread to Europe and Arabia

henceforth became the center of Christianity in the Middle East and a destination for pilgrims throughout the world.

Centuries after Jerusalem had become a center for Christian monotheism, it inspired a third religion, Islam. The founder, Muhammad, was born around 570 in the Arabian city of Mecca, halfway between Jerusalem and the ancient Sabean capital of Marib (where the temple of the moon god still functioned). He had grown disenchanted with the polytheism of his fellow Arabs and took an interest in the monotheism of Jews and Christians with whom he came into contact as a prosperous trader; he studied the Torah and the Gospel. After experiencing a mystical vision, he issued the doctrine of his new religion in the Koran. From among the many gods worshipped by the Arabs, he identified one called Allah as the one god of all humanity, including "Jews, Sabeans, and Christians" (Koran 5:69). To Muslims, followers of Islam, Muhammad is the last prophet, equal to Abraham, Moses, and Jesus. Muhammad was always drawn toward Jerusalem, which he referred to simply as the City of the Temple. Before he conquered Arabia and established his capital at Mecca in 630, he taught his followers to pray while facing in its direction. A legend even arose that before his death in 632 he was transported during a nocturnal reverie from Mecca to Mount Zion, where he was elevated temporarily into heaven. Thus when Muslim armies burst out of Arabia to conquer much of the Middle East during the seventh century, they were drawn irresistibly toward Jerusalem. In 638 the city fell to an Arab general and successor to Muhammad named Umar. He was taken to Mount Zion, where some sixteen hundred years earlier his fellow Arabian, the Queen of Sheba, had paid homage to Solomon's Temple. In 691, his successor, Caliph Abd al-Malik, completed the construction on this very site one of the most famous of all Muslim shrines, the Dome of the Rock.

Thus Jerusalem became a home to the three great monotheistic civilizations of the world, and as the centuries advanced, the holy city continued to be the object of strife among them. In 1099 it was conquered by a Roman

Catholic army during the first of the Crusades. For two centuries it changed hands between Europeans and Arabs, until it was annexed by the Ottoman Empire during the sixteenth century. After the creation of modern Israel in 1948, control of the city was contested by Arabs and Jews. Despite the continuation of these conflicts into the twenty-first century, the holy sites of Jerusalem still attract their monotheistic faithful from around the world.

See Also

VOLUME ONE: The Phoenician Trading Empire and the Spread of the Alphabet; The Greek Bronze Age: Minoan and Mycenaean Influence and Exchange; The Roman Empire and the Mediterranean World

VOLUME TWO: The Establishment and Spread of Islam; The Frankish Crusades and the Civilizations of the Eastern Mediterranean; The Ottoman Empire and European Civilization

Bibliography

Armstrong, Karen. *Jerusalem: One City, Three Faiths.* New York: Alfred A. Knopf, 1996.

Asali, Kamil J., ed. *Jerusalem in History.* 1st American ed. Brooklyn, N.Y.: Olive Branch Press, 2000.

Bevan, Edwyn R., and Charles Singer, eds. *The Legacy of Israel.* 1928. Reprint, Oxford: Clarendon Press, 1953.

Clapp, Nicholas. *Sheba: Through the Desert in Search of the Legendary Queen.* Boston: Houghton Mifflin, 2001.

Levine, Lee I., ed. *Jerusalem: Its Sanctity and Centrality to Judaism, Christianity, and Islam.* New York: Continuum, 1999.

Peters, F. E. *Jerusalem: The Holy City in the Eyes of Chroniclers, Visitors, Pilgrims, and Prophets from the Days of Abraham to the Beginnings of Modern Times.* Princeton: Princeton University Press, 1985.

Pfeiffer, Charles F. *Jerusalem through the Ages.* Grand Rapids, Mich.: Baker Book House, 1967.

—John Strickland

Primary Document
1 Kings 10:1–13 King James Version

During the illustrious reign of King Solomon, Israel's reputation as a great civilization in the Middle East extended to southern Arabia. In this passage from 1 Kings, the Queen of Sheba visits Jerusalem in about 950 B.C.E. to meet Solomon and to investigate the monotheistic religion practiced in the temple.

CHAPTER 10

1 AND when the queen of She-ba heard of the fame of Solomon concerning the name of the LORD, she came to prove him with hard questions.

2 And she came to Jerusalem with a very great train, with camels that bare spices, and very much gold, and precious stones: and when she was come to Solomon, she communed with him of all that was in her heart.

3 And Solomon told her all her questions: there was not *any* thing hid from the king, which he told her not.

4 And when the queen of She-ba had seen all Solomon's wisdom, and the house that he had built,

5 And the meat of his table, and the sitting of his servants, and the attendance of his ministers, and their apparel, and his cupbearers, and his ascent by which he went up unto the house of the LORD; there was no more spirit in her.

6 And she said to the king, It was a true report that I heard in mine own land of thy acts and of thy wisdom.

7 How best I believed not the words, until I came, and mine eyes had seen *it*: and, behold, the half was not told me: thy wisdom and prosperity exceedeth the fame which I heard.

8 Happy *are* thy men, happy *are* these thy servants, which stand continually before thee, *and* that hear thy wisdom.

9 Blessed be the LORD thy God, which delighted in thee, to set thee on the throne of Israel: because the LORD loved Israel for ever, therefore made he thee king, to do judgment and justice.

10 And she gave the king an hundred and twenty talents of gold, and of spices very great store, and precious stones: there came no more such abundance of spices as these which the queen of She-ba gave to king Solomon.

11 And the navy also of Hiram, that brought gold from O-phir, brought in from O-phir great plenty of al-mug trees, and precious stones.

12 And the king made of the al-mug trees pillars for the house of the LORD, and for the king's house, harps also and psalteries for singers: there came no such al-mug trees, nor were seen unto this day.

13 And king Solomon gave unto the queen of She-ba all her desire, whatsoever she asked, beside *that* which Solomon gave her of his royal bounty. So she turned and went to her own country, she and her servants.

Source: Excerpted from 1 Kings 10:1–13 King James Version.

Chavín Culture in Pre-Columbian Peru

900–200 B.C.E.

Around 900 B.C.E., in the numerous coastal river valleys of pre-Columbian Peru, vibrant, independent societies of farmers, priests, artisans, and traders suddenly fell into chaos. Large, cohesive lowland communities shattered into smaller, competitive units within the fertile valleys. No recognizable cause for this sudden collapse has become apparent, although archeologists have suggested massive crop failure, a natural calamity such as a tidal wave or deadly earthquake, or a profoundly disturbing celestial event that undermined the authority of existing religious leaders. At the same time, however, highland communities in Peru's mountains continued to prosper, with no interruption to temple construction or community cohesion. In an environment in which the highland and lowland peoples had frequent contact and trade, the stability of highland culture must have offered lowland peoples a new path to follow. Beginning around 750 B.C.E., the whole of ancient Peru became united under

The gateway to the temple complex at Chavín de Huántar. (The Art Archive/Dagli Orti)

3500–1800 B.C.E.	c. 3000	c. 2500	2500–1800
Pre-Ceramic Period in trans-Andes western South America	Grain agriculture develops in Andean highlands	Maize and bean agriculture develops in lowlands	Huaca Prieta, an early center of worship in pre-Columbian Peru, flourishes

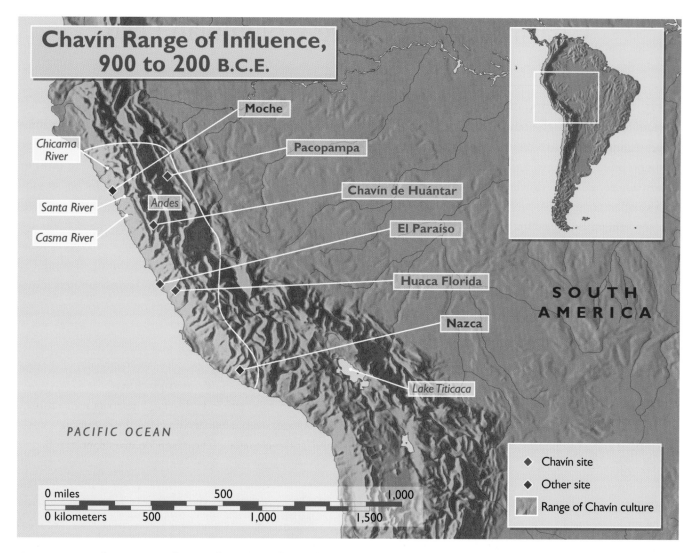

Chavín Range of Influence, 900 to 200 B.C.E.

Moche

Chicama River

Pacopampa

Chavín de Huántar

Santa River

Andes

El Paraíso

Casma River

Huaca Florida

Nazca

SOUTH AMERICA

Lake Titicaca

PACIFIC OCEAN

◆ Chavín site
◆ Other site
▨ Range of Chavín culture

0 miles · 500 · 1,000
0 kilometers · 500 · 1,000 · 1,500

Between 900 and 200 B.C.E., Chavín culture (named after the site at Chavín de Huántar) dominated pre-Columbian Peru and emerged as the first regional society in South America. Its influence would affect the development of other early societies on South America's western coast, including the Moche and Nazca (named after the sites at which these civilizations were centered). Source: Some data compiled from John Haywood, Atlas of World History (New York: Michael Friedman Publishing Group, 2000), 17.

one culture: the signs, symbols, and structures emanating from the highland religious center of Chavín de Huántar in the north.

Although little specific information has surfaced on Chavín culture, it is known that between 900 and 200 B.C.E., in a period frequently called the Early Horizon, an organized society thrived in Peru that had extensive commercial trade and cultural influence throughout Peru's

desert lowlands, its Andean highlands, and beyond. Chavín culture, a name derived from the supposed center of this culture at Chavín de Huántar, is the first known regional society in South America. It provided an important cultural foundation for subsequent precolonial peoples and societies, including the Moche and Nazca, on South America's western coast. Chavín culture also provided the first unifying cosmology and political culture

1800–900	900–200	100 B.C.E.	450–1250 C.E.
Initial Period in South America	Early Horizon Period in South America; dominance of Chavín culture	Growth and dominance of lowland Moche Empire	Tiwanaku and Wari dominate highlands

for western South America and influenced a series of societies that culminated with the empire building of the Inca in the fifteenth century C.E.

Origins of Chavín Culture

The relationship of geography and settlement along South America's western coast contributed to the growth and spread of Chavín culture. Central western South America consists of two zones: a lowland zone of deserts and a highland zone of lofty mountains. It is also divided into a northern region, composed of present-day Ecuador and northern Peru, and a southern region, consisting of southern Peru, Bolivia, and northern Chile. The lowlands are punctuated by fertile river valleys, of which five are suitable for year-round primitive irrigated agriculture. The highlands have lush valleys separated by imposing mountains. In these two zones and regions, different cultures, such as those centered at Paloma and Chilca (in present-day Peru), developed and remained in close contact with one another over a millennium.

Archeological evidence suggests that hunter-gatherers settled and exploited the highlands and lowland river deltas as early as 13,000 B.C.E. They had probably migrated into the area from Central America via the isthmus of Panama or perhaps by sea in primitive boats. In the highlands, hunter-gatherers relied on collecting tubers, such as primitive potatoes, for sustenance. In the lowlands, hunter-gatherers relied mainly on the acquisition of fish protein from the Pacific Ocean. They domesticated such animals as the alpaca and llama in the highlands and the guinea pig in the lowlands. (Guinea pigs, llamas, alpacas, dogs, turkeys, and bees were the only animals available for domestication in the Americas before colonial times.) Indeed, as archeological evidence from the densely populated area between the Casma and Huarmey rivers indicates, guinea pig hutches were some of the first permanent lowland structures not dedicated to religious purposes. Around 3000 B.C.E., highlanders developed grain agriculture (native quinoa, amaranth), which was probably imported from present-day Ecuador or Central America and practiced to supplement hunting

and gathering. Maize and lima beans appeared around 2500 B.C.E., spreading mainly in the lowland river valleys and providing a nutritional complement to meat and fish. In both areas, people lived in small, fixed villages and practiced the most primitive type of irrigation.

During the Pre-Ceramic Period (3500–1800 B.C.E.), agriculture and settled villages became common, and lowland and highland peoples began to build religious structures. In the subsequent period, the Initial Period (1800–900 B.C.E.), settled farmers learned crafts such as pottery, weaving, and stone carving. At sites along the coast and in the mountains, new kinds of villages appeared that were distinguished by innovative and more monumental architecture. By about 1800 B.C.E. at Huaca Prieta, a site along the Chicama River, the villagers had constructed underground houses with carved roof supports made of whalebone and wove non-loom ornamented textiles made of cultivated cotton. Around this time, population growth began to tax the land's ability to produce the necessary supplemental food products, forcing local peoples to turn to agricultural innovations, such as complex irrigation systems and land reclamation from riverside marshland.

The development of extensive irrigation, which supported the growing of lima beans and maize in the lowlands, encouraged greater social and political organization. In addition, the introduction of pottery between 2100 and 1800 B.C.E. created the ability to store excess food, resulting in a growing need to organize and distribute this agricultural surplus. Early in the Initial Period, irrigation management and distribution of surplus food became the purview of specialized management groups in the river valleys, including those at Moche and Casma (in present-day Peru). Similar innovations occurred in the highlands, but the highlanders relied less on intensive irrigation and more on gathered products and the herding of camelids (llamas and alpaca in particular). These groups in the river valleys had occasional contact with one another and with the highlanders through trade, but each had, as far as can be determined, distinct cultures.

In the context of concentrated populations, hierarchical societies, and strong social organization, a new

700	700–1100	1375–1475	1400s
Fall of Moche	Growth and dominance of lowland Sicán	Height of lowland Chimú state	Incas start to dominate western South America

administrative elite probably monopolized worship and trade in precious goods, and they increasingly dedicated labor and imagination to architectural innovation to confirm their power. The construction of ever more elaborate worship centers may have also been a form of competition between river valley societies. At El Paraíso, a site in the north of Peru dating from about 1800 B.C.E., there are small stone ceremonial structures and pyramids. At Huaca Florida (in present-day Peru), a site that originated in about 1700 B.C.E., temple construction expanded and moved inland from the coast to place it more centrally among the irrigated fields on which its community had come to rely for sustenance. The gradual enlargement and organizational intensification of these structures reveals the growth of organized religion and society.

By the end of the Initial Period, a distinguishing U-shaped center was a common feature of all these early sites and eventually became evident along the regional coasts and in the highlands around Lake Titicaca as well. Typically, three pyramids and a sunken court created the U-shaped courtyard, perhaps imitating a river valley. A much larger structure, such as a platform or flattened pyramid, sat behind the lower U and may have represented the mountains beyond the river valleys. However, sometime around 900 B.C.E., for unknown reasons, lowland architects of U-shaped ceremonial structures stopped building them, or maybe simply abandoned them, and lowland society appears to have collapsed.

Chavín's Highland Culture Spreads throughout Pre-Columbian Peru

Around 900 B.C.E., at the start of the Early Horizon Period, a people from the highland U-shaped complex of Chavín de Huántar descended and seized control of the struggling river valley communities of coastal Peru. Although the exact impetus for their descent remains unknown, the results are clear. In short order, Chavín cultural styles, ornamentation, and religious practices came to dominate coastal and some highland peoples.

Trading activity between lowlanders and highlanders contributed to the spread of Chavín culture. Some archeologists speculate that while highlanders based their diet on tuber agriculture and animal husbandry, they depended on the importation of dried fish and seaweed

from the coast to ensure a healthy diet. Likewise, the lowlanders, tightly confined to a few river valleys and ridges and surrounded by desert, relied on the importation of dried tubers and meat from the highlanders, even following the expansion of irrigation after 1800 B.C.E. This exchange of food and other products, including textiles and precious metals, existed between 2500 and 1800 B.C.E. and intensified through the Initial and Early Horizon periods.

In addition to the trade of agricultural products, highlanders and lowlanders exchanged cultural products as well. This exchange, when tied to well-organized political or religious leadership, encouraged the spread of dominant, regionwide cultures, such as that at Chavín. The wealth and prosperity of the Chavín may have attracted river valley dwellers to abandon their religion for that of Chavín, and community pressure or potential exclusion from irrigation access by the Chavín may have encouraged whole communities to "convert." In addition, Chavín priests seemed to have had impressive worship structures, including some that they could make roar with deft control of water flowing through specially carved channels in the temple complexes. Such dramatic rituals would have awed other precolonial societies in the region.

Coalesced from several trends exhibited throughout Peru, the great temple at Chavín, and subsidiary temples using the same motifs, provide a picture of the organization of Chavín society and religion. Although not a civilization—the Chavín cultural circuit lacked urbanization, an essential indicator of civilization—the Chavín sites in northern and southern Peru illustrate a common religion based on worship of animal spirits. Within the Chavín temple, pillars and lintels inside interior bays and galleries were adorned with bas-relief representing human, feline, and serpentine forms, and most importantly, with the Staff and Smiling Gods. The Staff God is half-human, half-feline, while the Smiling God (also called the Lanzón and believed to be the central deity in Chavín religion) has a broad face with what archeologists interpret as a smile. In this cosmology of animal and anthropomorphic spirits, priests attempted to contact, communicate with, and placate spirits in the world beyond. They did so through a number of rituals, often involving hallucinogens and animal sacrifice.

As a result of trade with the peoples of the Amazon on the eastern side of the Andes and with the tropical areas of Ecuador beginning as early as the Pre-Ceramic Period and continuing through the Early Horizon, tropical motifs appeared in the symbols of Chavín. While trade may have allowed the exchange of products between the tropical and more temperate zones of South America's western coast, the lasting impact of this exchange was cultural. For example, the jaguar, caiman (a species of alligator), and snake—dominant images along with humans in Chavín symbolic vocabulary—were not native to either the northern or southern Andes regions. The distant jungle provided powerful symbols for Chavín and inspired the artistic traditions of the whole Early Horizon Period.

Around 100 B.C.E., a northern coastal people known as the Moche absorbed the forms and styles of Chavín art and architecture, changed it, and became the dominant people in northern and central Peru. Although the Moche had large ceremonial structures and practiced the same type of agriculture (irrigated maize and bean fields, for example) and crafts (pottery and weaving, for example) as the people of Chavín de Huántar, the remains of Moche architecture suggest a much more violent and imperial people. Fortifications and evidence of *corvée* (tax) labor imply that the Moche added empire building to the religious dominance that had marked Chavín. The influence of Chavín ended, but its cultural forms endured.

Influence of the Pax Chavínensis

Enormous temples, large-scale trade, and a complex cosmology attest to the success of Chavín at satisfying the social, religious, and economic needs of the people of ancient Peru. The spread and dominance of Chavín culture via commercial trade and cultural exchange initiated a period sometimes known as the Pax Chavínensis (the Chavín peace), during which peace and prosperity became widespread and social organization became hierarchical and complex.

Although the influence of Chavín culture became predominant and, in one way or another infiltrated all precolonial cultures of the region, local innovations suggest that along the west coast of South America the Chavín did not have much political sway. Some of the cultures in lowland and highland Peru coexisted alongside Chavín culture. For example, between 2000 and 200

Cross-Cultural Exchange

↔ Common cultural vocabulary of animal symbols and worship practices spread throughout ancient Peru

↔ Flourishing artistic production in ceramics, metalwork, stone carving, and weaving

↔ Tight integration of coastal and highland Peru

↔ Conceptualization of Peru as a single cultural zone and treatment as a single polity

B.C.E., the Kotosh Religious Tradition, involving burning sacrificial animal bones and grain in shallow hearths within specially designed ceremonial rooms, endured in the Andean highlands and only slowly became subsumed by Chavín practices and symbols. Nonetheless, the cultural innovations that spread from Chavín de Huántar gave ancient Peru a unified society on which the subsequent civilizations of the Andes and coastal Peru were built.

Unlike its predecessors in Peru, the leadership of the Chavín, whether religious or secular, had the power and influence to organize huge labor projects. For instance, the site at Chavín de Huántar is remarkable for its massive, rectangular structure in stone, which must have required an enormous level of social and political organization to construct. With a common cultural language adopted across a broad area, which reduced hostility based on a lack of familiarity, the Chavín period seems to have sparked an economic boom in western South America. Aiding this process were the introduction of llama cargo trains, which vastly increased the amount of goods a small group of people could transport. These trains probably also improved nutrition by ensuring the speedy transit of preserved foodstuffs and enabled the quick transport of goods, such as precious stone, feathers, metals, and woven cloth.

Along with peace and improved nutrition, many of the various peoples of highland and lowland Peru who adopted Chavín culture also adopted its style of temple building and cosmology. Chavín took the earlier U-shaped temple of the Initial Period and imbued it with a more refined meaning. The Chavín temple duplicated a miniature river valley, with the sides of the temple shaped like mountains. Corridors within the temples may have imitated layers of the cosmos. The introduction of forest animals, an import from across the Andes and from the tropical north, distinguished Chavín worship from earlier religious practices. Through bright colors and elaborately carved stone images, these animals represented the recognition of a broader material world and a richer, more accessible spirit world where the spirits were exotic but recognizable. This viewpoint may have attracted people to adopt Chavín culture. While the core images and beliefs spread throughout much of coastal and highland Peru, however, local communities exercised significant latitude in their use and manipulation of Chavín symbols. For example, some groups embraced raptor (bird of prey) images and deemphasized caiman symbols.

After 200 B.C.E., Chavín culture became subsumed into a series of new cultural zones in the lowlands and highlands. In the lowlands, the Moche peoples disrupted whatever political unity the Chavín may have inspired. After 700 C.E., ecological factors destroyed Moche influence. Strong, state-oriented societies, such as the Sican from 700 to 1100 C.E. and the Chimú from 1375 to 1475 C.E., followed the Moche in the lowlands. In the highlands near Lake Titicaca, the Chiripa and Pukara cultures, which were independent of Chavín, had developed from 1400 to 200 B.C.E. Beginning in about 450 C.E., subsequent peoples known as the Tiwanaku and Wari spread a Pukara-based culture northward throughout the highlands, even though after 1000 C.E. the unity of the Tiwanaku and Wari shattered into a series of petty states. In the lowlands and highlands, increasingly strong state-centered societies tended to compete violently with one another. Ultimately, after the late 1300s, the Inca, a people from a small region northeast of Lake Titicaca, absorbed the highlands and lowlands of western South America into one huge empire. In a sense, the Inca were the inverse of the Chavín because they conquered by consciously adapting local forms suited to their needs. The Chavín, however, had dominated only those local cultures that were compatible with their own in a way that promoted and encouraged peace.

See Also

VOLUME THREE: Christopher Columbus and the Columbian Exchange

Bibliography

Burger, Richard L. *Chavín and the Origins of Andean Civilization*. London: Thames & Hudson, 1995.

———. *The Prehistoric Occupation of Chavín de Huántar, Peru*. Berkeley: University of California Press, 1984.

Kano, Chiaki. *The Origins of the Chavín Culture*. Washington, D.C.: Dumbarton Oaks, 1979.

Moseley, Michael E. *The Incas and Their Ancestors: The Archaeology of Peru*. Rev. ed. New York: Thames & Hudson, 2001.

———. *The Maritime Foundations of Andean Civilization*. Menlo Park, Calif.: Cummings, 1975.

—David W. Del Testa

Primary Document
Relief Sculpture at Chavín de Huántar

Chavín culture, named after the large temple complex of Chavín de Huántar in the Andes of Peru, became widespread in the highlands and lowlands of the central part of western South America between 900 and 200 B.C.E. Rather than being imposed by conquest, Chavín culture spread through trade, with various societies adopting it as a strong component of their own cultural vocabulary. The Chavín fascination with animals and a particular style of representing them is evident on this relief sculpture depicting snakes and pumas. What is not so evident is that some of the animals portrayed, such as the snake, do not exist in the Andes, indicating that the Chavín had contact with the tropical forests and appreciated the power of their forces.

Source: © Charles and Josette Lenars/Corbis.

The Persian Empire of Darius

521–486 B.C.E.

One day in the first years of the rule of Darius I (r. 521–486 B.C.E.), the emperor of Persia (present-day Iran), a man named Syloson presented himself at the gates of the royal palace. Syloson insisted that the king owed him a favor because he had once presented Darius

with a gift from Egypt, which he had helped to conquer for Persia under Cambyses II (r. 529–522 B.C.E.), Darius's predecessor. Upon seeing him, the king indeed granted the favor: to send a royal force to recapture the Aegean island of Samos, just off the west coast of Anatolia

Persepolis was the site of one of Darius's greatest building works. This wall relief from the ruins of the royal palace depicts a Medes officer standing with two Persian guards before Darius. The Medes were an ethnic group of the Persian kingdom. (© Gianni Dagli Orti/Corbis)

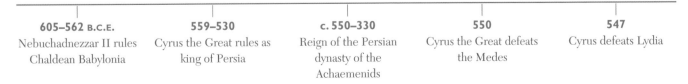

605–562 B.C.E.	559–530	c. 550–330	550	547
Nebuchadnezzar II rules Chaldean Babylonia	Cyrus the Great rules as king of Persia	Reign of the Persian dynasty of the Achaemenids	Cyrus the Great defeats the Medes	Cyrus defeats Lydia

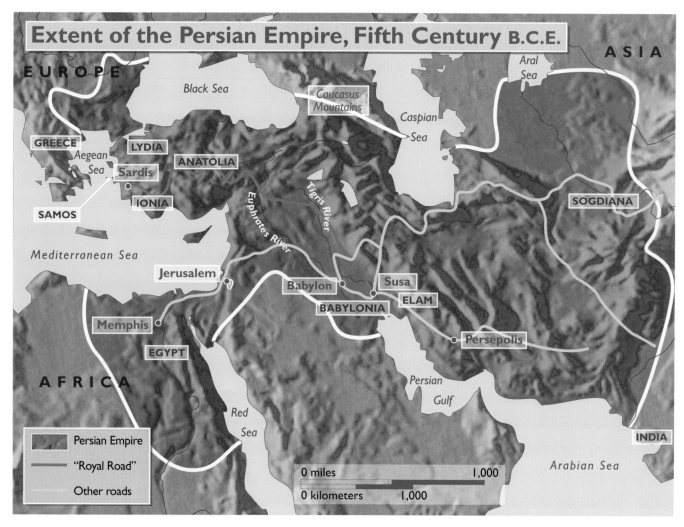

Extent of the Persian Empire, Fifth Century B.C.E.

EUROPE

ASIA

Black Sea

Aral Sea

Caucasus Mountains

Caspian Sea

GREECE

Aegean Sea

LYDIA

ANATOLIA

Sardis

SAMOS

IONIA

Mediterranean Sea

Euphrates River

Tigris River

SOGDIANA

Jerusalem

Babylon

BABYLONIA

Susa

ELAM

Memphis

Persepolis

EGYPT

AFRICA

Persian Gulf

Red Sea

INDIA

Arabian Sea

Persian Empire
"Royal Road"
Other roads

0 miles — 1,000
0 kilometers — 1,000

At the height of the Persian Empire, under Darius in the fifth century B.C.E., *the Persians ruled an extensive territory in the Middle East, creating the largest empire in the world at the time. As a result of its expansion, the empire instituted new administrative methods, influenced religious and cultural ideas, and established communication networks like the "Royal Road" across the Middle East. Source*: Some data compiled from Gerald A. Danzer, *Atlas of World History* (London: Laurence King, 2000), 33.

(modern-day Turkey), and turn it over, intact, to Syloson. The expedition was successful and Syloson was installed as the ruler of Samos.

The defeat of Samos and the grant of rule to Syloson was just one of hundreds of diplomatic, economic, military, and administrative encounters that took place under Darius; similar events would continue under subsequent Persian kings. Such encounters were a normal part of life during the Achaemenid Dynasty (named after Achaemenes, the great-great-grandfather of Cyrus the Great who ruled from 559 to 530 B.C.E.) and a necessary component of historical change and stability. Darius spread the borders of the kingdom far beyond the boundaries established by his predecessors and therefore transmitted Persian ways farther than ever before. His rule also brought stability to most of the regions over which the Persians extended their control and solidified that control through a system of administration that for the most part minimized uprisings among the peoples whom the Persians ruled.

546	539	529–522	521–486
Cyrus defeats the Greek cities of Ionia	Cyrus defeats Chaldean Babylonia	Cambyses II rules as king in Persia and defeats Egypt	Darius I rules as king of Persia

Rise of the Achaemenid Dynasty

From the middle of the sixth century B.C.E. until 330 B.C.E., when the Greek Empire under Alexander the Great (356–323 B.C.E.) defeated Persia, the Achaemenid Dynasty (c. 550–330 B.C.E.) ruled a wide swath of territory in the Middle East. At the dynasty's height, its territorial holdings were vast, including several modern-day countries: from Egypt in the southwest; Syria along the eastern Mediterranean Sea; Turkey, Bulgaria, and Greece in the northwest; Armenia, southern Russia, and Iraq in the Caucasus Mountains between the Black and Caspian seas; through Iraq and Iran along the Persian Gulf and extending to parts of India in the east. This was the largest empire in the world at the time. The Assyrians had been the great power in the region until the seventh century B.C.E. when they were supplanted by the next great power, the Chaldeans, whose most distinguished leader was Nebuchadnezzar II (r. 605–562 B.C.E.). Babylon, the splendid capital of Chaldean Babylonia (modern-day Iraq), would be defeated by the most influential of Darius's Persian predecessors, Cyrus the Great.

The Babylonians had defeated and taken captive, among other ancient peoples, the Jews of Jerusalem and the surrounding area. After defeating the Babylonians in 539 B.C.E., Cyrus released the Jews and allowed them to return to Jerusalem and rebuild their holy city. The books of Ezra and Nehemiah, among other texts from the Hebrew Bible that address this period of Jewish history, speak of the release and relatively humane treatment of the Jews by Cyrus and of the travails of the Jews to rebuild the Jerusalem Temple, the center of ancient Jewish worship. This treatment was in stark contrast to that meted out by Nebuchadnezzar II, which is discussed in the Book of Daniel from the Hebrew Bible, among other ancient sources.

The return of the Jews to their ancestral land by Cyrus was consistent with one of the general principles of all the Achaemenid leaders: ruling through local elites and respecting local customs, rather than establishing wholly new ruling institutions or structures. Cyrus, for instance, obtained the goodwill of the priesthoods in the conquered lands by, as in the case of the Jews, allowing for the restoration of temples and for the conquered peoples to practice their chosen religions. He also used members of the native populations to govern them. He had a reputation for being merciful, which led to many different peoples acknowledging him as their legitimate ruler. When he built his palaces, he incorporated Lydian (from modern-day eastern Turkey), Egyptian, Assyrian, and Babylonian methods and influences, reflecting his genuine respect for the ancient cultures and peoples over which he ruled. Adopting the practices of conquered peoples, the Achaemenid rulers frequently used their encounters with surrounding peoples to their advantage. This incorporation of foreign ideas provided the Achaemenid Dynasty with one of its greatest achievements: highly stable and consistent rule.

Cyrus was worthy of the epithet "the Great" in many respects. Under his leadership, the Achaemenid Dynasty, based in the southern region of modern Iran, developed as a major power and spread extraordinarily under his leadership. He led it in 550 B.C.E. to victory over the Medes, an ethnic group closely related to the Persians, and made the Medes the first province, or *satrapy*, of the Persians. That was followed by defeats of other kingdoms and people and by the establishment of new satrapies, such as the kingdom of Lydia in 547 B.C.E. and the Greek city-states along the western coast of Ionia (modern-day western Turkey) near the Aegean Sea in 546 B.C.E. On the eastern part of the Persian plateau, the dynasty next defeated western India and the Sogdians, a group of Buddhist Persians who engaged in the Silk Roads trade and who were responsible for disseminating Buddhism all the way into China. In 539 B.C.E., the Achaemenids conquered the Mesopotamians, the inhabitants of the region between the Tigris and Euphrates rivers, and Babylon, their capital.

Cambyses II, Cyrus the Great's son, succeeded his father and had some successes such as adding major parts of Egypt to the holdings of the Achaemenid Dynasty. Upon Cambyses's death, however, there was a struggle for power. Darius took the throne from an impostor, or pretender to the throne, named Gaumata (d. 522 B.C.E.), a Persian Magian Zoroastrian priest who claimed to be the brother of Cambyses. Darius developed into the most important and successful of the Achaemenid rulers.

c. 517	330
Darius revises the provincial satrapy system	Alexander the Great defeats the Achaemenids, ending the dynasty

The Expansion of Persian Rule

Darius was a leader of great energy and talent. This enabled him not only to reorganize the dynasty into an efficiently run empire encompassing dozens of different peoples, but to also create a better administrative and tribute system. Darius successfully undertook many important improvements essentially simultaneously, such as building new cities or developing new laws for the vast reaches of his domain, all while continuing to conquer more lands. Just as important for the long-term survival of the dynasty, he manipulated and changed the dynastic system to avoid future succession crises like the one he had faced at the death of Cambyses, limiting future kings to the descendants of a single family. While this may have been motivated by personal ambitions, it still helped minimize future struggles over the throne and created stability.

Change of Organization

As the dynasty developed under Darius, the administration of the kingdom changed significantly. Although there is some question among historians about how similarly Cyrus and Darius organized their administrations, Darius not only incorporated some very important changes, but also solidified those changes in ways that enabled Persian methods to spread much farther than during the reign of Cyrus.

Very early in Darius's reign, Darius and his advisers determined that new royal palaces would be built in Susa (Shush, in present-day Iran) and Persepolis (its ruins are at Takht-i Jamshid, about 35 miles northwest of the present-day city of Shiraz, in Iran). The relocation of the empire's court by different Achaemenid rulers often reflected the needs of the particular regimes and the whim of the ruler. Darius chose Susa as his principal capital because it was accessible to other major cities and was also close to the original Persian homeland. Located just 65 miles from the Persian Gulf up the Tigris River, Susa was more advantageous as a trading and business center in comparison to, for instance, Babylon, which was 365 miles up the Euphrates River. Susa was well protected by the mountains that surrounded it and had fertile soil. Previously, Susa was the capital of Elam. The city was ruled by the Elamites, a people whose origins extend back to the sixth millennium B.C.E. and who are probably

the biblical people said to be from "Shushan," and featured splendid Elamite craftsmanship. Darius incorporated these cultural treasures into the construction of his palaces, and the ruins of Susa today offer valuable information about these two important ancient civilizations.

Persepolis was constructed to serve as the spiritual capital of the empire, and craftsmen from all across the known world were brought in to construct its magnificent palaces and temples. Built on a high plain against a mountain, its huge columns supported massive buildings constructed of black mountain stone. Long stairways embellished with artistic relief carvings brought majesty to the structures. To this day, Persepolis's ruins serve as a testimony to the history of the Persians.

Darius replaced the tribal organization of the armies with an army composed of professional troops. The army comprised different contingents drawn from the various ethnic groups of the kingdom (i.e., Lydians, Medes, Egyptians). There was a large cavalry, numbered at 10,000 men, and another 10,000 served as elite infantrymen. Not only was the military impressive and intimidating to its enemies, it was also ethnically diverse, adding to the stability of Persian rule by showing that no one ethnic group had enough control to oppress the others. To be sure, in many ways the Persians were privileged in the empire, but the tolerance shown by Darius toward cultural, ethnic, religious, and linguistic differences also illustrated to non-Persians that the empire was not based upon the oppression of other peoples.

To increase the efficiency of the empire's financial system, Darius revised the satrapy system and set up 20 provincial satrapies to assess taxes on each, probably beginning in 517 B.C.E. Darius replaced Cyrus's tribal tribute system with an administrative system in which governors, called *satraps*, administered the provinces and, therefore, the kingdom. Thereafter, the use of satraps spread and improved. The satraps under Darius were generally ethnic Persians, and he made sure that the satraps of the most important regions came from the royal family, probably to maintain stability. (Although it was normal to be respectful of local ways and traditions, the king still had to have control and oversight at the highest level of the governing of the kingdom, something made much easier by limiting the people who served as satraps.) In the future, those satrapies that were not reserved for the royal family evolved into hereditary offices, which would bring corruption and some level of incompetence. Darius, however, was able to appoint talented people and keep an eye on them through royal spies. The provinces themselves were apparently no longer populated by people of the same tribe, but grouped by ethnicity, or by a number of ethnicities. These groups would then pool their tribute, and pay it through the satrap.

The satraps were not just collectors of taxes and tribute; they were active agents in cross-cultural exchange by virtue of their central role in governing the kingdom. Satraps also had civil and military duties, being responsible for justice and security, commanding the military forces within their provinces, and raising military levies for the army. Darius's successors would begin to hoard wealth and overtax, even though Darius's policies had been agreeable enough with his subjects and not considered to be overly extractive.

Expanding the Communication System

As important as these administrative changes were to the governing and expansion of the dynasty's dominions, so too was the development of the communication system. The relatively sophisticated system of roads facilitated these improvements in communication networks. The most famous network was the highway from "Susa to Sardis," called variously the "road to the king," the "King's Road," and the "Royal Road." This road, as well as other "royal roads," was wide enough to be accessible to chariots used by civil and military personnel. Such roads were not necessarily paved, but were still characterized by their well-maintained status. Along this and the many other roads were towns, hostels, military garrisons, and bridges. Many other roads, although not nearly as prominent, developed throughout the dominions and contributed to the administration of the kingdom. Although scholars do not know with certainty the extent of these transportation routes or the number of workers who were responsible for constructing and maintaining them, the predominance of references in ancient sources to such an extensive system of roads makes it clear that significant resources would have been devoted to the task.

Cross-Cultural Exchange
- ↔ Persian administrative methods spread throughout the Middle East
- ↔ Egyptian, Lydian, Babylonian, and Assyrian architectural methods and artistic forms are brought to Persia
- ↔ The Lydian use of coins, replacing in-kind payments, is adopted by the Persians
- ↔ An effective postal courier system spreads throughout the kingdom
- ↔ The use of several official languages exposes peoples throughout the kingdom to other cultures and languages

The empire's communication system also included a courier system, which allowed the king to receive direct news from most places in the dominions within a week. The courier system would have encompassed hundreds of stations and used hundreds of riders. The well-maintained roads and highways, which would have included a "highway patrol" force, tied together imperial outposts and the empire itself. This system of roads and highways also allowed for speedy troop mobilization.

An elaborate system of archives and administrators also allowed the king to be kept informed with accurate information regularly chronicled by well-trained scribes. Darius's regime communicated with its subjects throughout the dominions, increasingly in a number of different languages. Persian was the language of the court and the language in which government was conducted. The empire, however, published official announcements and other administrative documents in up to three languages, a practice that would continue even up to the time of Jesus, having been adopted by the Romans when the sign that was placed on the cross calling Jesus the "King of the Jews" was written in three languages.

Justifying Greatness through Religion and Architecture

The Achaemenids were relatively tolerant of other cultures and religions. Darius in particular, however, justified his rule and sovereignty over the many different peoples of his empire in terms of the state religion, Zoroastrianism. This religion, based upon the teachings of a prophet, Zoroaster, who lived and taught during the seventh century B.C.E., believed in a supreme creator called Ahura Mazda, or "Lord Wisdom," who was destined to triumph over a supreme evil being. This dualistic religion, which acknowledged the existence of good and evil, held that people possessed free will and therefore should be held responsible for their own actions. Darius asserted that he was king by the will of the only deity, Ahura Mazda. Persian rulers justified such claims in elaborate court ceremonies during which the ruler acted as priest. In Darius's time, the king and the priests, or *magi*, propagated Zoroastrianism as a monotheistic (single god) faith system. Subsequent kings and priests would allow it to evolve into a polytheistic (many gods) system, incorporating older Persian theological notions as well as the beliefs of many of the peoples in the kingdom.

Persian rulers also glorified themselves in very impressive architecture. Darius, for instance, ordered that marvelous buildings be built portraying not only his connection with divinity, but the connection of his servants and protectors with divinity by showing them in regal poses with angel wings on their backs. The religious claims of the rulers, coupled with the military successes of the dynasty, seemed to support Darius's claims of royal status and divine authority. Even so, and perhaps influenced by Cyrus's practice of ruling through local elites and the sheer size of the areas ruled, Persian rulers tolerated local religion, custom, and other practices as long as they did not inspire rebellion.

In Susa, archeological evidence indicates that the city plan did not change much until Darius. The changes made were typical of the new energy of Darius and his desire to leave his mark. In fact, with these changes, virtually all traces of the influence of Susa's previous builders and rulers, the Elamites, were erased, a good example of how cross-cultural encounters sometimes result in outright destruction. In the case of Susa, the rebuilding of the Elamite city proclaimed to all of Darius's subjects that such influences had been eradicated and that the great Persian king now held control of the city, and in effect, the entire empire.

Economy and Trade

The Achaemenid economy was one more avenue of cross-cultural exchange. Whereas coins had been introduced earlier, apparently borrowed from Lydia, under Darius coins would replace in-kind payments (payment given in goods and commodities) as compensation for workers. This encouraged the reemergence of banking operations and a relatively sophisticated monetary system, which included loans, leases, and capital investment in property, canals, shipping, and various commodities. Similarly, a fairly complicated agricultural system existed as well, including the use of canals where water for irrigation was scarce.

The Significance of the Persian Empire of Darius

The Persian Empire under Darius successfully organized and administered a kingdom of great size with much cultural, religious, and linguistic diversity. Part of its success was due to the Persian habit of allowing a high degree of local autonomy, as evidenced by the Persian tolerance for foreign customs and ideas. It was precisely this tolerance that enabled Darius to build a stable and efficient army and administration that was diverse, but also loyal. No ruler or kingdom would surpass the Persians' efficiency in this regard until the Romans, several centuries later.

Even some of the things the Persians did not necessarily excel at, such as artistic and intellectual developments, also contributed to cross-cultural exchange. For instance, because the Persians were not as experienced as other peoples within the empire in the building arts, influences from outside Persia were imported, showing that sometimes conquest is not just about imposing, but also about receiving. As in the case of the building of Persepolis, Darius brought in architects and craftsmen from places and regions like Lydia, Mesopotamia, Egypt, and Assyria to build great temples and palaces. The result was a magnificent, multicultural complex of architectural and artistic styles showing that even "conquered" peoples and their cultures live on after military defeat. This exchange testifies to the cross-cultural component of historical change, demonstrating the power and continuity of cultural practice. Sometimes even perceived weaknesses (for example, the absence of advanced Persian architectural engineering) on the part of conquering peoples promulgate the continued existence of other cultural influences. In the case of the Persian Achaemenid Dynasty, this cross-cultural evolution is evident.

See Also

Bibliography

Briant, Pierre. *From Cyrus to Alexander: A History of the Persian Empire.* Translated by Peter T. Daniels. Winona Lake, Ind.: Eisenbrauns, 2002.

Culican, William. *The Medes and Persians.* London: Thames & Hudson, 1965.

Georges, Pericles. *Barbarian Asia and the Greek Experience: From the Archaic Period to the Age of Xenophon.* Baltimore: Johns Hopkins University Press, 1994.

Lorentz, John H. *Historical Dictionary of Iran.* Lanham, Md.: Scarecrow Press, 1995.

Wiesehöfer, Josef. *Ancient Persia: From 550 BC to 650 AD.* Translated by Azizeh Azodi. London/New York: I. B. Tauris, 1996.

—*John Patrick Farrell*

Primary Document

Darius's Account of Building the Palace at Susa

This inscription was uncovered from remains at Susa, one of Darius's great palaces (the other one being Persepolis). Note not only what he is reported to have thought, but the ways in which it is clear that the building incorporated materials from faraway places and building methods from other cultures.

. . . This is the palace which I built at Susa. From afar its ornamentation was brought. Downward the earth was dug, until I reached the rock in the earth. When the excavation has been made, then rubble was packed down . . . On that rubble the palace was constructed. And that the earth was dug downward, and that the rubble was packed down, and that the sun dried brick was moulded, the Babylonian people, it did (these tasks). The cedar timber, this—a mountain by name Lebanon—from there was brought; the Assyrian people . . . brought it to Babylon; from Babylon the Carians and the Ionians brought it to Susa. The yak timber was brought from Gandara and from Carmania. The gold was brought from Sardis and from Bactria, which here was wrought. The precious stone lapis-lazuli and carnelian which was wrought here, this was brought from Sogdiana. The precious stone turquois, this was brought from Chorasmia, which was wrought here. The silver and the ebony were brought from Egypt. The ornamentation with which the wall was adorned, that from Ionia was brought. The ivory which was wrought here, was brought from Ethiopia and from Sind and from Arachosia. The stone columns which were here wrought—a village by name Abiradus, in Elam—from there were brought. The stone cutters who wrought stone, these were Ionians and Sardians. The goldsmiths who wrought the gold, these were Medes and Egyptians. The men who wrought the wood, these were Sardians and Egyptians. The men who wrought the baked brick, these were Babylonians. The men who adorned the wall, these were Medes and Egyptians. Saith Darius the king: At Susa a very excellent [work] was [brought to completion]. Me may Ahuramazda protect, and Hystaspes, my father, and my country.

Source: Excerpted from Albert M. Craig et al, *The Heritage of World Civilizations*, 6th ed. (Upper Saddle River, N.J.: Prentice Hall, 2003), 125.

Nok Culture and the Spread of the Bantu Peoples

500 B.C.E.–500 C.E.

Early in the fifth century C.E., in the highlands of southern Africa (present-day South Africa, Tanzania, Zambia, and Zimbabwe) peoples whose livelihood, appearance, and cultural ways differed significantly from local peoples suddenly appeared. These peoples, who spoke Bantu languages, had a culture derived extensively from ancestral practices in southern Nigeria and had attained a relatively high level of agricultural and technological development. They migrated into and settled widely across southern Africa's fertile plains and river valleys. Their culture and society differed extensively from that of the Khoisan-speaking hunter-gatherer peoples who had settled across sub-Saharan Africa for millennia. As several archeological sites in the region indicate, the Bantu migrants decorated pottery and iron castings with strong parallel lines, chevrons (V-shaped figures stacked on one another), and other geometric patterns in ways resembling practices in southern Nigeria. They farmed with iron-tipped instruments, shaved with iron razors, and hunted with iron weapons. Altogether, the common cultural language and technological advantages of these Bantu migrants enabled them to form the backbone of Africa's early sub-Saharan civilizations.

Only a few traces of the early Bantu migrations remain, hence much of the scholarship about these Bantu-speaking bearers of Nok culture remains speculative. Archeologists first found evidence of this culture near the village of Nok, in Nigeria, so it is called Nok culture. The distribution of these traces and their dating through Carbon-14 analysis, however, tell a rich story. Despite Africa's large land area, varied topography, and often dense vegetation, Bantu society spread from a small section of tropical west Africa all across the sub-Saharan portion of the continent between 500 B.C.E. and 500 C.E. The Bantus' strong culture, adaptability, and advanced technology in combination with fertile farmland and the wide availability of iron ore in sub-Saharan Africa facilitated this rapid expansion.

Development of Bantu Society in West Africa

Around 2000 B.C.E., peoples whose farming and herding ancestors had migrated from eastern Africa and who spoke Bantu languages began to dominate the forests, plains, and highlands of West Africa. The ability of these Bantu speakers to manipulate the environment to suit their nutritional needs and engage in trade across a broad area gave them a competitive advantage over West Africa's Khoisan-speaking hunter-gatherers. As the Bantu became more populous throughout West Africa, they

Nok terra-cotta mask from Nigeria. (© Werner Forman/Art Resource, NY)

2000 B.C.E.	900	700–600	500
Farmers and herders migrate from East Africa to West Africa	Evidence of iron smelting in North Africa	Evidence of iron smelting in the Sahara	Evidence of iron smelting in West Africa; Nok culture begins period of great vibrancy

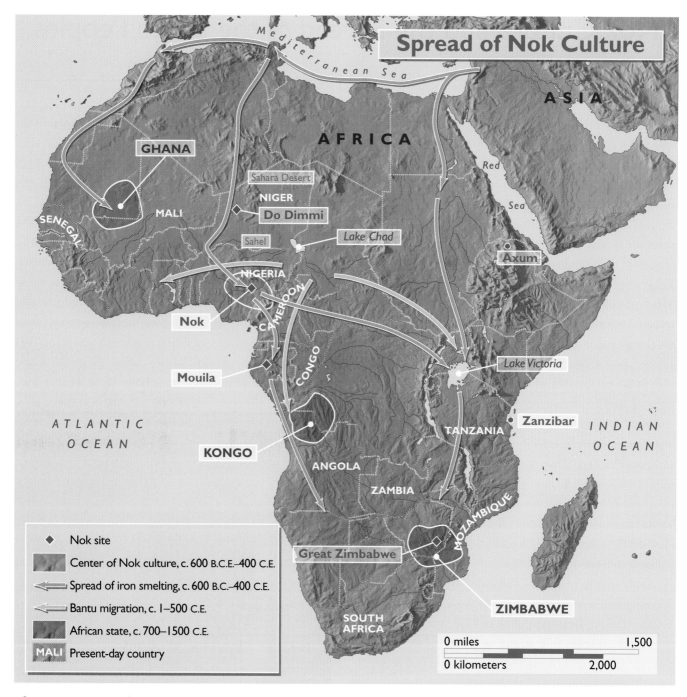

Spread of Nok Culture

Legend:
- ◆ Nok site
- Center of Nok culture, c. 600 B.C.E.–400 C.E.
- Spread of iron smelting, c. 600 B.C.–400 C.E.
- Bantu migration, c. 1–500 C.E.
- African state, c. 700–1500 C.E.
- MALI Present-day country

The Bantu in West Africa began smelting iron around 500 B.C.E. as a result of cross-cultural contact with the peoples of North Africa, who had obtained knowledge of this skill from trading peoples around the Mediterranean. Beginning in about 1 C.E., the Bantu began migrating across sub-Saharan Africa, carrying Nok culture—named after the site at Nok— and developing complex trading societies in new regions.

Sources: Some data compiled from Albert M. Craig et al., *The Heritage of World Civilizations*, 3rd ed. (New York: Macmillan College Publishing, 1994), 181; and John Haywood, *Historical Atlas of the Ancient World: 4,000,000–500 B.C.* (New York: MetroBooks, 2001), 1:16.

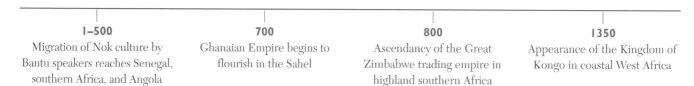

1–500	700	800	1350
Migration of Nok culture by Bantu speakers reaches Senegal, southern Africa, and Angola	Ghanaian Empire begins to flourish in the Sahel	Ascendancy of the Great Zimbabwe trading empire in highland southern Africa	Appearance of the Kingdom of Kongo in coastal West Africa

expelled, absorbed, or destroyed many of the other peoples they encountered.

By 1000 B.C.E., the Bantu speakers had organized themselves into many complex but stateless societies with a relatively high population density across tropical West Africa, especially in the area encompassing present-day Cameroon, Congo, and Nigeria, between the Atlantic coast and Lake Chad. The Bantu formed villages of up to several hundred individuals led by a headman or council. These villages may have in turn showed loyalty to a higher group, such as a clan, whose leaders met only occasionally to organize cooperative projects, such as clan warfare or the resolution of land conflicts. The ability of the Bantu to organize effectively beyond the level of the village distinguished them from the Khoisan speakers alongside whom they often lived. The Bantu society shared the same cosmology (belief system), which stressed a single, disinterested creator, a panoply of lesser gods identified with various spirits or elements of nature, and a clergy of shaman or diviners interested in curing and protecting from evil.

Around 500 B.C.E., Bantu-speaking peoples in south central Nigeria (and perhaps, independently, in the Lake Victoria area) began smelting iron for the production of hand tools, farming implements, and weapons. It appears that at the same time they also acquired knowledge of copper smelting, which remained an almost purely ornamental craft. The acquisition of these technologies resulted in an increase in food production and political competition among the Bantu peoples, which in turn encouraged migrations of excess population.

The practice of iron smelting began as a result of cross-cultural exchanges between the peoples of North Africa and West Africa. Archeologists have found evidence of iron smelting among Berber peoples in North Africa from at least 900 B.C.E.; the Berbers must have learned it from trading peoples, such as the ancient Greeks or Phoenicians, who had contact with the originators of iron smelting, the Hittites of Anatolia (present-day Turkey). Archeologists and historians assume that Berbers traveled from North Africa to West Africa across the Sahara in search of relatively plentiful West African gold and brought iron smelting with them. A slightly more temperate climate at this time made trans-Saharan travel easier than it would be in later years; evidence of horse-drawn wheeled chariots, now impossible to use in the arid, sandy Sahara,

has been found at archeological sites at many oases. There is also evidence of iron smelting at Do Dimmi, in the central Sahara (in present-day Niger), from 700 to 600 B.C.E. Indeed, archeological evidence of the chariots used in trans-Sahara trade as well as evidence of iron smelters illustrates the progress of iron smelting from North Africa to West Africa over a period of five hundred years.

Along with iron smelting came increased social and cultural complexity. In an area of particularly high population density between the coast of Nigeria and Lake Chad, Bantu speakers achieved a common cultural language and an advanced level of technological development. In this broad area, Bantu speakers possessed common artistic and technological traits, based on the farming of yams and millet, animal husbandry, sculpted clay figurines, and iron work. Naturalistic representation of humans with proportional limbs but exaggerated facial features and animal figures, typify Nok artistic representation.

Spread of Nok Culture across Sub-Saharan Africa

Sometime around 1 C.E., perhaps because of overpopulation, competition, or simply a desire for new lands, Bantu speakers began to migrate across sub-Saharan Africa, carrying Nok culture with them. It appears that Nok culture arose within West Africa based on local innovations and cultural and social norms brought from East Africa thousands of years before. However, neither the increase in population nor the dispersal of Bantus carrying Nok culture across sub-Saharan Africa encouraged them to form state societies. Social organization remained based on the village. Only after the conclusion of these great Bantu migrations did states and empires form out of the scattered remnants.

Many Bantu speakers traveled east and then south. They spread Bantu language and Nok culture into the highlands of present-day Mozambique, South Africa, Tanzania, and Zimbabwe, retracing the steps their ancestors had taken across Africa several thousand years before. The Bantu group that crossed through the tropical rainforests and mountains of central Africa toward East Africa created an arc of Bantu-speaking peoples across the whole of subequatorial Africa. There is evidence of iron smelting near Lake Victoria in present-day Tanzania by the fourth century C.E., and in Broederstroom, in South Africa, by the fifth century C.E. (although some archeologists claim that iron smelting began concomitantly in West Africa and East Africa). This group inhabited the uplands of central and southern East Africa and began vibrant trade with the coastal peoples of mixed Khoisan, Arab, Indian, and Malay backgrounds. The Bantu speakers traded upland products, especially gold and hides, for salt and manufactured items. In so doing they developed a vibrant trade-based economy and began to influence coastal culture with Bantu-based languages and cultural traits. The descendants of these peoples established, for example, the trading empire in southern Africa centered at Great Zimbabwe.

Some Bantu traveled directly south, into the rainforests of Congo and Cameroon and on to the coastal plains of Angola. There is evidence of iron smelting by 200 C.E. at Mouila, in Cameroon. The societies they formed eventually developed complex kingdoms involved in trade with Bantu cousins to the north in West Africa and across the continent in highland East Africa. Much later (c. 1400–1500 C.E.), kingdoms deeply involved in the trade of slaves, such as the Kingdom of Kongo (present-day Angola and part of Congo), developed out of these early Bantu societies.

Other Bantu groups traveled to the northwest, into the Sahel region of Niger, Mali, and Senegal. (The Sahel is the fertile grassland between the savannas in the south and the Sahara in the north.) Less evidence exists for the spread of Bantu cultures to the Sahel, even though many of West Africa's greatest societies and civilizations appeared here after 500 C.E. The early Kingdom of Ghana (700–1100 C.E.) encompassed many peoples, including Bantu migrants, Ife, and Benin, and enjoyed a great deal of prosperity derived from the trans-Sahara trade. Like the trade of the east coast of Africa, this trade relied on exchanging African gold for products manufactured in the Mediterranean Basin. After 500 C.E., the introduction of camels reinvigorated trans-Sahara trade, which had been weakened in previous centuries by desertification and disruption of the Mediterranean Basin during the collapse of Roman authority in North Africa. The growth and strengthening of Islam, with its thriving tradition of trade, further improved trans-Sahara trade after 650 C.E.

Nok culture provided a unifying cosmology for West Africa's Bantu speakers, while iron smelting provided them with the technology to efficiently manipulate the various environments and people they encountered during their migrations. In East Africa, despite their ability to thrive in new, unfamiliar lands, the Bantu speakers remained restricted to the highlands and coasts. At no point did the complex Bantu societies compete with the organized states and civilizations of East Africa (such as Axum and Zanzibar) even when they had organized into powerful trading societies, such as that at Great Zimbabwe farther south after 800 C.E. In western Africa, states did develop, but only in regions where no competition existed (such as at Ghana after 700 C.E.) or much later (such as at Kongo after 1350 C.E.).

By 500 C.E., the Bantu speakers had reached the Atlantic coast of Senegal, the highlands of southern Africa, and the coast of Angola. Although the Bantu were not a particularly violent people, their expansion disrupted existing societies throughout Africa. As in West Africa, the Bantu speakers absorbed, pushed back, or destroyed the hunter-gatherer peoples whom they encountered. Although competition existed between the Bantu and the Khoisan hunter-gatherers, oral tradition recounts mutual assistance as well. The spread of the Bantu contributed to the language distribution of contemporary Africa. Today, Khoisan speakers remain isolated in the desert regions of southwest Africa.

Factors Contributing to the Spread of Nok Culture

The spread of Nok culture served as the underlying cultural base for much of the social and cultural development of sub-Saharan Africa, but the nature of the migration of Bantu speakers meant that Nok culture did not become a unifying political identity. After the migration concluded, local Bantu speakers developed their own unique cultures and societies on the foundations that Nok culture and the Bantu language had provided them. A number of different factors, some cultural and some material, helped contribute to the success of the Bantu in spreading across sub-Saharan Africa. Because of a lack of historical evidence, however, much of the significance of the Bantu expansion is based on circumstantial information, but that evidence reveals some very compelling trends.

Perhaps most important, the flexibility and adaptability of the Bantus' social and economic structure made them ideal migrants; these traits remained significant in the societies that succeeded the first Bantu migration. The political organization of the Bantu, structured in family-based hierarchies, allowed for cohesive units, rather than just individuals, to migrate and maintain traditions while adapting to new environments. Their religious organization was controlled by a shaman attached to the smallest unit of political organization, the village. As a result, the Bantu did not need to maintain costly material structures or links to an ancestral homeland in order to maintain worship; rather, their societies were portable. The Bantu based their economy on farming, cattle, small craft production, and trade, providing each village with a variety of sources from which to derive its sustenance and income and ensuring the ability of the Bantu to adapt to new environmental conditions during their migrations. Finally, the Bantu had a great deal of experience in cross-cultural contact and trade, which exposed them to different geographical zones and made them more receptive to the knowledge of others. Yet throughout their migrations and exchanges, the Bantu were able to maintain their basic cultural identity.

One of the more interesting factors that permitted the Bantu to expand into and thrive in East Africa originated with a cross-cultural exchange related to nutrition. Around 300 C.E., bananas had become widely available across tropical sub-Saharan Africa after being brought to East Africa by Malay traders a few hundred years before. The tremendous nutritional benefit of the banana encouraged the Bantu to venture deeper into the tropical forests of the Congo and West Africa in search of equally rich crops (in an expansion they had previously avoided because these forests did not provide a suitable environment for growing either yams or millet, the Bantus' main foodstuffs).

The material elements of Bantu culture certainly provided them with the tools necessary for taming new environments. The relatively low cost of iron smelting done at small, wood-fired foundries gave migrating Bantu the ability to forge tools easily as they moved and thus engage in relatively intensive farming as they colonized new land. Beyond their local settlements, this ability to work with metals created powerful catalysts for economic development across much of Europe, Asia, and Africa.

The Bantus' abilities to work with metals and practice primitive mining transformed cross-cultural links into very profitable trade relations when, between 400 and 1200, the metal-based economies of the Mediterranean Basin, Persian Gulf, and South Asia developed an insatiable demand for gold that only the underdeveloped mines of

---

Cross-Cultural Exchange

↔ Spread of common Nok culture (artistic and social forms) across highland sub-Saharan Africa

↔ Migration of Bantu speakers across highland sub-Saharan Africa

↔ Use of smelted iron and copper across highland sub-Saharan Africa

↔ Development of complex societies into trading kingdoms in Congo, Zimbabwe, and the Sahel

↔ Development of new languages, such as Swahili, which retains Bantu structures but reflects Arabic, Persian, and Indonesian influences

↔ Retreat of Khoisan speakers into arid southwest Africa

Africa could meet. At the same time as the foundation of the Roman Empire in 27 B.C.E., the Romans began to send vast quantities of gold and silver abroad for luxury products and, late in the empire (180–350 C.E.), as protection against barbarian invasions. This metal often ended up in central and eastern Asia, depriving Europe and the Middle East of the gold it needed for its sophisticated trade-based economy. Likewise, after the fall of the western part of the Roman Empire in 476 and the growth of new trading empires in the Middle East, metal-based currencies provided the easiest (although certainly not the only) method for conduct trade across many cultures and countries.

In response to these demands, the Bantu peoples of West Africa and Zimbabwe developed extensive gold-mining operations, sending gold across the Sahara and to the coast of Tanzania for export in exchange for manufactured products. This gold kept the economies of the Mediterranean Basin and the Middle East alive during a time when war and hoarding elsewhere could have destroyed them. Even early in the first millennium C.E., the Bantu of Zimbabwe adapted new methods for engaging in this trade. There is evidence in Zimbabwe and Tanzania of gold mines that used South Asian techniques and probably were operated by Indian sub-contractors or by Bantu speakers who had learned the technique from Indians. The Bantu revealed a remarkable adaptability that permitted them to thrive across all of sub-Saharan Africa and would provide the foundation for the evolution of complex states, such as at Ghana, Kongo, and Great Zimbabwe.

One example of the enduring legacies of the Bantu is from their language. As they migrated, the Bantu took with them various dialects, which evolved over time and region but retained the basic grammatical and syntactic structure. Swahili is a language that came to dominate the East African coast after the ninth century C.E. (The word *swahili* is a corruption of *sawahil*, the Arabic term for coastlands.) It retains Bantu structures, but includes words from Arabic, Persian, and Indonesian, and other languages as well. Swahili is written using Arabic letters. This overlay reflects perfectly the nature of the Bantu migration: the duration of cultural traits brought with the Bantu from West Africa and adapted to local cultures. This situation is repeated in religion (early West African Islam had many elements of animism) and political structure (the trading empire of the Great Zimbabwe may have imitated the chief-based structure of traditional Bantu culture). The adaptability of Nok culture and the Bantu language also created zones of cross-cultural contact, such as in East Africa, transforming Africa into a vibrant environment of trade and exchange throughout the period of classical and medieval civilizations of Europe, the Middle East, South Asia, and China.

See Also

VOLUME ONE: The Phoenician Trading Empire and the Spread of the Alphabet

VOLUME TWO: The Great Zimbabwe Trading Empire; The Spread of Islam to Sub-Saharan Africa

Bibliography

Chittick, H. Neville, and Robert I. Rotberg, eds. *East Africa and the Orient: Cultural Syntheses in Pre-Colonial Times.* New York: Africana Publishing, 1975.

Davidson, Basil. *The Lost Cities of Africa.* Rev. ed. Boston: Little, Brown, 1970.

Fage, J. D., with William Tordoff. *A History of Africa.* 4th ed. London: Routledge, 2002.

Mokhtar, G., ed. *Ancient Civilizations of Africa.* Berkeley: Heinemann/University of California Press, 1981.

Vansina, Jan. *Paths in the Rainforests: Toward a History of Political Tradition in Equatorial Africa.* Madison: University of Wisconsin Press, 1990.

—*David W. Del Testa*

Primary Document
History of the Mukema of Talagwe

The anthropologist Thomas Beidelman collected this creation myth of the Kaguru people of present-day Tanzania. The story describes the migration of the Bantu people from west to east and then to southern Africa.

The Mukema clan is among the clans which came from far away into the land of Ukaguru. The Mukema came from Irangi. They had stayed there for many years along with other clans. Later that land of Irangi was entered by two other groups and those groups were fierce, the Masai and the Little-People.

Because of their fierceness those people made people afraid to stay in that land, so they deserted group by group and went down from out of the north. . . . During that journey the group of people was led by three female elders for even though there were males, those were youths.

The first of those people was Old Woman Lugode and she was the eldest and she was with her younger sister who was called Nechala but the name of their third comrade is not known. They marched like that back again to Ifunda. When they left Ifunda they reached Chimagai Swamp and then they reached Igombo. There at Igombo they settled for some time. Then they climbed up into the Itumba Mountains and then passed through Munyela Pass.

When they left Munyela they reached Munhindili in Uponela. There they didn't spend much time but continued on with their journey to find a good land in which to settle. Then they entered Itungo in the land of Maundike. From Itungo they went to Malmdike but they didn't like that land, so they soon left and went to Ikonde in the land of Mamboya. There they stayed for five years and some of their comrades remained there but all of that [Mukema] group left and passed along the way to Chimhinda at Mugugu and so they reached the land of Talagwe.

At that time the land of Talagwe had no clans which had reached there and so Old Woman Lugode and her comrades climbed Talagwe Mountain and then they made a fire in order to show that they themselves where the first to arrive. . . .

The others who appeared later passed through to go ahead to find lands on which to settle. Consequently even today the land of Mukundi is the land of the Mukema. . . .

Source: Excerpted from Paul Spickard, James V. Spickard, and Kevin M. Cragg, eds., *World History by the World's Historians* (Boston: McGraw-Hill, 1998), 1:18.

India's Cultural Expansion to Southeast Asia

500 B.C.E.–900 C.E.

In 671 C.E., a Chinese monk named Yi Jing (635–713) began 25 years of travel throughout India and Southeast Asia to improve his understanding of Buddhism. His return journey to China brought him through Southeast Asia, which he found alive with fellow Buddhists and the study of Buddhism. In his account of his journeys, *A Record of the Buddhist Religion as Practised in India and the Malay Archipelago* (published after 695), Yi Jing recommended that future Chinese students of Buddhism first travel to Palembang, the capital of the Kingdom of Srivijaya (in present-day Indonesia), for a year or two before pressing on to India to acquaint themselves with India's customs. By Yi Jing's time, the influence of India on religious thought was already quite strong throughout Southeast Asia, although local customs and needs in the region tempered its influence.

View of stupas at Borobudur, the great Buddhist monument in Indonesia. (© Borromeo/Art Resource, NY)

1500–500 B.C.E.	1000	800–500	c. 586–466	c. 500	273–232
Vedic Age in South Asia	Dong Son culture emerges in Southeast Asia	Period of contemplation in India	Life of the Buddha, Gautama Siddhartha	First Indian traders travel to Southeast Asia	Reign of King Asoka in India

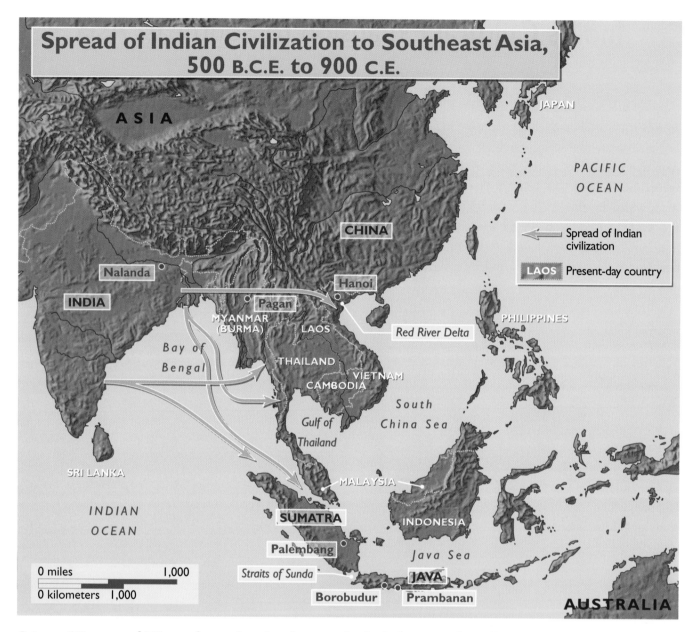

Spread of Indian Civilization to Southeast Asia, 500 B.C.E. to 900 C.E.

Between 500 B.C.E. and 900 C.E., the people and civilizations of India had a tremendous effect on Southeast Asia. Important trading regions, such as northern Vietnam and Srivijaya (with its center of trade located at Palembang), served as sites of cultural exchange between Indian merchants and indigenous peoples from Southeast Asia and would facilitate the spread of India's religious ideas, including Buddhism and Hinduism.

Source: Some data compiled from Gungwu Wang, *The Nanhai Trade: The Early History of Chinese Trade in the South China Sea* (Singapore: Times Academic Press, 1998), 4.

Southeast Asia as a geopolitical entity has existed in name only since World War II, when the British and Americans designated it as a zone of military operations.

Prior to this, Europeans called Southeast Asia the Indies or the Spice Islands. The ancient Indians called parts of it Suvarnobhumi, or "the Land of Gold." The

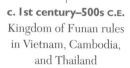 **c. 1st century–500s C.E.** Kingdom of Funan rules in Vietnam, Cambodia, and Thailand	**1st century–800s** Kingdom of Pyu rules in Myanmar	**192–1720** Kingdom of Champa rules in Vietnam	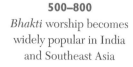 **500–800** *Bhakti* worship becomes widely popular in India and Southeast Asia	 **670–1025** Buddhist Kingdom of Srivijaya rules in Sumatra, Malaysia, and Java

Chinese referred to it as Nanyang, "the Southern Seas." Although there are no intrinsic geographical reasons to consider Southeast Asia as a region with any particular unifying characteristics, these older names often hint at the common elements that characterize the region. Scholars generally agree that Southeast Asia consists of the regions east of India, south of China, and north of Australia where Indian and Malay cultures had a strong cultural influence. Because of its multiplicity of cultures, the accessibility it offers to so many different peoples, and its importance as a center for rare spices, Southeast Asia has served as a crossroads for millennia. One of its most important influences was the people and civilizations of India.

The Peoples and Religions of Southeast Asia and India

The various peoples of Southeast Asia practiced different subsistence patterns, with nomadic hunter-gatherers living in close proximity to settled civilizations. The region's first complex society was Dong Son culture, which originated independently from other civilizations in Vietnam in about 1000 B.C.E. and spread quickly across the region. Dong Son culture consisted of seafaring peoples organized in chiefdoms that practiced wet-rice agriculture and used bronze for weapons and ritual items. Dong Son states participated in extensive trade with each other. For example, the tin used in the manufacture of bronze in northern Vietnam may have originated in present-day Malaysia.

Between 500 B.C.E. and 150 C.E., much of Southeast Asia came under the influence of Indian culture. Beginning around 500 B.C.E., Indian merchants seeking spices and gold in Southeast Asia spread their religious beliefs, specifically Buddhism and Hinduism, throughout the region. Buddhism and Hinduism grew from the same religious tradition. They both emerged out of Vedic Age religion, which the Aryan peoples brought to India when they migrated into the area after 1500 B.C.E. from the Eurasian steppe. Vedic Age religion revolved around priests performing elaborate rituals and sacrifices. The

core of its beliefs is contained in four Vedas (Wisdoms), collections of stories and religious instructions. By 800 B.C.E., the Aryans had spread out over much of South Asia and had absorbed the indigenous Dravidian culture (which worshiped spirits of nature and fertility). They imposed a fourfold social classification on society called Varna (colors), which linked an individual's profession to their place in a divine moral hierarchy. The Varna consisted of priests, warriors, artisans, and farmers. Over time, these divisions evolved into the caste system. Between approximately 800 and 500 B.C.E., many spiritually minded people dissatisfied with Vedic Age religion retreated into India's forests and lived in contemplation as hermits. Out of this period of contemplation emerged an inwardly focused religious practice, as well as religious texts (the Upanishads) and epic literature (especially the epic poem the Bhagavad Gita) that soon swept across South Asia. The main reforms of the post-500 B.C.E. period included the internalization of sacrifice as a spiritual practice. The religions that emerged, including Buddhism and Hinduism, also emphasized reincarnation (*samsara*) along a path toward eventual release (*moksha*) from earthly existence.

As part of the period of contemplation in the late Vedic Age, Siddhartha Gautama (c. 563–483 B.C.E.), a prince of northeastern India, founded Buddhism and eventually became known as the Buddha. As a young man, he renounced his power and wealth and began a life of wandering in search of enlightenment. He practiced extreme asceticism and self-mortification. One day, while meditating under a pipal tree, Gautama realized that there were Four Noble Truths and became enlightened. These truths were that existence is pain, that desire creates pain, that pain and therefore desire must end, and that the Eightfold Path, which consisted of eight behaviors that ended desire, was the way to end suffering. Buddhism teaches that anyone who gives up the material world, believes in the Four Noble Truths, and follows the Eightfold Path can realize *nirvana*, the Buddhist place of release. After the Buddha's death, his religious philosophy developed into a series of schools,

700–1000s	750–800s	802–1431	1196
Islam becomes gradually influential in Malaysia and parts of Indonesia	Shailendra kingdom rules in Java	Khmer Empire rules in Cambodia, Thailand, and Laos	Sack of Buddhist center at Nalanda by Turkish Muslims destroys Buddhism in subcontinental India

the two most important of which are Theravada (Way of the Elders; also known pejoratively as Hinayana, or "Lesser Vehicle") and Mahayana (Greater Vehicle). The adherents of the former believe that only those who become monks and dedicate their lives to Buddhism might achieve nirvana. Adherents to the latter believe that anyone might achieve nirvana through the acquisition of merit (through good works, in particular) or heartfelt appeals to saintlike *bodhisattvas* (almost-Buddhas). King Asoka (r. 273–232 B.C.E.) of the Maurya Dynasty in India converted to Buddhism and encouraged its spread throughout the known world.

Hinduism emerged alongside or in reaction to the individual nature of salvation in Buddhism and continued to develop after Asoka's reign despite the popularity of Buddhism. At its base, Hinduism revolves around the worship of one divine spirit that manifests itself in many forms, such that Hinduism appears to be polytheistic but in fact reflects heavily on the relationship of the individual's microcosm (*atman*, meaning "soul") to the macrocosmic whole (*brahman*, meaning "universe") in a state of oneness (like cells to a body). In practice, Hinduism at this time tied the possibility of advantageous reincarnation to the effective performance of duty (*dharma*) appropriate to one's moral/vocational class (*jati*, a subdivision of the Varna). In about 500 C.E., *bhakti*, a personal and emotional form of devotion often accomplished through singing that was facilitated but not controlled by priests, became popular. With bhakti, which resembled Mahayana Buddhist worship, a devotee, usually of a cult of Vishnu or Shiva, prayed for the fulfillment of desires and the preservation of the good qualities that one already possessed. According to some scholars, Hinduism gained in popularity in India because its new personalism probably made the enduring and rigid religious-based social structure of the Varna more bearable.

Indian culture would have associations with the wider world because of the sweeping influence of its religions throughout Asia and the powerful spirituality behind those religions. Its influence would more profoundly affect those states closer to it (present-day Myanmar, formerly Burma, and the islands of Indonesia) and along common trade routes (southern Vietnam) than it would those in far-flung regions (such as the

Philippines). Southeast Asian leaders first came into contact with Indian culture through their interactions with Indian merchants. In addition to using the profits from trade to create stronger, consolidated states, they also adopted Indian religions, rituals, and statecraft to enhance their prestige and power. Around 150 B.C.E., these leaders invited Brahmans (Hindu priests who are members of India's highest caste, or social grouping) and Buddhist monks to Southeast Asia in order to learn more about Indian culture. Religion was the most important element in Indian influence, but with religion came a whole set of values, politics, and material expressions that also influenced Southeast Asia. Although Indian religions influenced Southeast Asia's leadership more quickly than it did the common peoples, these groups gradually adapted Indian culture to their own.

Spread of Indian Civilization

Because trade routes spread Hinduism and the culture associated with it from India to Southeast Asia, and Southeast Asian leaders invited Brahman to their courts, it is not surprising that the major centers of trade in Southeast Asia adopted a Hinduized culture before Buddhism. For its part, Buddhism and Buddhist culture spread from India to Southeast Asia in three distinct movements. The first was to peninsular Southeast Asia (present-day Myanmar, Thailand, Cambodia, Laos, and southern Vietnam). Missionaries sent by King Asoka spread Buddhism across this region, and there were certainly Buddhist kingdoms in Myanmar, Cambodia, and southern Vietnam by the first century C.E. The second was to insular Southeast Asia (present-day Malaysia and the major Indonesian islands of Sumatra and Java). Java became the first place where Buddhism dominated in Southeast Asia, and by the seventh century, Sumatra also had a significant Buddhist population. The third movement was to northern Vietnam. All of Vietnam gradually became associated with Chinese Buddhism, losing its connection to Southeast Asian Buddhism after the eighth century.

Peninsular Southeast Asia

In peninsular Southeast Asia, Indian-influenced states developed almost simultaneously in several places. The first known Indianized kingdom in Southeast Asia was

Funan, located on the coast of present-day Vietnam, Cambodia, and Thailand. The name Funan is a Chinese corruption of the word *bnom* (mountain) in the old Khmer language, spoken by Cambodians. The establishment of Funan sometime during the first century C.E. is ascribed to an Indian Brahman named Kaudinya, who, according to legend, defeated the daughter of the king of the cobras and married her, starting a new dynastic line. The legend illustrates the blend of Indian and local traditions (such as snake and water worship). Funan became an important trading center and endured until the end of the sixth century C.E. The leaders of Funan called themselves *rajas* (kings) in the Indian manner, used Sanskrit (a language of Aryan origin used for religious purposes), and adopted an Indian-style bureaucracy.

Like Funan, the Kingdom of Champa, located on the central coast of Vietnam, was also Indianized, even though its founder was a Chinese official exiled from his homeland in 192 C.E. Champa shows the distinct influence of the Amaravati architectural style from India, which incorporates towers in temple designs. Champa endured the longest of all of Southeast Asia's Indianized kingdoms, from the second through the eighteenth centuries (although Vietnam, in its slow expansion southward from the Red River Delta, had greatly reduced Champa's size and influence after the fourteenth century).

Geographically closer to India, Myanmar experienced a long period of Indianization. Buddhist missionaries reached Myanmar in the third century B.C.E., and its peoples remained in continual contact with the important Theravada Buddhist centers in Sri Lanka long after Buddhism had faded from India itself. Between the first and the ninth centuries C.E., the Pyu people, native inhabitants of southern and central Myanmar, organized a stable, Indianized state. The Pyu rejected violence to the point that they would not wear silk because its manufacture involved the killing of silkworms. The Mon and Burman, peoples from the northern region of Myanmar who are related to the Cambodians, conquered the Pyu. The Burmans migrated southward from Myanmar's northern mountains sometime in the second century C.E. and adopted Mahayana Buddhism. They founded the highly syncretic (of mixed origins) Pagan Kingdom (849–1287) and made the city of Pagan

> ### Cross-Cultural Exchange
> ↔ Buddhism and Hinduism spread from India to Southeast Asia
> ↔ Southeast Asia adapts Indian political systems (*mandala* state, *chakravartin*)
> ↔ Indian epics and architectural forms combine with local Southeast Asian traditions
> ↔ International centers for study of Buddhism develop at Palembang

an important religious center that blended Buddhism with local spirit (*nat*) worship. Much later, when the Burmans formed a political alliance with the Mon and created a syncretic Mon-Burman society, they adopted Theravada Buddhism and Indian forms of kingship, administration, and court ritual.

Other peninsular Southeast Asian states exhibit profound Indian influences as well, although they adopted the syncretic blend of Hinduism, Buddhism, and local religious and cultural elements already practiced throughout the rest of the region. The great Khmer Empire (802–1431), built in part on the ruins of Funan and located in present-day Cambodia, Thailand, and Laos, began to expand during the reign of Yasovarman I (r. 889–900). Yasovarman was the first Khmer leader to build temples to the worship of Buddha and of the Hindu gods Shiva and Vishnu at Angkor Wat in present-day Cambodia, and he began a series of conquests that made the Khmer Empire powerful. Beginning in the thirteenth century, other Indianized states arose in Thailand, Myanmar, and Laos that challenged the Khmer state until they triumphed over it in 1431.

Insular Southeast Asia

Indianized states developed in insular Southeast Asia somewhat later than they did in Myanmar, Cambodia, and southern Vietnam. Srivijaya, with its capital at Palembang, was the most important of the insular Southeast Asian states. Located on the Straits of Sunda in eastern Sumatra and encompassing parts of Java and Malaysia, Srivijaya served as an important point of shipment for goods traveling between China and the Indian Ocean and from the rest of Southeast Asia to China, between the seventh to eleventh centuries. The Srivijayan capital at Palembang was not only an administrative center but also one of the preeminent places outside of India to study Buddhism. Although Palembang had a powerful fleet that served as Srivijaya's navy and customs collection service, and although its kings could muster a powerful army, it relied mainly on alliances with neighbors to ensure its security and prosperity. Interestingly, Srivijaya collapsed in 1025, when the southern Indian state of Chola invaded, conquered, and temporarily administered it in a bid to end Srivijayan control of trade.

Another powerful state developed in insular Southeast Asia alongside Srivijaya. The Shailendra family, exiles from Funan, acquired a Javanese kingdom around 750 C.E., established a prosperous state, and became strong patrons of Mahayana Buddhism. The Shailendras built their power on agricultural wealth and to some degree on trade, but not nearly as much as Srivijaya. At the end of the eighth century, their power even extended to the area once controlled by Funan, although the Khmer stamped out this colony in 802.

Northern Vietnam

Northern Vietnam served as an important stop on the trade routes between China and Southeast Asia and received missionaries and practitioners of many religions. Because of the colonial presence of the Chinese in northern Vietnam, however, Chinese religious practices such as Buddhism were most influential here. (When referring to Vietnam during this period, it is important to distinguish between the lands of the Vietnamese, which consisted of what was occupied by the Chinese between 111 B.C.E. and 939 C.E. and is today northern Vietnam, and the rest of Vietnam, which the Champa controlled.)

Beginning late in the third century, the area around Hanoi became an important center of Buddhist learning, and historians assume that this Buddhism was more Theravada than Mahayana in tendency. By the fifth century, however, Mahayana Buddhism, because of its personal and individual nature, had become popular and widespread throughout northern Vietnam. This attraction to Mahayana Buddhism may have been caused by the alienation the Vietnamese felt as a result of the continuing Chinese colonial occupation.

Rather than existing alongside other religions as in China, Buddhism in Vietnam fused with other religious expressions to become a highly syncretic mix that has endured into the twenty-first century. Often called the "three religions," Vietnamese Buddhism linked the populism of Mahayana Buddhism with a worship of Chinese Confucian figures, Daoist mysticism (a religion that promotes a natural and simple way of life), and enduring pre-Chinese traditions, such as spirit possession. Although continuously linked with Southeast Asia by trade, northern Vietnam's close identification with Chinese culture and the satisfactory and accommodating nature of the three religions caused Vietnamese Buddhism to remain more closely identified with China than with Southeast Asia or Indian religions. By contrast, Champa, to the south of premodern Vietnam, practiced a mixture of Indian Hinduism and Theravada Buddhism.

Synthesis of Indian and Southeast Asian Culture

Southeast Asian leaders did not adopt all aspects of Buddhism, Hinduism, or other elements of Indian civilization. Although highly respectful of different faiths, they often embraced the forms of these religions but modified the various beliefs and rituals to their individual needs. For example, the people of Southeast Asia accepted Hinduism and Buddhism, but rejected the Indian caste system.

The kind of Hinduism imported to Southeast Asia tended to revolve around the worship of Shiva, especially in ceremonies honoring Shiva's phallus, known as a *linga* (a symbolic representation of the male sex not to be associated directly with the penis). Followers focused on a personal relationship with Shiva through bhakti, or devotion. Existing religious and cultural practices facilitated the spread of Hinduism throughout much of Southeast Asia. In Indonesia, Malaysia, and Vietnam, shamanistic cults (believing nature is the source of spiritual life) conducted worship at terraced mountaintop temples ringed by megaliths (large stone edifices). These megaliths were easily transformed in a symbolic sense from being the focus of shamanistic ritual into *lingam*, and worshipers replaced shamans with Brahmans, whose meditative rituals may have resembled the trances into which pre-Hindu shaman placed themselves. Likewise, some Southeast Asians believed water that flowed from their sacred mountains had a purifying or healing quality. Hinduism had a similar respect for water. Using and consuming water in the worship of Shiva, especially water run over the linga, may have seemed familiar. Thus, in many places, Hinduism resembled existing religious practices, which made its adaptation relatively easy.

Buddhism of Southeast Asia blended the ideas of many schools, including Theravada and Mahayana, but in particular favored Tantric Buddhism, with its emphasis on the mystical and magical powers of faith and the Buddha. (Vietnam was an exception because of its close affiliation with Chinese Buddhism and the unity of Confucianism, Daoism, and Buddhism into a single faith.)

Hinduism and Buddhism both provided a powerful source of spiritual development for the peoples of Southeast Asia, although their individual impact depended to a great extent on social class. Southeast Asian leaders adopted both as a way to monopolize political and religious power. In the context of Buddhism, Southeast Asian leaders presented themselves as bodhisattvas on earth. Inscriptions from Palembang, dating from the eighth century, show images of rulers helping common people toward salvation. This suggests that leaders were interested in Buddhism as a way to distribute spiritual wealth to their followers, since encouraging spirituality and harmony was one of the hallmarks of Buddhist leadership. This distribution had its origins in earlier systems of leadership in Southeast Asia, where leaders redistributed taxes to curry favor with subjects. In more Hindu-dominated areas, kings often represented themselves as connected directly to Shiva. In both cases, kings, not priests, had the responsibility of ensuring the ability of all subjects to worship. Whether this was a self-conscious bid to destroy the rival power of shamans or merely a consequence of the adoption of Hinduism and Buddhism remains unknown.

Many of the laws and moral codes for Southeast Asian kings developed out of Hinduism. The leaders of Southeast Asia adopted the Indian court ceremony and relied on such cultural influences as Indian legends, lore, and mathematics. On the other hand, Southeast Asian leaders used the influence of Buddhism to suggest that they possessed powerful magic and mysticism; they also used the concept of the *chakravartin* (the secular counterpart of the Buddha and universal king who struggled for justice) to their advantage. Together, the two religions gave Southeast Asian rulers a powerful identity and politico-religious system by which they might effectively rule their subjects. The relationship between king and subject fit into a broader, Indian-influenced notion of state power called a *mandala*, in which the intensity of rule waned the farther a person found themselves from the king's court. Mandala might overlap, with lesser leaders having greater influence in a locality but still falling under the control of a distant king.

The Shailendras' Buddhist temple at Borobudur (built between about 778 and 850) in Java, which unified indigenous and imported styles, demonstrates the union of Buddhist and Hindu practices in Southeast Asia. Pre-Hindu hilltop temples in Southeast Asia often used stone megaliths as the focus of worship. Borobudur retains this feature but in the form of an artificial stone mountain (103 feet high at its peak with almost 2 million cubic feet of stone). This "mountain" serves as a Buddhist *stupa* (a structure for worship) and as an artificial representation of Mount Meru, a mythological location important in Hindu legends. According to Buddhist practice, stupas often contained relics, particularly originating with the body of the Buddha; instead, the structure's patron, a member of the ruling Shailendra family, used it as a burial site to signify his union with the Buddha. Likewise, its design affirms the Mahayana Buddhist conceptualization of the world (an earthly square sitting on the circle of the universe), but at the same time incorporates Javanese styles, such as numerous statues that represent important scenes in the life of the Buddha. In the ninth century, quite close to Borobudur, other important Javanese leaders built Prambanan, a huge temple complex dedicated to the Hindu god Shiva whose walls illustrate the Indian epic *Ramayana* (The Romance of Rama). The images and motifs of religions of an Indian origin blend with local forms and practices to create a new religion and aesthetic.

In addition to strictly religious values, India provided Southeast Asia with important legends and symbols. Two great Indian epics, the *Ramayana* and the *Mahabharata* (Great Epic of the Bharata Dynasty), provided models of "correct behavior" to the leaders of

Southeast Asia, and the stories in them were popularized and adapted to local artistic forms. Finalized in its current form around 400 C.E. but with origins far earlier than that, the *Mahabharata* consists of about 100,000 instructional and inspirational couplets that chart the struggle between the Kauravas and Panadavas clans for political supremacy in northern India of the early Vedic Age. The *Ramayana*, which offered moral guidance, celebrates the god Rama's exploits on earth. Southeast Asian artists adapted these epics to local characters, with Javanese, Sumatrans, or Cambodians taking the place of Indians in the stories. The *Ramayana* is retold in a classical Cambodian dance, known as Reamker. Parts of the *Mahabharata* are frequently retold in *wayang kuli*, Indonesian shadow-puppet performances. Images of both epics were frequently reproduced in carvings on Southeast Asian temples.

After the tenth century, Southeast Asia began to chart a more independent cultural path based on local initiative rather than the direct influence of India. The decline of Buddhist influence in India contributed to this shift, although contact between Myanmar and Thailand and the Theravada Buddhist centers in Sri Lanka remained influential. Some scholars believe Buddhism was so accepting of other faiths that a revivified Hinduism overwhelmed it. The destruction of the great Buddhist center at Nalanda in northern India by Turkish Muslims in 1196 added to Buddhism's demise, although some scholars believe that by the time Nalanda was destroyed, Indian Buddhism had already became so isolated in monastic communities that it no longer appealed to the average person.

In Southeast Asia, Hinduism and Buddhism had became so firmly linked by the end of the millennium that distinctions between them were sometimes difficult to make. As had happened in India some 1,800 years before, many Southeast Asians had begun to worship the Buddha as an *avatar*, or incarnation, of the Hindu god Shiva, through bhakti. Soon, proselytizing Brahmans incorporated most Buddhists into the more personal Hinduism that had evolved. This system developed to the point where the followers of the Javanese king Kertanagara (r. 1268–92) revered him as the Shiva-Buddha, a union of two systems that had split in India. Although of different origins and intentions, Hinduism and Buddhism in Java and elsewhere in Southeast Asia became fused. The Hinduism of Java demanded strict personal worship of the god Shiva, but incorporated the mysticism and magic associated with Tantric Buddhism.

The direct influence of classical India ended with the appearance of Islam in Southeast Asia. Islam had reached the area in the eighth century, and had slowly begun to influence local cultures because of its simplicity. Islam was first popular in ports because it facilitated trade as the common bond between Arab and Persian merchants transporting goods from Southeast Asia to the Mediterranean Basin. By the end of the eleventh century, it had spread across present-day Malaysia and Sumatra. Unlike in India, where Hinduism and Islam remained fairly distinct, Southeast Asia absorbed Islamic practices to add yet another layer to their complex cultural fabric.

See Also

VOLUME ONE: Indo-European Migration to the Indus Valley; China's Contact with Southeast Asia
VOLUME TWO: Buddhism in China; The Establishment and Spread of Islam; Chinese and Islamic Empires in Central Asia; Vietnam's Southward Expansion

Bibliography

Adshead, Samuel Adrian M. *China in World History.* New York: St. Martin's Press, 2000.

Benda, Harry J., ed. *The World of Southeast Asia: Selected Historical Readings.* New York: Harper & Row, 1967.

Codès, George. *The Indianized States of Southeast Asia.* Translated by Susan Brown Cowing. 3rd ed. Honolulu: East-West Center, 1968.

———. *The Making of South-East Asia.* Translated by H. M. Wright. Berkeley: University of California Press, 1966.

Marr, David G., and A. C. Milner, eds. *Southeast Asia in the 9th to 14th Centuries.* Singapore: Institute of Southeast Asian Studies; Canberra, Australia: Research School of Pacific Studies, Australian National University, 1986.

Osborne, Milton E. *Southeast Asia: An Introductory History.* Boston: Allen & Unwin, 1979.

SarDesai, Damodar R. *Southeast Asia, Past and Present.* Boulder: Westview Press, 1997.

Schafer, Edward H. *The Vermilion Bird: T'ang Images of the South.* Berkeley: University of California Press, 1967.

—*David W. Del Testa*

Primary Document
The Shwegugyi Pagoda Inscription

In this selection from 1141 C.E., King Lansu I (1112–87 C.E.; also known as Aluangsithu), Burmese king of Pagan, discusses his rule. The multiple influences of Indian culture are clear. He references many aspects of Buddhist practice and belief, for Pagan was a kingdom dominated by Theravada Buddhism. There is, however, also a reference to Mount Meru, a mythical location important to Hindus.

. . . I would fulfil hereafter, great and small,
Those rules the Teacher gave for our behoof.
Borne through the element the spotless moon
Outdazzles all the constellated stars:
So I delighting in the Master's lore,
The saint's religion, virtuously yoked,
Would shine among disciples. I would know
Sutta [passages or chapters in Buddhist scriptures],
And Abhidhamma [transcendent doctrine],
Vinaya [rules of the order],
The Master's mind, his ninefold doctrine fraught
With words and meaning. By the Conqueror's Law
I would do good to others and myself.
What the Great Sage forbids I would not do.
May I be always conscious and aware
Of kindness done me. Union of ill friends
Be far from me. Beholding man's distress
I would put forth mine energies and save
Men, spirits, worlds, from seas of endless change.

By merit of this act I would behold
Mettayya, captain of the world, endued
With two and thirty emblems, where he walks
Enhaloed on a rainbow pathway fair
Like Mèru King of mountains, and sets free
Samsara's captives by his holy words.
There might I hear good Law, and bending low
Offer the four things needful to the Lord
And all his monks, till clad in virtues eight,
Informed by such a Teacher, I become

A Buddha in the eyes of spirits and men.

Tathagata by men and spirits adored
Shines bright in virtues manifold; so I
Would shine and be by men and spirits adored.

The twenty four infinities he saved
From bondage of Samsara, compassed all
A Buddha's duties, mercifully taught
The fourscore and four thousand points of Law
For good of all hereafter, blazed abroad
With his disciples like a ball of fire,
Set forth the transcience of conditioned things,
Wrecking the notion of dull fools who deemed
"All thing are stable," and at last attained
the city of Nirvana, safe retreat
Where is not age nor death.—O might I thus
Compass a Buddha's duties and attain
That city lavish of abounding bliss! . . .

This is the stone inscription of the king
Siritibhuvanadiccapavaradhammaraja
Brave, thoughtful, keen, and prudent, who ensues
The elements of wisdom, the Three Gems
Adores, and seeks Nirvana. He began
On Sunday the fourth waxing of Kason
In the five hundred and third year to build
At an auspicious moment. That same year
On Thursday eleventh waning of Nadaw
'Twas done, with effigies of guardian spirits.

Source: Excerpted from Harry J. Benda, ed., *The World of Southeast Asia: Selected Historical Readings* (New York: Harper & Row, 1967), 34–37.

The Silk Roads

400 B.C.E.–900 C.E.

In 629 C.E., a 27-year-old Buddhist monk by the name of Xuanzang left Chang-an, the capital of Tang China, and followed the Silk Roads westward to central Asia and India. Unlike the numerous merchants who had preceded him in earlier centuries, Xuanzang intended to study and retrieve authoritative texts to strengthen Chinese Buddhism. By the time of Xuanzang's travels,

Bactria, an area encompassing much of today's Afghanistan and Pakistan, and the Silk Roads had become the conduits for cultures from Europe and Asia and the center of many schools of Buddhism and other religions before their popularization across Eurasia. When Xuanzang finished his epic journey of about 10,000 miles in 645, he returned to Chang-an with

Two female statuettes, dating from about the second century C.E., from Hatra, a religious and trading center of the Parthian Empire and a standing Buddha, in gilt bronze, produced by the Northern Wei in China in 477 C.E. All three figures, with their draping robes and realistic postures, reflect Greco-Roman styles from the Mediterranean region that traveled to Asia along the Silk Roads. (Left, © Scala/Art Resource, NY; right, Metropolitan Museum of Art, John Stewart Kennedy Fund, 1926 [26.123], Photograph © 1983 The Metropolitan Museum of Art)

336–323 B.C.E.	273–232	221–206	206 B.C.E.–220 C.E.	138 B.C.E.
Alexander the Great amasses an empire from Anatolia to India	Indian ruler King Asoka of the Maurya Dynasty converts to and patronizes Buddhism	Qin Dynasty rules in China	Han Dynasty rules in China	Zhang Qian begins his travels to Bactria (in parts of contemporary Afghanistan, Uzbekistan, and Tajikistan), which contributes to the opening of the Silk Roads

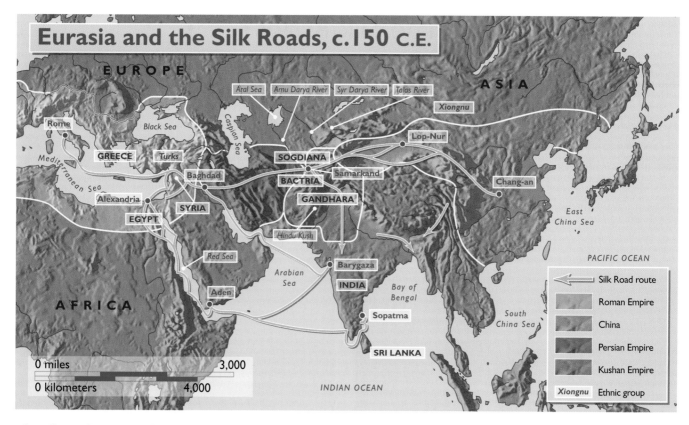

Eurasia and the Silk Roads, c. 150 C.E.

The Silk Roads, a series of trade routes stretching from the Mediterranean region to East Asia, facilitated many cultural, religious, and artistic exchanges between 400 B.C.E. and 900 C.E.

Source: Some data compiled from Luce Boulnois, *The Silk Road* (New York: Dutton, 1966).

scrolls filled with translated Buddhist texts, sandalwood images, and relics that enlivened Chinese Buddhism for the next two centuries.

No route has inspired so much interest or encouraged so much contact among the peoples of the world as have the Silk Roads. The term Silk Roads primarily refers to the many land routes between East Asia and the Mediterranean that developed across central Asia beginning in about 400 B.C.E. and lasting until about 900 C.E. They are best thought of as a corridor, up to 8,000 miles long, along which traders, pilgrims, conquerors, refugees, and curious travelers trekked between early empires of the Mediterranean Basin and East Asia such as the Roman Empire (27 B.C.E.–476 C.E.) and China's Han Dynasty (206 B.C.E.–220 C.E.). In general, the Silk Roads consisted of well-delineated paths connecting

fortified towns between 20 and 60 miles apart. At almost every point, the Silk Roads skirted or traversed some of the world's most punishing environments: broiling deserts, airless mountain passes, and endless plains. The cultural encounters that occurred along the Silk Roads reverberated throughout Europe, Asia, and Africa, creating new cultural traditions and facilitating or hindering the growth of empires.

The Empires in Europe and Asia along the Silk Roads

The Silk Roads had the most impact on China. Although the Silk Roads had come into use during the Warring States Period (403–221 B.C.E.), when up to seven Chinese states competed against one another, it was during the Qin (221–206 B.C.E.) and Han dynasties

50 B.C.E.–150 C.E.	224–651	651	843–45
Height of trade between the Roman Empire and Han Dynasty China	Sassanid Empire rules in Persia; increasing restrictions on Silk Roads traffic	Islam triumphs in Persia	Tang persecution of Buddhists and followers of other "foreign" religions; ebbing of religious exchange on Silk Roads

that they became a focus of political, cultural, and economic importance. The Qin united the "Warring States" under one ruler and a single bureaucracy. The succeeding Han Dynasty built on the strength of the Qin Dynasty, but relied on less totalitarian measures to rule China and encourage its economy and culture. Throughout the course of their rule, the Han worked hard at creating a prosperous, ordered, and unified state. Like many dynasties in Chinese history, however, the Han faced two great problems: the constant threat of neighboring "barbarians" (nomadic pastoralists with strong military traditions), who were eager to take advantage of China's unparalleled prosperity, and Chinese peasants who rebelled against the ever-growing taxation needed to pay for the repression of barbarian invasions. Although periods of chaos and reunification followed the collapse of the Han in 220 C.E., it remained the model for subsequent dynasties, including those of the Sui (589–618 C.E.) and Tang (618–907 C.E.). Likewise, the Silk Roads remained important after the Han. In fact, the Tang Dynasty supported the greatest cultural activity along the Silk Roads (even if its rulers eventually brought about their demise as a vital route of trade and exchange).

At the other end of the Silk Roads, the Romans held an important and powerful role in encouraging the use and extension of the routes by creating the demand for the goods carried on the roads. The Roman Empire expanded so successfully not only because of the superiority of its military and its expertise in administration, but also because it effectively afforded the peoples of its conquered regions the status of allies and, eventually, full citizenship. A united Roman Empire endured in theory until 476 C.E. in the western Mediterranean, although in actuality its authority in the West had evaporated by 400 C.E. The eastern Roman Empire became known as Byzantium, and survived in greatly reduced form until 1453.

The Sassanid Empire of Persia (present-day Iran), which grew between 224 and 651 C.E. out of the older Seleucid and Parthian empires, derived significant income from the trade of the Silk Roads and provided a filter for cultural exchange along these routes. Persia, however, restricted travel across its lands and, for the most part, proved an uneasy middle ground for the Silk

Roads. At the same time, however, Persia became the source of some of the most important cultural traditions transmitted along the route.

Other empires and peoples also had important roles to play in the development and exchanges along the Silk Roads. In India, Emperor Candragupta (c. 348–298 B.C.E.) of the Maurya Dynasty had created a defensive alliance against the Greek-Macedonian invader Alexander the Great (356–323 B.C.E.; king of Macedonia, 336–323 B.C.E.) and used this alliance to unify much of India. Most significantly for the Silk Roads, King Asoka (r. 273–232 B.C.E.), the third emperor of the Maurya Dynasty, adopted and promoted Buddhism and served as one of its important patrons. Although a relatively minor figure in India's history, Asoka's conversion to and support of Buddhism initiated a period of increased cultural exchange along the Silk Roads, and Buddhist India was the destination of many travelers.

Neighboring India to the north were two important states that developed into the nerve center of the Silk Roads. The first was Kushan, which ruled over most of the northern Indian subcontinent, Afghanistan, and parts of central Asia between the first and the third centuries C.E. The Kushans became affluent through trade, particularly with Rome, and were renowned for their tolerance and syncretism (fusion of different belief systems) in religion and art. Within the Kushan Empire, the Sogdian people played an increasingly important role. The Sogdians came from higher in the Hindu Kush mountains than the majority of the Kushans, at the vital crossroads between the Amu Darya and Syr Darya rivers in the northern part of present-day Pakistan and Afghanistan. A seminomadic group, they were the great translators, traders, interpreters, and craftspeople of the Silk Roads. Until Islam became profoundly influential in the region after 730 C.E., the Sogdians served as the ideal intermediaries for the Silk Roads.

Finally, the Silk Roads were bordered on the north by a whole series of nomadic and seminomadic peoples, such as the Xiongnu (commonly referred to as the Huns in the West) and the Turks, who often adopted religions they drew from the Silk Roads and played politics along the trade routes, to the chagrin of all the peoples and societies mentioned above. The Silk Roads provided profound cultural influences and important trade goods to these peoples, as well.

Rise and Decline of the Silk Roads

The Silk Roads developed in part from the need of the Han Dynasty's leadership to resist "barbarian" invasions, such as by the Xiongnu, without raising taxes. In order to defend themselves against the threat of barbarians, the Han Chinese hoped to ally themselves with the Yuehzi in Bactria against the Xiongnu. The Yuehzi had strong horses, which the Chinese needed to battle the Xiongnu. In 138 B.C.E., the Han emperor Wudi (r. 141–87 B.C.E.) sent commander Zhang Qian as an envoy to Bactria. Early in his travels, Zhang Qian was captured by the Xiongnu. After 10 years of captivity, he finally found the Yuehzi in Bactria, but they were no longer interested in fighting the Xiongnu. They did, however, show interest in trading with the Han. When Zhang Qian returned to China after his 13-year journey, he reported that in order to ensure the safe flow of Bactrian horses in exchange for Chinese trade goods, the Han should open a road between the hostile Xiongnu in the north and the Indian empires in the south. Between 104 and 98 B.C.E., Wudi sent large expeditions to Bactria to both capture horses and to begin the process of pacification of the corridor between Bactria and Han China. Until around 180 C.E., when the weakened Han state abandoned it, the corridor, watched over by a series of guard towers and garrisons, served as a route for the exchange of Bactrian horses for Chinese trade goods.

While living in Bactria, Zhang Qian noticed bamboo and silk for sale in the region's markets that had come by sea from southern China via the Bay of Bengal and thence to India. People throughout Africa, Asia, and Europe prized trade goods from East, South, and Southeast Asia. The demand was high for such spices as cinnamon, pepper, and sandalwood from India and for silk from China. Prior to the opening of the Silk Roads to regular travelers, these products traveled a maritime "Spice Roads" from China to India, then from India to Red Sea ports, and thence to trading centers in the Middle East (specifically in western Persia, Syria, and Egypt). Finally, merchants, especially Greeks and Jews, would purchase the goods for resale throughout the Mediterranean. In return, the Romans sent, through intermediary traders, colored glass, amber, furs, asbestos, and a great quantity of gold to the peoples of central Asia and China.

Beginning with the defeat of the Carthaginian Empire (centered in present-day Tunisia) in 146 B.C.E. by the Roman Republic (509–27 B.C.E.), Roman power grew steadily until finally, in 29 B.C.E., Augustus (63 B.C.E.–14 C.E.), Rome's first emperor, annexed Egypt, and Rome gained control of the entire Mediterranean region from Spain to Syria. The unity and security provided by Rome, the concentration of wealth of many countries into the hands of relatively few Romans, and the increasingly ostentatious display of Roman social status encouraged a luxury market, which rested firmly on the availability of Chinese silk. Silk became a highly fashionable and sought-after material, with a 10,000 percent markup from producer to final buyer. So much gold flowed out of Rome to purchase silk that the Emperor Augustus made silk illegal for men to wear and significantly limited its use for women.

The Silk Roads operated as a trade route between the Roman Mediterranean and Han China between about 50 B.C.E. and 180 C.E. The Chinese and the Romans had always been curious about each other and had tried to make contact directly across the Eurasian landmass. The Han Chinese knew about the existence of the Roman Empire as the rich and vast land beyond the unfriendly borders of Seleucid and Parthian Persia. The first official Roman mission to reach China arrived during the reign of Emperor Marcus Aurelius (r. 161–80 C.E.); the first Chinese mission did not reach Byzantium until 634 C.E. So although official exchange between the extremities of the Silk Roads remained severely limited, unofficial exchange through trade was rich and frequent. After 150 C.E., the Han had faced increasing difficulty in ensuring security along the route. The Kingdom of Wei, one of the states that emerged from the component parts of the disintegrated Han Dynasty, reestablished Chinese contact with central Asia beginning in 440 C.E. In 618 C.E., through a government bureau called the *sarthavaha* (Sanskrit for "caravan leader"), the Tang Dynasty began to assure the safety of travelers from China to central Asia and reinitiated the exchange of Chinese silk for Bactrian horses. Yet despite this renewed security, the Silk Roads languished as the favored route for transcontinental trade.

Other factors contributed to the Silk Roads' decline as a transcontinental trade route. Beginning in about 70 C.E., luxury trade between Asia and the Roman Empire had become gradually more focused on maritime routes between the Red Sea and Sri Lanka or the west coast of India. Later, in the third century C.E., the Romans could no longer afford silk because of the economic impact of the barbarian invasions in Europe. The transformation of the Roman Empire into a collection of impoverished small states in western Europe and a wealthy authoritarian state in the eastern Mediterranean occurred within the context of larger disruptions along the Silk Roads. Chinese demand for Roman trade products declined precipitously when Roman expatriates taught central Asian people how to make colored glass. The chaotic Six Dynasties Period (220–589 C.E.) in China seriously hindered the production of goods for the Silk Roads. Conversely, by 550 C.E., Emperor Justinian (r. 527–65) of the Byzantine Empire had learned how to produce silk, thereby eliminating the need for continued trade with China.

Restriction of travel across Persia's borders also impeded trade along the Silk Roads. The Sassanid Empire, for instance, became increasingly strict in its interpretations of its state religion, Zoroastrianism (which contains monotheistic and dualistic features) and equally strict in permitting travelers to cross its lands freely. Subsequently, the political, cultural, and religious triumph of Islam in Persia in 651 C.E. promoted a strategic homogenization of culture and society within the Umayyad (661–750 C.E) and Abbasid (750–1258 C.E) dynasties that succeeded the Sassanids and further restricted travel between the Mediterranean and China across Persian territory. Whereas products of the Silk Roads had previously arrived regularly at many ports and trading centers, Rome, Byzantium, and the changing empires of Persia often selected by treaty a single city through which the trade of the Silk Roads could pass.

Two events exacerbated this process of decline along the Silk Roads. First, in 751 C.E., a Chinese army lost a major battle to the Islamic forces at the Talas River (near Dzhanbul in modern Kazakhstan). The Battle of Talas led ultimately to a less fluid religious and philosophical

Cross-Cultural Exchange
- ↔ Gandharan School of religious art synthesizes Greco-Roman humanism into Buddhist symbols
- ↔ Knowledge of China and the Roman Mediterranean about each other endures throughout first millennium through exchange between the Han Dynasty and Roman Empire
- ↔ Mahayana Buddhism spreads throughout East Asia
- ↔ Greco-Roman frescoes are created in central Asia
- ↔ Silk cloth and brocade are exported to the Mediterranean Basin

environment in central Asia, with the Abbasid, Indian, and Chinese empires abutting one another and having hostile relations. Second, between 843 and 845, in an effort to solidify central control over the Chinese people, the Tang emperor Wu Zong (r. 841–46) closed all of the many and powerful Buddhist monasteries in China and expropriated their property for the state. Subsequently, in 845, he outlawed all foreign religions. With Islam becoming socially dominant in western central Asia and with religious intolerance taking hold in eastern central Asia, the power of the Silk Roads to bring peoples and ideas together was greatly reduced.

Legacy of the Silk Roads: Religious and Artistic Transformations

Although trade formed the core of the development of the Silk Roads, its enduring legacy originated in the powerful cultural exchange and religious transformations engendered by the kind of contact it facilitated. Language and cultural and artistic forms instrumental in religious expression were transformed as a result of interactions along the corridor. In particular, the exchanges led to the solidification of the different schools of Buddhist thought, as well as transmitting Buddhism to China and Japan, where it continues to have an enormous social, cultural, and religious impact.

Buddhism originated in about the sixth century B.C.E. with the Buddha Siddhartha Gautama (c. 563–483 B.C.E.), an Indian aristocrat who at the age of 29 renounced his privileged life to pursue a path of spiritual enlightenment. The Buddha's teachings led to several schools of interpretations. The populist Mahayana Buddhism, which emphasizes the inherent possibility of enlightenment in everyone, especially embodied the cosmopolitan and international spirit of the Silk Roads and may possibly have originated at the cultural cross-roads of Bactria. Other schools of Mahayana Buddhism, such as the less orthodox Pure Land Buddhism (which emphasizes faith as a prerequisite for enlightenment), Tantric Buddhism (which emphasizes chanting as a path to enlightenment), and Chan ("Zen" in Japanese; which reflects upon paradoxes called *koans* as a path to enlightenment), also became important in China and Japan because of the travel facilitated by the Silk Roads.

Beyond its philosophical and religious attraction, Buddhism served the travel needs of the people who used the Silk Roads. It provided Silk Roads travelers and traders with a distinctive cultural identity whereby they could recognize one another and locate sympathetic communities to which they could turn to for assistance and guidance during their travels. Until the Chinese, Indian, and Persian empires foreclosed on the presence of "foreign" religions, including Buddhism, toward the end of the first millennium, local Buddhist communities, especially in Bactria and Kushan, provided a refuge for travelers and traders all along the Silk Roads. In addition, practitioners of Mahayana Buddhism built large and powerful monasteries in which travelers could lodge throughout Bactria. In a mixed cultural world, practicing Buddhists, merchants, and people residing at the intersections of the Silk Roads felt safe.

One of early Christianity's most vibrant communities, the Nestorians, also made the Silk Roads its home and created an active Christian network that stretched, by the 800s, from Baghdad in Iraq to Chang-an in China. The Nestorians, who stressed the human rather than the divine nature of Jesus Christ, resided along the Silk Roads. Exiled by the Byzantines and the Roman Catholic Church from the remnants of Byzantium and the western Roman Empire after 489 C.E., the Nestorians remained influential all along the route until Islamic and Chinese rulers began a severe repression of their faith at the end of the millennium. Certain nomadic Turkish communities to the north of the Silk Roads had converted to Nestorian Christianity before that time. Similar to other religions along the route, Nestorianism stressed inclusiveness, which was attractive for communitarian, nomadic peoples, and incorporated many cultures into

their practices and displays. For example, a 10-foot-high Nestorian monument erected in China's capital, Chang-an, in 781 C.E. was adorned with a cross resting on a Buddhist lotus leaf. In addition to Buddhism and Christianity, the Silk Roads carried other equally important religions, such as Zoroastrianism, Manicheism, and, eventually, Islam. Greek Orthodox Christians also roamed the route, and a significant number of Jews spread across Asia via the Silk Roads, creating trading and religious communities.

Much like the Kushan Empire and Sogdiana did for Buddhism, Parthian and especially Sassanid Persia served as a melting pot of religious and cultural exchange near the western terminus of the Silk Roads. A stable standardized coinage, a network of well-established and newly built roads, and access to the seas made Persia a busy center of trade. Although not a missionary religion, the indigenous Persian religion, Zoroastrianism, influenced cultures and religions along the corridor. All the monotheistic religions of the Middle East—Judaism, Christianity, and Islam—incorporated Zoroastrian ideas of a final judgment by a supernatural being, rewards for good works, and punishment for evil. In central Asia and China, where Zoroastrians traveled in trade caravans along the Silk Roads, they were highly valued for their knowledge of astronomy and magic. The Silk Roads later became a route to exile, when many thousands of Zoroastrians fled the Islamization of Persia after 651, despite their status as a *dhimmi*, or protected community.

The most visible and demonstrable effect of the exchange made possible by the Silk Roads came in the visual arts, especially the influence of Hellenistic and Roman art on Buddhist religious forms. For example, the early adherents of Buddhism had represented themselves and the teachings of the Buddha through a series of stylized symbols, including a footprint (to represent the passage of monks), a pipal tree (under which the Buddha sat), an empty throne (to signify the worldly life the Buddha surrendered), and a wheel (representing law). Toward the end of the first century C.E., artists in Gandhara, an area that encompasses present-day northern Pakistan and Afghanistan, began to portray the Buddha as a human figure rather than through symbols. These figures combined elements from many different sources, but the type of human pose used by the artists is the most striking feature. The draping of the robes on the Buddha, the sense of confidence the artist portrays in the figure, and the realistic posture of the body originated with Greco-Roman styles of the Mediterranean Basin. Good examples of these figures can be seen in extreme western China at Lop-Nur. In addition, the medium through which Gandharan painters expressed themselves, frescoes, is a Mediterranean form of painting. What attracted the artists to this particular form of representation remains a point of scholarly inquiry. The artists may have found the humanity of Greco-Roman style appropriate to the nature of the Buddha they wanted to portray or they may have trained with Roman exiles or expatriates living in central Asia. What is clear, however, is that this kind of synthesis between Europe and Asia occurred repeatedly along the Silk Roads and profoundly influenced the political, religious, and cultural development of its peoples and empires.

In mid-2001, at Bamiyan in the Hindu Kush, the Taliban, an oppressive and intolerant regime in Afghanistan, blew up two large statues of the Buddha hewn from living rock that the traveling monk Xuanzang had viewed in 630 C.E. Bamiyan straddles one of the branches of the Silk Roads leading from Kushan toward Persia. It was only one site of intense religious devotion in a topography of relative tolerance and rich exchange that characterized the Silk Roads during the height of their use, between approximately 400 B.C.E. and 900 C.E. The legacy of the Silk Roads is not just the exotic trade and fruitful exchanges it facilitated, but the tolerance and cultural exchange it supported.

See Also

VOLUME ONE: Indo-European Migration to the Indus Valley; The Roman Empire and the Mediterranean World
VOLUME TWO: Buddhism in China; Nestorian Christianity and the Civilizations of Asia; The Establishment and Spread of Islam; Chinese and Islamic Empires in Central Asia; The Mongols and the Civilizations of Eurasia; Marco Polo in Asia

Bibliography

Adshead, Samuel Adrian M. *China in World History*. 3rd ed. New York: St. Martin's Press, 2000.

Bentley, Jerry H. *Old World Encounters: Cross-Cultural Contacts and Exchanges in Pre-Modern Times*. New York: Oxford University Press, 1993.

Boulnois, Luce. *The Silk Road*. New York: Dutton, 1966.

Foltz, Richard. *Religions of the Silk Road: Overland Trade and Cultural Exchange from Antiquity to the Fifteenth Century*. New York: St. Martin's Press, 1999.

Liu, Hsin-ju. *The Silk Road: Overland Trade and Cultural Interactions in Eurasia*. Washington, D.C.: American Historical Association, 1998.

Ruysbroeck, Willem van. *The Journey of William of Rubruck to the Eastern Parts of the World, 1253–55*. Translated and edited by William Woodville Rockhill. Columbia, Mo.: South Asia Books, 1998.

Whitfield, Susan. *Life along the Silk Road*. Berkeley: University of California Press, 1999.

—*David W. Del Testa*

Primary Document

Xuanzang's Description of the Famous Buddhas at Bamiyan

Between 629 and 645 C.E., Xuanzang, a Chinese monk, traveled from China to central Asia and India to collect Buddhist texts so that he might help improve Chinese Buddhism. During his 10,000-mile journey, Xuanzang visited many sites important to early Buddhism and mentioned them in his account of his trip, Buddhist Records of the Western World. Here, Xuanzang describes Bamiyan, a site in Afghanistan that had two giant Buddhas carved into the living rock of the area's mountains until their destruction by the Taliban in 2001.

This kingdom is about 2000 li [one li equals 0.3 mile] from east to west, and 300 li from north to south. It is situated in the midst of the Snowy Mountains. The people inhabit towns either in the mountains or the valleys, according to circumstances. The capital leans on a steep hill, bordering on a valley 6 or 7 li in length. On the north it is backed by high precipices. It (*the country*) produces spring-wheat and few flowers or fruits. It is suitable for cattle, and affords pasture for many sheep and horses. The climate is wintry, and the manners of the people hard and uncultivated. The clothes are chiefly made of skin and wool, which are the most suitable for the country. The literature, customary rules, and money used in commerce are the same as those of the Tukhâra country. Their language is a little different, but in point of personal appearance they closely resemble each other. These people are remarkable, among all their neighbours, for a love of religion (*a heart of pure faith*); from the highest form of worship to the three jewels [Buddha, Dharma, and Sangha], down to the worship of the hundred (*i.e., different*) spirits, there is not the least absence (*decrease*) of earnestness and the utmost devotion of heart. The merchants, in arranging their prices as they come and go, fall in with the signs afforded by the spirits. If good, they act accordingly; if evil, they seek to propitiate the powers. There are ten convents and about 1000 priests. They belong to the Little Vehicle, and the school of the Lôkôttaravâdins (Shwo-ch'uh-shi-pu).

To the north-east of the royal city there is a mountain, on the declivity of which is placed a stone figure of Buddha, erect, in height 140 or 150 feet. Its golden hues sparkle on every side, and its precious ornaments dazzle the eyes by their brightness.

To the east of this spot there is a convent, which was built by a former king of the country. To the east of the convent there is a standing figure of Sâkya Buddha, made of metallic stone (*teou-shih*), in height 100 feet. It has been cast in different parts and joined together, and thus placed in a completed form as it stands.

To the east of the city 12 or 13 li there is a convent, in which there is a figure of Buddha lying in a sleeping position, as when he attained *Nirvâna*. The figure is in length about 1000 feet or so. The king of this (*country*), every time he assembles the great congregation of the Wu-che (*Môksha*), having sacrificed all his possessions, from his wife and children down to his country's treasures, gives in addition his own body; then his ministers and the lower order of officers prevail on the priests to barter back these possessions; and in these matters most of their time is taken up.

Source: Excerpted from Hiuen Tsiang (Xuanzang), *Si-Yu-Ki: Buddhist Records of the Western World*, translated from the Chinese of Hiuen Tsiang (629 C.E.) by Samuel Beal (London: Kegan Paul, Trench, Trübner, 1909), 49–52.

The Greek Empire: The Creation of the Hellenistic World

327 B.C.E.–600 C.E.

In 334 B.C.E., Alexander the Great (356–323 B.C.E.), king of Macedonia and the future conqueror of a vast Greek Empire, began his ultimately successful campaign against Emperor Darius III (r. 336–330 B.C.E.) of the Persian Empire (present-day Iran). He defeated the Persian army in two major battles and destroyed Gaza and the Phoenician city of Tyre, two of Persia's important port cities, in 332 B.C.E. That same year, he marched his army into Egypt, where he was welcomed as a liberator from hated Persian rule. After being proclaimed pharaoh by the leading Egyptian priests in the capital city of Memphis, Alexander founded a new city on the delta of the Nile River. Named Alexandria after the great Macedonian ruler, the city's purpose was to become a new port that would replace Tyre as the center of maritime trade in the eastern Mediterranean.

Alexandria would eventually emerge as one of the most important cities in Egypt, but it was only the first of many "Alexandrias" founded by the Macedonian king as he continued his spectacular conquests across western Asia into northern India. Although many of them were founded simply as military outposts, some developed into cities from which Greek culture spread and interacted with the indigenous population, creating the Hellenistic world. (Hellas is the ancient name for Greece.)

The Rise of Alexander the Great and the Persian Empire

Alexander was the ruler of Macedonia, a state in the southern Balkans heavily influenced by Greek culture but ruled by a monarchy, rather than its citizenship, as was the case in Athens and other Greek city-states of the Classical Era. Alexander was born in the northern Balkan Peninsula, son of King Philip II of Macedon

(r. 359–336 B.C.E.). He was tutored by the philosopher Aristotle (384–322 B.C.E.), absorbing Greek culture, and was groomed for military leadership by his father, who was an adroit military strategist. At the age of 16, Alexander was appointed regent while his father conducted almost continual military campaigns, and he also became a commander in his father's army. When his father was assassinated in 336 B.C.E., Alexander assumed the throne as Alexander III. (The Romans added "the Great" to his name many years later.) Alexander built his empire on a Macedonian kingdom

Seventeenth-century painting The Battle of Granicus, *by Charles Le Brun, depicting Alexander the Great in battle against Persian emperor Darius III. (© Réunion des Musées Nationaux/Art Resource, NY)*

559–530 B.C.E.	521–486	500–479	486–465	356	334
Reign of Cyrus the Great in the Persian Empire	Reign of Darius I in the Persian Empire	Persian Wars	Reign of Xerxes in the Persian Empire	Alexander the Great is born	Alexander initiates the conquest of the Persian Empire

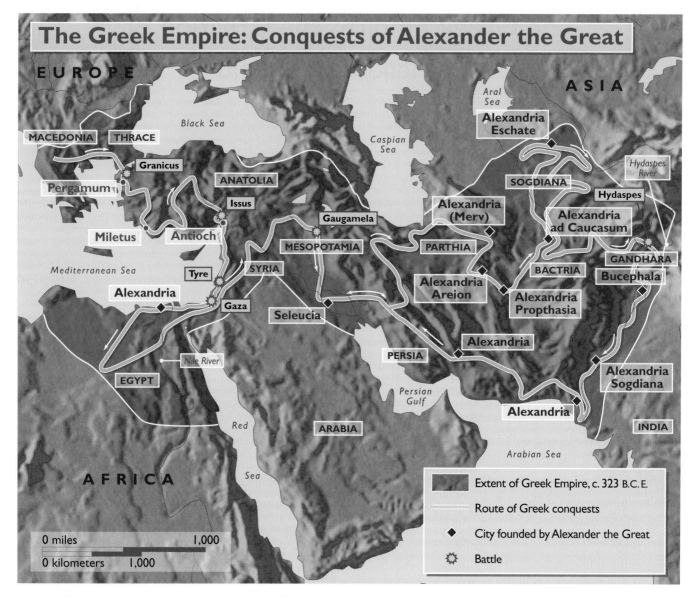

The Greek Empire: Conquests of Alexander the Great

EUROPE

ASIA

Aral Sea

Alexandria Eschate

Black Sea

Caspian Sea

MACEDONIA **THRACE**

Granicus

ANATOLIA

Hydaspes River

Pergamum

SOGDIANA

Hydaspes

Issus

Alexandria (Merv)

Alexandria ad Caucasum

Miletus **Antioch**

Gaugamela

MESOPOTAMIA

PARTHIA

GANDHARA

Mediterranean Sea

Tyre

SYRIA

BACTRIA

Bucephala

Alexandria

Gaza

Seleucia

Alexandria Areion

Alexandria Propthasia

Alexandria Sogdiana

Nile River

Alexandria

PERSIA

EGYPT

Persian Gulf

Red Sea

ARABIA

Alexandria

INDIA

Arabian Sea

AFRICA

	Extent of Greek Empire, c. 323 B.C.E.
	Route of Greek conquests
◆	City founded by Alexander the Great
✺	Battle

0 miles 1,000

0 kilometers 1,000

During the reign of Alexander the Great, the Greek Empire expanded into Egypt, northern India, and western Asia through a series of successful battles and conquests. Alexander founded many "Alexandrias" throughout the empire, which contributed to Greek interactions with the indigenous populations of these cities, the spread of Greek culture, and the creation of the Hellenistic world.

Sources: Some data compiled from Gerald A. Danzer, *Atlas of World History* (London: Laurence King, 2000), 35; and C. Warren Hollister, *Roots of the Western Tradition: A Short History of the Ancient World*, 6th ed. (New York: McGraw-Hill, 1996), 133.

consolidated and strengthened by his father. In 334 B.C.E., after suppressing rebellions against Macedonian rule arising among the northern tribes and the Greek city of Thebes, Alexander decided to launch an invasion of the Persian Empire, the traditional Greek enemy. His stated reason was to avenge the invasion of Greece by the Persian emperor Xerxes (486–465 B.C.E.) in the early fifth century B.C.E.

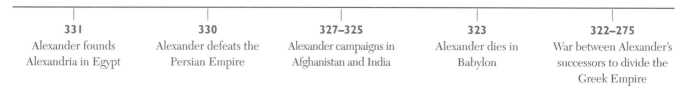

331	330	327–325	323	322–275
Alexander founds Alexandria in Egypt	Alexander defeats the Persian Empire	Alexander campaigns in Afghanistan and India	Alexander dies in Babylon	War between Alexander's successors to divide the Greek Empire

At this time, the great Persian Empire dominated western Asia from the Indian border to the coast of the eastern Mediterranean. It was founded in the sixth century B.C.E. by Cyrus the Great (r. 559–530 B.C.E.), who founded the long-lasting Achaemenid Dynasty. In a 20-year period, Cyrus expanded from his base in southwestern Iran and conquered states and territories in Anatolia (present-day Turkey), central Asia, Bactria (present-day Afghanistan), and Mesopotamia (present-day Iraq). After his death, his successors expanded the empire to include Egypt, the northern Indian kingdom of Gandhara, along with Thrace (present-day Bulgaria) and other lands in southeastern Europe.

The early Achaemenids were also successful administrators, constructing a centralized government to administer a diverse and far-flung empire, but allowing local laws and customs to remain in place. To administer and tax each district more efficiently, Darius I (r. 521–486 B.C.E.) divided the empire into 23 *satrapies* (provincial governments), governed by *satraps* (governors) who were prevented by imperial agents from gaining independence from central rule.

The official policy of tolerance ended in the fifth century with the reign of Darius's son Xerxes, causing deep resentment among his many non-Persian subjects, especially the Greeks who lived in Ionia on the western coast of present-day Turkey. The Ionian Greeks had already begun to rebel against their satraps in 500 B.C.E., initiating a 20-year conflict between Persia and the Greek states known as the Persian Wars (500–479 B.C.E.). Twice, in 490 and 480 B.C.E., Xerxes sent an invasion force to conquer and absorb the Greek city-states into his empire, and twice he was defeated, creating an atmosphere of hostility between the Greeks and the Persians that would last another 150 years and end only with Alexander's Persian campaign.

The Battle of Granicus in 334 B.C.E. initiated Alexander's conquest of the Persian Empire. From there he marched into Syria, where his well-disciplined troops defeated the Persian army, led by Emperor Darius III, at the Battle of Issus in 333 B.C.E. Darius

fled eastward, leaving Alexander in control of the western half of the Persian Empire. In 332 B.C.E., Alexander turned south, along the Mediterranean coast, and after long and arduous sieges, destroyed Tyre and Gaza, both important port cities for the Persian fleet. After taking control of Egypt, he returned eastward to face Darius again at the definitive Battle of Gaugamela (in present-day Iraq). Alexander's bold and creative battlefield tactics continued to defeat the Persians, and Darius once again fled the battlefield, his authority among his own people in tatters. Eventually, Darius was murdered by one of his own satraps, enabling Alexander to proclaim himself emperor.

Having defeated the Persians, Alexander declared himself heir to the Achaemenids and "Lord of Asia." Soon he adopted Persian ceremonials, appointed Persian officials, married a princess from the Persian province of Sogdiana, and began to wear Persian dress. Although he sought to combine Greek and Eastern cultures, his primary goal was to continue his military campaign eastward to what he believed was the edge of Asia. (Geographical knowledge at the time radically underestimated the extent of lands stretching beyond the Indus River in northern India.) In 327 B.C.E., Alexander conquered present-day Afghanistan and in 326 B.C.E. defeated King Porus (d. c. 321), ruler of the Jhelum region in northern India on the Hydaspes River. In 325 B.C.E., Alexander was forced by his weary troops to retreat. He died, most likely of malarial fever, in Babylon in 323 B.C.E. Alexander the Great's distant conquests spread Greek culture throughout much of western Asia and Egypt, during what is known as the Hellenistic Era.

The Spread of Greek Culture and the Development of the Hellenistic World

Alexander's vast empire did not survive his death. It was soon replaced by several successor states ruled by his generals, called the Diadochi (successors). From 322 to 275 B.C.E. they went to war with each other to determine how to divide the imperial lands. In Egypt, Ptolemy I

c. 155	64	30	476 C.E.	c. 600s
Parthians gain control of Persia and parts of Mesopotamia	Romans conquer the Seleucid Empire	Ptolemaic Egypt is absorbed into the Roman Empire	Fall of the Roman Empire in the West	Islamic forces from Arabia destroy the Greek Empire in the East

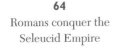
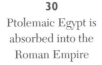

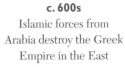

(r. 323–283 B.C.E.) founded a long-lasting dynasty, which came to an end only with the death of Cleopatra in 30 B.C.E. Seleucus (r. 323–280 B.C.E.) obtained most of the former Persian Empire, and Antigonus (r. 323–301 B.C.E.) gained control of Macedonia. Except in Macedonia, the majority of whose population remained Greek, the new rulers of these successor kingdoms immediately faced the challenge of ruling as a tiny Greek minority among potentially hostile indigenous populations. The consolidation of their power began in the cities they founded or controlled. Alexander founded possibly up to 70 new cities or military outposts—one, founded in present-day Tajikistan, was called "Alexandria-the-Furthest" for its remote location at the extreme boundary of the Alexandrian conquests.

Each new dynasty adapted its method of rule to the local circumstances. Imitating the pharaohs who previously ruled Egypt, Ptolemy I had himself proclaimed "Savior God" upon his death, and his successors took the additional step of self-deification while still alive. The Ptolemies also continued the pharaonic practice of strictly controlling the economy, adapting it to the Greek money economy. While Ptolemy excluded native Egyptians from serving in the army and allotted land to Greek and Macedonian soldiers, his successors eventually allowed native Egyptians into the military because not enough Greeks were immigrating to fill the ranks. These Egyptians adopted Greek culture, some more deeply than others. The city of Alexandria was transformed into an important center of trade with a harbor, marketplaces, shipyards, and banks. Its population reached approximately one million residents. Not long after Alexander died, his corpse was retrieved by Ptolemy to be buried in Alexandria, the new capital of Egypt. Not only a center of trade, Alexandria, with its famous library and museum (which also served as a sort of research university), became a cultural magnate for Greek scholars and other intellectuals. The expanded cultural interaction led to advances in science, mathematics, astronomy, philosophy, and other fields. Alexandria's prestige and cosmopolitanism influenced other Hellenistic cities.

In Seleucid Persia (312–64 B.C.E.), the new rulers maintained Achaemenid administration and infrastructure, founded new cities and colonies, and enticed Greek colonists to populate them. These cities, islands in a sea of different ethnic groups, were designed to resemble the classical Greek cities and featured gymnasiums, traditional Greek schools to train the local elite, among many other Greek institutions and traditions. Antioch (in present-day Turkey), while not able to rival Alexandria in wealth and splendor, became the greatest city of the Seleucid Empire.

In Seleucid lands, new and old cities were transformed into provincial capitals serving their particular kingdoms. They were built according to the so-called Milesian plan, after Miletus, an Anatolian city in which the design was pioneered. Built on a plain instead of a large hill, this type of city plan consisted of a functional rectangular pattern, a gridiron of streets of uniform size oriented according to the coordinates of the compass, and surrounded by walled fortifications. Rich and poor districts were separated by quadrant, each of which possessed a marketplace, but with narrow streets in the poor districts and wider, more comfortable streets in the rich ones. The most important of these cities displayed public buildings and monuments lavishly funded by either the central royal government or by wealthy merchants. City-states that were once independent political entities were absorbed into the kingdom and transformed into administrative, manufacturing, and commercial centers for each imperial province.

The cities of the Hellenistic world formed the central points of Hellenistic culture; their inhabitants adopted Greek patterns of government, institutions, and economic life. Educational, artistic, and intellectual activities flourished, and trade was expanded to include Arabia, India, and China. A new ruling elite was formed, mostly of Greeks and Macedonians who migrated in large numbers to the new cities. They served as bureaucrats, who used the Greek language, law, calendar, and coinage to administer their provinces. Those members of the indigenous population who wanted to rise in this new bureaucracy or take part in its economy learned to adopt at least a veneer of Hellenistic culture. In the process, Greek identity became more associated with adherence to Hellenistic culture than to a particular region or city-state in Greece, which underpinned the previous concept of identity and citizenship in classical Greece. Each successor state's increasing demand for professionals, such as physicians, engineers, scholars, bureaucrats, actors, musicians, and athletes, meant that foreigners could now become Greek by adopting the Greek culture and speaking the Greek language. As a result, Greek customs and language spread, especially to elite Persian and Egyptian families. A dialect of Greek, Koines, became—along with the Semitic language, Aramaic—a common tongue (*lingua franca*) of the eastern Mediterranean region.

The Transformation of Greek Religion and Science

Two aspects of Greek culture—religion and science—were especially affected by the new cosmopolitan age. In Greece, each city-state worshipped its particular god (e.g., Athenians worshipped Athena, the goddess of war), as part of its civic and public life. In the new polyglot cities of the Hellenistic world, however, immigrants from the four corners worshipped a bewildering number of gods, with no single entity prevailing. Immigrants also understood that the local gods worshipped by the indigenous population must be respected. Religious belief became more individual, stressing personal fulfillment and salvation rather than civic identity. One result was syncretism: the fusion of traditional gods (of classical Greece) with other (Eastern) gods underpinned by the belief that the gods of different peoples actually manifested the same divine spirit. For example, the god Serapis was a fusion of the Egyptian god Osiris and Apis, a divine bull calf in Greek mythology. He was considered a kind and gentle god who nevertheless ruled over the earth.

Mystery cults, involving intense private ceremonies stressing salvation and resurrection, also gained popularity. These religions seemed to blend Jewish monotheism with Egyptian and Middle Eastern polytheism. Mystery cults usually revolved around a savior-god, who would protect its worshipers from evil, or a loving mother-goddess, who would greet the faithful in the afterlife. The most popular of these cults involved the worship of the god Osiris, who was killed, reborn, and then passed judgment on the dead. The cult of Mithras, which emerged in Persia, stressed the battle between good and evil and the coming of a savior who would redeem humankind and save it from the forces of darkness. Many more such cults existed, along with belief in

Cross-Cultural Exchange
- ↔ Greek (Hellenistic) culture and language, centered in the provincial cities, spreads to western Asia
- ↔ Religious traditions from East and West merge to form new practices and beliefs
- ↔ Spread of Hellenistic culture promotes scientific advances in astronomy, mathematics, engineering, and medicine

sorcery, witchcraft, and magic. An individual could and did participate in more than one cult.

The increased contact between Greece and the civilizations of the East also expanded the horizons of science. The Hellenistic dynasties encouraged scientific study, establishing libraries not only in Alexandria, but also in Antioch, Pergamum (in present-day Turkey), and other locations. These libraries served as research institutions for scholars from all over the Hellenistic world. Particular achievements occurred in astronomy and mathematics, as well as in engineering and medicine. Astronomers calculated the length of the lunar month (with a level of accuracy that rivals modern precision), proposed a heliocentric model of the universe (where Earth revolves around the sun), and theorized that Earth rotated on its own axis. Mathematicians developed geometry and integral calculus, calculated the value of π (pi), and established other mathematical principles. Engineers developed, among other devices, catapults that operated on compressed air, the compound pulley, and devices that improved irrigation and mining operations. In medicine, researchers based in Egypt's Alexandria conducted dissections and discovered that the brain is the center of the nervous system and of intelligence and that blood flows through arteries pumped by the heart. Dissections also revealed more about the female reproductive system, including the function of ovaries and possibly of the fallopian tubes. These discoveries influenced the development of science and medicine in western Europe into modern times.

Despite the stimulation of new ideas in the Hellenistic world, many members of the indigenous populations in Egypt and the East either could not or would not assimilate into Greek culture. They stood fast by their own traditions and viewed the Greeks as colonial overlords. Only a tiny proportion of the indigenous population, those who sought positions in government and the military, fully embraced a Greek way of life. When the dynasties of the successor states began to weaken, indigenous leadership, supported by peasants and others exploited by the Hellenistic dynasties, took back control of their lands. In Persia, one of these groups was the Parthians. Originally a seminomadic people from the eastern Persian satrapy of Parthia, the Parthian Empire (247 B.C.E.–224 C.E.) progressively overthrew Seleucid rule in the East and by about 155 B.C.E. had gained control of Persia and parts of Mesopotamia.

In 64 B.C.E., the Romans, the new imperialists, conquered what was left of the Seleucid Empire. In 30 B.C.E., Ptolemaic Egypt was also absorbed into the emerging Roman Empire. However, the destruction of the successor dynasties diminished but did not destroy the influence of ancient Greek culture, which was spread so widely by Alexander. The Romans also adopted much of Greek culture with greater enthusiasm than the peoples of the East, and the eastern half of the Roman Empire reaffirmed its Greek identity with the fall of the western Roman Empire in 476 C.E. The arrival of Islamic forces from Arabia in the seventh century eventually destroyed the Greek Empire.

See Also

VOLUME ONE: The Roman Empire and the Mediterranean World; Barbarians in the Roman Empire

VOLUME TWO: The Establishment and Spread of Islam

Bibliography

Ellis, Walter M. *Ptolemy of Egypt*. London: Routledge, 1994.

Green, Peter. *From Alexander to Actium: The Historical Evolution of the Hellenistic Age*. Berkeley: University of California Press, 1990.

Grimal, Pierre. *Hellenism and the Rise of Rome*. London: Weidenfeld & Nicolson, 1968.

Kuhrt, Amélie, and Susan Sherwin-White, eds. *From Samarkhand to Sardis: A New Approach to the Seleucid Empire*. Berkeley: University of California Press, 1993.

———. *Hellenism in the East: The Interaction of Greek and Non-Greek Civilizations from Syria to Central Asia after Alexander*. Berkeley: University of California Press, 1987.

—*Florence Lemoine*

Primary Document

Dio Chrysostom Extols Alexandria's Cultural and Economic Amenities

Dio Chrysostom (c. 40–110 C.E.) was a Greek philosopher during the era of the Roman Empire. He traveled widely giving speeches on a variety of topics. In the speech from which this excerpt is taken, Dio Chrysostom urges Alexandrians to fulfill the promise of their splendid city.

. . . For your city is vastly superior in point of size and situation, and it is admittedly ranked second among all cities beneath the sun. For not only does the mighty nation, Egypt, constitute the framework of your city—or more accurately its appanage—but the peculiar nature of the river, when compared with all others, defies description with regard to both its marvellous habits and its usefulness; and furthermore, not only have you a monopoly of the shipping of the entire Mediterranean by reason of the beauty of your harbours, the magnitude of your fleet, and the abundance and the marketing of the products of every land, but also the outer waters that lie beyond are in your grasp, both the Red Sea and the Indian Ocean, whose name was rarely heard in former days. The result is that the trade, not merely of islands, ports, a few straits and isthmuses, but of practically the whole world is yours. For Alexandria is situated, as it were, at the crossroads of the whole world, of even the most remote nations thereof, as if it were a market serving a single city, a market which brings together into one place all manner of men, displaying them to one another and, as far as possible, making them a kindred people.

Source: Excerpted from Dio Chrysostom, *Works*, translated by J. W. Cohoon and H. Lamar Crosby (Cambridge: Harvard University Press; London: William Heinemann, 1932), 3:205–207.

Barbarians in China

206 B.C.E.–907 C.E.

During the Three Kingdoms/Six Dynasties Period (220–589 C.E.), China fell into a period of chaos and struggle. Initially, during the Three Kingdoms, the authority of the Han Dynasty (206 B.C.E.–220 C.E.) devolved into a three-way division of China between the kingdoms of Wei, Shu Han, and Wu. No one kingdom could overpower the others to reunite China, and by 290, the disunity worsened.

Because of the chaos and collapse of frontier defenses, "barbarian" nomadic peoples of the Eurasian steppe north of China began to migrate south for better pastureland and plunder. They established mixed, Chinese-barbarian kingdoms in northern China that eventually agglomerated into the dynasty of the Northern Wei (386–534 C.E.). At the same time, many native Chinese in northern China fled

The Great Wall of China, built by the Qin Dynasty to serve as a defensive wall against the nomadic Xiongnu, known in the West as the Huns. (© Keren Su/Corbis)

2200–1766 B.C.E.	1766–1122	1122–256	403–221	221–206
Xia Dynasty rules in China	Shang Dynasty rules in China	Zhou Dynasty rules in China	Warring States Period in China	Qin Dynasty (ethnic Chinese) rules in China

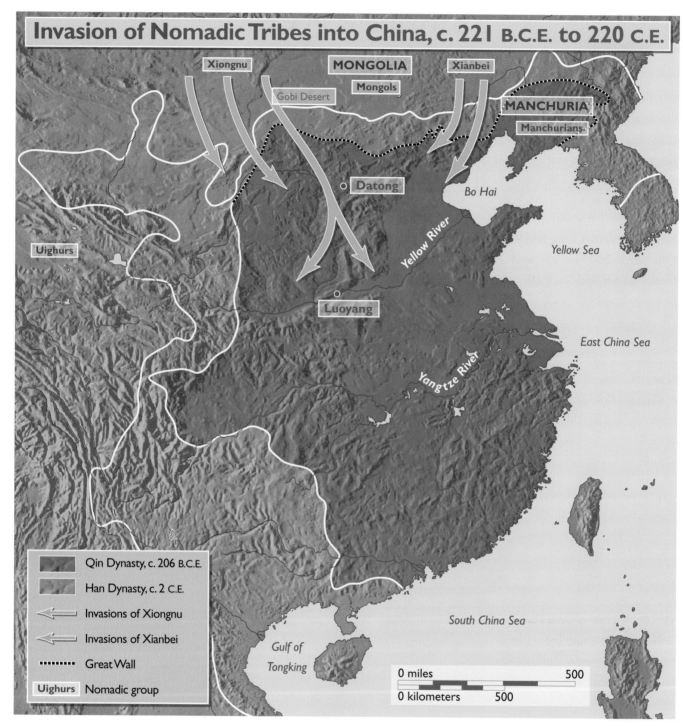

Invasion of Nomadic Tribes into China, c. 221 B.C.E. to 220 C.E.

Xiongnu

MONGOLIA

Xianbei

Mongols

Gobi Desert

MANCHURIA

Manchurians

Datong

Bo Hai

Uighurs

Yellow Sea

Yellow River

Luoyang

East China Sea

Yangtze River

South China Sea

Gulf of
Tongking

Qin Dynasty, c. 206 B.C.E.

Han Dynasty, c. 2 C.E.

Invasions of Xiongnu

Invasions of Xianbei

Great Wall

Uighurs Nomadic group

0 miles 500

0 kilometers 500

During the Qin and Han dynasties in China, nomadic peoples (referred to as "barbarians" by the Chinese) who spoke Turko-Mongol languages formed an arc around China and began flowing across its borders. As a result of these interactions, nomadic groups such as the Xiongnu and Xianbei adopted Chinese writing, customs, and political structures, and would eventually unify China under their rule following the collapse of the Han Dynasty in 220 C.E.

Source: Some data compiled from Gerald A. Danzer, *Atlas of World History* (London: Laurence King, 2000), 42.

209–174	**206 B.C.E.–220 C.E.**	**220–589**	**386–534**	**494**
Reign of Maodun, who establishes the Xiongnu confederation	Han Dynasty (ethnic Chinese) rules in China	Three Kingdoms/Six Dynasties Period in China	Northern Wei Dynasty (syncretic Chinese-nomad) rules in China	Northern Wei Dynasty moves its capital from Datong to Luoyang

southward. In the south, six successive dynasties attempted to reunify China by establishing their authority over southern China. The hybrid, Chinese-barbarian Sui Dynasty (581–618 C.E.), however, would succeed in doing so from the north in 589.

The English word *barbarian* originated from a term that described someone who did not know the Greek language and thus, to the Greeks, was incomprehensible. To the Chinese, a barbarian came to signify someone who lacked civilization, in the sense of not living in cities or possessing the morals and customs of the Chinese. Much of the cultural exchange that occurred during the Qin (221–206 B.C.E.) and Han dynasties and the medieval Sui and Tang (618–907 C.E.) dynasties flowed in one direction, with nomadic peoples adopting or adapting Chinese writing, personal habits, and leadership structures to suit their needs. Because of the comparative comfort of settled life, nomadic peoples became more sinicized (that is, acculturated to Chinese customs) the longer they interacted with Chinese civilization. The exchange between the Chinese and their nomadic neighbors, however, had a much deeper and more important impact. Nomadic society had a disregard for tradition and an enthusiasm for innovation that repeatedly rejuvenated a China badly divided between warring factions. Since the beginning of China's Classical Age in 206 B.C.E. until the founding of the Qing Dynasty in 1644 C.E., nomads served as the primary agents for political and perhaps cultural change in China.

Rise of the Dynastic System in China

Scholars generally divide the history of China into periods called dynasties, which denote the reign of a series of hereditary emperors who unified the Chinese people under a common political and cultural system. The first recognized dynasty is that of the Shang (1766–1122 B.C.E.), although some scholars claim the existence of an earlier dynasty, the Xia (2200–1766 B.C.E.). In these early dynasties, kings justified their rule through their monopoly of important rituals, prognostication (foretelling), and bronze smelting after its introduction

around 1600 B.C.E. (thus controlling the availability of advanced weapons, chariot axles, and ritual vessels). Early kings governed lowland agricultural centers along the capricious Yellow River; these centers were expanded by the Shang Dynasty, which organized town leaders into a decentralized government. Although the common view of China is often one of isolation and cultural homogeneity, it appears that during the early dynasties, there must have been a fair amount of willingness to absorb outsiders and their ideas into the dominant culture. Lowland Chinese probably had frequent contact with highland dwellers and steppe nomads, who resembled them but were ethnically and culturally distinct. Likewise, through steppe nomads and their own merchants, lowland Chinese probably had contact with cultures beyond East Asia. Through this cross-cultural contact, for example, the Chinese learned about bronze smelting and chariots.

The Zhou Dynasty (1122–256 B.C.E.) initially began ruling one region of the Shang kingdom. It was able to take over from the Shang after perfecting its military capabilities in skirmishes with the nomadic peoples on its borders. The Zhou Dynasty also centered on the Yellow River and continued to use a relatively decentralized system of government to rule. The dynasty expanded the area of the Shang considerably.

Two factors challenged Zhou leadership. First, in 771 B.C.E., unknown nomadic peoples from the west of China (probably Eurasian steppe peoples) invaded the Zhou Dynasty. The success of these invasions damaged the loyalty of local chiefs to the Zhou leadership and the ability of the Zhou to rally support to resist future invasions. This began a long period of incursions on the Zhou from nomadic peoples living on the Eurasian steppe to China's north and west. Culturally distinct, these horse-mounted nomads outmaneuvered Zhou chariots and infantry, initiating a period of decline for the Zhou Dynasty. By 403 B.C.E., these challenges became so frequent and widespread that China fell into a period of chaos known as the Warring States Period (403–221 B.C.E.).

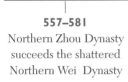

557–581
Northern Zhou Dynasty succeeds the shattered Northern Wei Dynasty

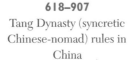

581–618
Sui Dynasty (syncretic Chinese-nomad) rules in China

618–907
Tang Dynasty (syncretic Chinese-nomad) rules in China

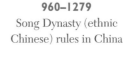

960–1279
Song Dynasty (ethnic Chinese) rules in China

1279–1368
Yuan (Mongol) Dynasty (syncretic Chinese-nomad) rules in China

Curiously, during the Warring States Period, lowland Chinese began to assert a consciously unique identity that became important in their dealings with other peoples. The great philosophical and moral systems of China—Confucianism, Legalism, and Daoism (which stressed a simple and natural way of life)—developed and became widely influential. (Buddhism would not be influential until after the Han Dynasty, even though it had developed prior to that point.) Confucianism, with its emphasis on morality, virtue, hierarchy, and leadership by example, became particularly important and formed the definition of leadership for the Chinese.

After 221 B.C.E., with a disciplined army and salaried bureaucrats, King Zheng (r. 238–221 B.C.E. as king; 221–210 B.C.E. as emperor) completed the process of reuniting all the Chinese states under a single ruler and founded the short-lived Qin Dynasty. King Zheng, who called himself Shi Huangdi (the First Emperor), followed the tenets of Legalism, a political philosophy that stressed harsh punishment for even the most minor infractions and rich rewards for obedience. It is during the Qin that China's emperors began to actively resist their barbarian neighbors. This stance reflected Legalist doctrine as well as a strong Chinese identity based on morality, virtue, appropriate behavior, education, and the superiority of agriculture as the basis of the economy. The Chinese character for "writing" also doubles as the character for "civilized," thus reflecting negative Chinese attitudes toward nomadic cultures.

As ruler of the Qin Dynasty, Shi Huangdi built roads, united separated defensive earthworks into the Great Wall, and standardized the Chinese script and legal code as well as its system of weights, measures, and currencies. Together, these commonalties demarcated what it meant to be Chinese. The construction of the wall established the zone where China ended and the steppe of the nomadic peoples began. In addition, a negative motivation may have contributed to this sense of cultural unity. Shi Huangdi ordered the burning of all books not dealing with medicine, divination, and agriculture. Their reconstruction during the Han Dynasty from scraps, hiding places, and memory may have helped to form the Chinese intellectual sphere, since the intellectual tradition that dominated China after the Qin, Confucianism, was based on the recovered texts. The Qin Dynasty's intellectual, cultural, and political legacy would become the foundation for all Chinese dynasties for the next two thousand years.

Early Exchange between Han China and the Xiongnu

Xiongnu

Settled, agricultural China had probably always faced harassment from the nomadic peoples who lived on the steppe and in the deserts that ringed much of agricultural China. Over time, nomads (Manchurians, Mongols, Turks, Uighur, Xiongnu, and Xianbei) who spoke Turko-Mongol languages figured most strongly in China's barbarian problem. By the time of the Qin Dynasty in the third century B.C.E., the nomadic peoples had developed distinct identities and formed an arc around China. The first group with whom the Chinese had a relationship was the Xiongnu, known in the West as the Huns.

Like other nomads, the Xiongnu consisted of a variety of peoples who practiced pastoralism and some agriculture. Like many of the nomadic peoples, Xiongnu men practically lived their lives on horseback, and they were highly effective warriors when they used their mobility as a weapon. They subsisted on herding sheep and goats, but augmented their economy with trade, plunder, and the receipt of gifts. The nomadic peoples normally lived on the open steppe in small separated chiefdoms, each ruled by a hereditary leader who maintained his position through his generosity in the redistribution of resources. The Xiongnu practiced a shamanistic religion.

A Xiongnu leader named Maodun (r. 209–174 B.C.E.) unified the various Xiongnu peoples and clans into a gigantic confederation that stretched from the Aral Sea to Manchuria. Maodun declared himself *chanyu* (the Son of Heaven), an appellation derived from the title traditionally used by the Chinese emperor. Like the Chinese dynasties, this confederation set a pattern that repeated itself until the Qing Dynasty came to power in 1644 C.E. and the pressure from nomadic peoples essentially disappeared. Loosely ruled, Maodun's confederation profited from trade passing along the early Silk Roads from China to Rome, raids on Chinese settlements, and cash payments that Chinese leaders often sent to mollify the northerners. As long as China was prosperous, so was the Xiongnu confederation.

The Xiongnu confederation faced stiff opposition from the Qin Dynasty's armies and Shi Huangdi's relentless pursuit. Knowing they could not easily oppose Qin armies face to face, the Xiongnu simply retreated into the deserts and steppes. With the threat of the Xiongnu temporarily abated, Qin officials invested heavily in the construction of the Great Wall of China to serve as a defensive wall against the Xiongnu.

Han Dynasty

In 206 B.C.E., a general in the Qin army, Liu Bang (256–195 B.C.E.), established the Han Dynasty and began the dynasty that, by bringing together the political legacy of the Qin and the cultural elements of the Warring States Period, would form the Classical Age of Chinese history. With the help of brilliant advisors, Liu Bang maintained Qin political unity. Rather than choosing between the brutality of the Qin or the ruinous decentralization of the earlier Zhou, Liu Bang created provinces over which administrators held considerable power but in which imperial administrative penetration was quite low. Instead of relying on bureaucratic or aristocratic leadership, he depended on volunteer community leaders who led through moral persuasion and customary Confucian deference to authority.

As opposed to the entirely punitive policy of the Qin, the Han emperors adopted a mixed policy when dealing with their nomadic neighbors, especially the Xiongnu confederation. The Han Dynasty generally sought to expand its borders to the size of China during the Qin Dynasty, capture the Tarim Basin (a large desert area in central Asia famous for its horses), and divide the nomads against one another. To achieve their goals, the Han developed an implicit understanding with the Xiongnu. In return for peace and respecting China's territory, the Xiongnu could expect that the Han would send them annual payments of silk, wine, and grain, as well as Han princesses for marriage alliances; that the Han would treat the Xiongnu as political equals; and

Cross-Cultural Exchange

- ↔ Nomadic peoples absorb Chinese cultural traits, such as Chinese dress and political organization
- ↔ Challenges by nomadic peoples force a consolidation of Chinese culture by philosophers and political leaders
- ↔ "Barbarian" dynasties of the Sui and Tang become receptive to foreign ideas and cultural influences
- ↔ Buddhism becomes popular in China through the Tang Dynasty because of the influence of nomadic peoples

that the Great Wall would serve as the main boundary between the Han and Xiongnu. Through this arrangement with the Xiongnu, China placed itself in opposition to the barbarians, which helped the Chinese define themselves culturally and enabled the nomads to assert a distinct identity of their own.

Sometimes, however, these negotiated relationships did not serve the strategic needs of the Chinese emperors. For example, Han ruler Wudi (r. 141–87 B.C.E.) lashed out against China's nomadic neighbors during his rule. Wudi campaigned so vigorously that he captured the far western Tarim Basin and forced the Xiongnu into retreat. Likewise, after 80 C.E., armies of the Han Dynasty may have crossed the Gobi Desert (in present-day Mongolia and western China) and placed pressure on the Xiongnu to the point that the Xiongnu began to migrate westward in such numbers as to threaten the Roman Empire after 350 C.E.

While the Han emperors temporarily resolved the problem of invasions, they could not, however, raise enough revenue to support the empire. In a pattern that typified most Chinese dynasties, the Han had large military expenses related to border patrols that they mitigated through unpopular taxes. Throughout the latter half of the Han Dynasty, rebellions from strong families and palace intrigues rocked the dynasty, and by 184 C.E., mass revolts of peasants led by religious leaders completely disrupted the country. With little tax revenue flowing in, the dynasty collapsed with the death of the last Han emperor in 220 C.E. As became typical in China at the end of dynasties, the field generals of the Han armies became rulers of their military districts.

Sinicized Nomadic Groups Rule China

The Three Kingdoms/Six Dynasties Period following the collapse of the Han Dynasty was incredibly chaotic and destructive. In fact, there are decades in which no historical records exist. With the collapse of Han authority, the nomadic peoples became the unifiers of China. Such unification began in China's north in 386 C.E. with the founding of the Northern Wei Dynasty. The Northern Wei had evolved out of a group of sinicized Turko-Mongolian nomads (specifically, the Toba tribe of the Xianbei people) who had migrated from the steppe to north China and had pushed back other groups. They retained their powerful military traditions but consciously adopted Chinese dress, customs, names, and, in the case of male Toba, ethnic Chinese wives. By 494 C.E., the Northern Wei had moved their capital from Datong, in northern Shanxi province, to the more centrally located capital of the former Han Dynasty at Luoyang. Eventually, in 534, the Northern Wei Dynasty fell apart and was replaced by a series of short-lived successor states, but it had set a precedent for strong, unified Chinese-barbarian leadership.

In 581, Yang Jian (541–604), a general of mixed Chinese and Xianbei blood, overthrew the non-Chinese dynasty (known as the Northern Zhou) that had governed northern China since 557, and by 589, after more than three hundred years of chaos and division, reunited all of China under the Sui Dynasty. The Sui leaders held China together until 618. Another leader of mixed Chinese-barbarian background, Gaozu (r. 618–26), overthrew an overextended Sui Dynasty and founded the long-lasting Tang Dynasty, recognized by scholars as a high point in imperial China's 2,200-year history. The Sui and Tang dynasties marked the blending of cultures (syncretism) that had become important for China and would remain so until the fall of the Tang in the tenth century.

During this period, the nomadic barbarian peoples, particularly the Xiongnu, Uighur, and Xianbei, adopted significant portions of Chinese culture as they migrated into northern China and gradually asserted leadership over the Chinese. Despite the incursion of nomadic peoples into China, this occupation signified the beginning of a remarkable synthesis of culture. The newcomers adapted to the Chinese customs, married into Chinese families, and became settled farmers. Xianbei leaders began to research the great Chinese philosophers and moralists to seek out strategies for governing settled peoples. In short, they became sinicized.

The presence of the barbarian peoples transformed Chinese society and culture. In a pattern that in retrospect seems quite predictable, a Chinese dynasty would rise up, enjoy a period of prosperity, and then collapse as it expended its vitality on defending the empire from the incursions of barbarians. Subsequently, nomadic peoples, often already partially involved in Chinese politics, would invade and establish a new dynasty, and the pattern would then repeat itself. Historians argue that this dynastic cycle undermined the resources and authority of the Chinese emperors as they attempted to resist the nomadic invaders. Each change in dynasty, whether to a nomad-influenced leadership or a return to an ethnic Chinese one, created new opportunities for cultural expression and philosophical exploration. Likewise, the influence of these nomadic peoples periodically transformed intellectual fashions in China, whether they permanently changed China or not.

In an environment in which the nomadic peoples considered personal relationships and respect more important than reverence of institutions and tradition, many Tang leaders maintained an openness to outsiders and foreign ideas that the previous leaders or subsequent dynasties lacked. In part, this had to do with how the Tang mixed the famous hospitality of steppe dwellers, who offered comfort to strangers, with their governing of China. For example, until late in the dynasty, the borders of the Tang were open to the representatives of the world's religions, and trade with foreign lands flourished. The mixture of barbarian curiosity and Chinese inquisitiveness also contributed to this increased tolerance, as did the profitability of receiving visitors eager to trade. During their rule, the Tang temporarily revived the thriving trade of the Silk Roads that had stopped late in the Han Dynasty.

In some ways, the Tang leadership already had a predilection for cultural openness. The steppe dwellers had been among the first peoples outside of South Asia to adopt Buddhism as it spread westward from India during the first century C.E. Through their allies and fellow nomads, they controlled a broad area that connected India and China via the Tarim Basin. Buddhism was a universal religion that fit the egalitarianism of steppe society and distinguished the nomads from the Chinese, whose religious tendencies favored Daoism and whose moral system emanated from Confucianism. Buddhism also linked the nomads to the Chinese of southern China who embraced Buddhism beginning in the fifth century as solace from the chaos and strife of the Three Kingdoms/Six Dynasties Period.

Prosperity returned to China during the Tang Dynasty, initiating the period during which China was most open to foreign ideas and trade. In 618, when the Tang Dynasty came to power, the first two emperors, Gaozu and Tai Zong (r. 626–49), borrowed influences from their nomadic background as guides to government. Much like the redistribution of wealth in nomadic societies that maintained harmony and bound herdsmen to chieftains, the early Tang conducted a land reform that gave all males equal access to land. Stability brought greater trade, and greater trade meant new agricultural techniques arrived in China from abroad. These innovations, such as fertilization, fast-growing rice, and artificial irrigation, vastly increased agricultural yields. The Tang Dynasty also produced many innovations in production, including porcelain ceramics, coke-fired iron, gunpowder, paper, and woodblock mass printing. Trade improved, especially with Southeast Asia and central Asia, and China's commercial sector created more efficient ways to do business, including the use of banking and paper money. The Tang embraced the values that made their nomadic society function but added to it Chinese elements and practices that encouraged the state to serve its people through bureaucracy and law.

The activity of the Tang Dynasty developed alongside or encouraged a great deal of contact with foreign cultures, especially through religion. Zoroastrians fleeing Muslim persecution in Persia, Manicheans escaping persecution in Europe, Persia, and North Africa, as well as Nestorian Christians and Jews, found homes in China, at least until the end of the Tang Dynasty. Buddhism, which had flourished during the Three Kingdoms/Six Dynasties Period, became extremely important. Foreign music, clothing fashions, and philosophy also spread to Tang China. For example, flute music of the steppe nomads became popular at the Tang court. The Tang Dynasty received these new groups and customs with relative openness.

Ironically, in trying to fight against internal revolt and threats to the government's power, the Tang emperor in 843 abandoned the earlier openness of the dynasty and began to brutally repress Buddhism. In 845, the dynasty outlawed "foreign" religions to the point that no institutional religion resurfaced as an important cultural force again in China (although the Chinese people still practiced many religions quietly). Throughout Tang rule, Confucian scholars and bureaucrats had bristled against the permissiveness of the Tang leadership and the influence of foreign philosophies (especially Buddhism, whose powerful monasteries and egalitarian philosophy seemed to oppose the social hierarchy and state-centered ideas of the Confucians). After the Tang, China once again fell into chaos, but was soon revived by the ethnic Chinese Song Dynasty (960–1279). Although the Song certainly had extensive contacts with foreigners, only the Yuan Dynasty (1279–1368), whose leaders came from the nomadic Mongols, would have a similar openness and embrace foreign ideas so fully.

See Also

VOLUME ONE: Eurasian Trade and Migration; Indo-European Migration to the Indus Valley; The Silk Roads; Barbarians in the Roman Empire
VOLUME TWO: Buddhism in China; Nestorian Christianity and the Civilizations of Asia; Chinese and Islamic Empires in Central Asia; The Mongols and the Civilizations of Eurasia

Bibliography

Barfield, Thomas J. *The Perilous Frontier: Nomadic Empires and China.* Cambridge: Basil Blackwell, 1989.
Bentley, Jerry H. *Old World Encounters: Cross-Cultural Contacts and Exchanges in Pre-Modern Times.* New York: Oxford University Press, 1993.
Elvin, Mark. *The Pattern of the Chinese Past.* Stanford, Calif.: Stanford University Press, 1973.
Lattimore, Owen. *Inner Asian Frontiers of China.* New York: American Geographical Society, 1940.
Loewe, Michael. *Everyday Life in Early Imperial China during the Han Period, 202 BC–AD 220.* New York: Putnam, 1968.

—*David W. Del Testa*

Primary Document
Tomb Figure

A sancai (lead-glazed earthenware pottery) tomb figure with a camel and a foreign rider, produced in the eighth century C.E. during the Tang Dynasty. The figure has an exaggerated nose, which means that it probably depicts a non-ethnic Chinese, such as a member of the "barbarian" nomadic peoples who migrated into China from the Eurasian steppe.

Source: © Werner Forman/Art Resource, NY.

The Spread of Chinese Script throughout East Asia

200 B.C.E.–1200s C.E.

Around 400 C.E., scribes from the Korean Kingdom of Paekche (c. 18–663 C.E.) traveled to Japan and introduced the Chinese writing system to the Japanese, who hitherto did not have a system of written communication. Along with Buddhism, which traveled to Japan at about the same time, the Chinese script introduced to Japan by the

Oracle bone from the Chinese Shang Dynasty with an early writing system etched on it. The bone was used to carry out divination rituals. (© Werner Forman/Art Resource, NY)

1766–1122 B.C.E.	**250 B.C.E.–250 C.E.**	**221–206 B.C.E.**	**213**
Shang Dynasty rules in China, during which Chinese script is frequently used	Yayoi Culture Period in Japan	Qin Dynasty rules in China	Li Si begins standardization of the many Chinese scripts into one national system

99

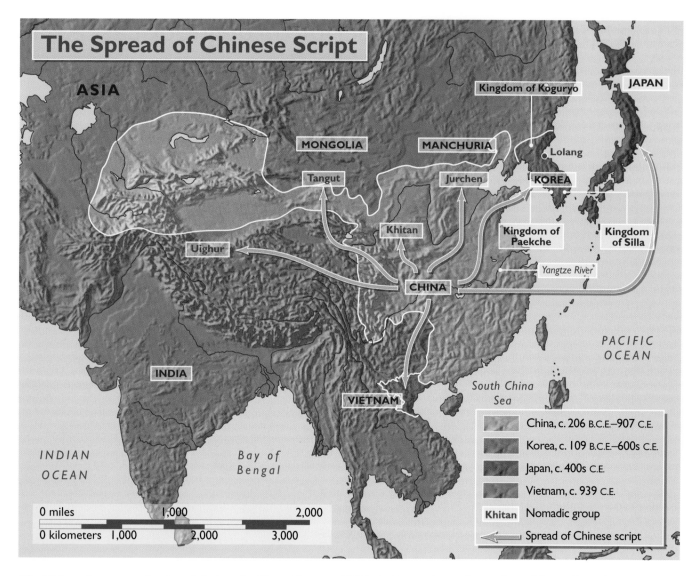

The Spread of Chinese Script

The Chinese language, developed during the Shang Dynasty (1766–1122 B.C.E), was later adapted by such civilizations as Korea, Vietnam, and Japan, as well as by various nomadic groups, including the Jurchen, Khitan, Tangut, and Uighur. The Chinese writing system served as the basis for the exportation of important cultural ideas and philosophies, including Confucianism, Buddhism, and Legalism, throughout East Asia.

Source: Some data compiled from Gerald A. Danzer, *Atlas of World History* (London: Laurence King, 2000), 50.

Koreans linked the Japanese to a great cultural sphere then expanding throughout East Asia and built on Chinese writing. East Asia's leaders adopted Chinese writing because it provided the symbolic breadth to express the ideas of the increasingly complex societies in Korea and Japan, proved sufficiently adaptable to local languages, and was associated with the dominant power and civilization of the region.

In many ways, Chinese writing was not the best possible structure for the languages of East Asia. Adapting Chinese to the Japanese and Korean languages was an arduous process and required some significant modifications. First, Chinese is monosyllabic, in which individual syllables strung together produce complex ideas. Second, Chinese is tonal; that is, the same word might have different

206 B.C.E.–220 C.E.	111 B.C.E.–939 C.E.	109 B.C.E.	18–663 C.E.	220-64
Han Dynasty rules in China	China occupies northern Vietnam	Chinese colonies are established in Korea	Kingdom of Paekche rules in Korea	Wei Dynasty rules in China

meanings depending on its pronunciation. Vietnamese is monosyllabic and tonal like Chinese, but has elements of many different languages, including words from Malay and Polynesian vocabularies. Japanese and Korean are not tonal like Chinese, and while Korean is monosyllabic, Japanese is polysyllabic (meaning, syllables are brought together in the same word to form a complex word). The other languages to which Chinese was adapted (Khitan, Mongol, and Uighur from present-day Mongolia and Central Asia) also had peculiarities that did not lend themselves to the structure of Chinese. The foundation provided by the Chinese language, however, enabled those who adapted it to their own language to continue to read Chinese and maintain access to China's culture and the rest of the Chinese-language sphere. China's most important export to the peoples of East Asia has been its philosophies and religions—Confucianism, Buddhism, and Legalism (a political philosophy that stresses harsh punishment for even the most minor infractions and rich rewards for obedience)—all of which have served as a basis for the politics, societies, and cultures throughout East Asia. The key to exporting these ideas was the Chinese writing system.

Development of China's Writing System

The Chinese writing system was developed to carry out divination rituals during or just before the Shang Dynasty (1766–1122 B.C.E.), a kingdom centered north of the Yangtze River in China. During divination rituals, shamans (diviners) etched ideographs and pictograms (images directly representing beings, objects, or actions) and some phonograms (pictograms or ideograms with modifying marks for sounds) onto tortoise shells or the scapulae (shoulder blades) of oxen. These etchings asked the gods their opinion on various topics, such as hunting, crops, war, and the weather. The shamans then applied a heated rod to the etchings. The way the scapulae or shells split as a result of the application of heat determined the answer to the question etched into the bone or shell. After the divination ceremonies, shamans also recorded on the cracked bones or shells the results of

their divinations and stored them. These caches of stored bone and tortoise shells have provided archeologists with a valuable record of early Chinese civilization. Shang-era kings had a very important role in divination through writing, for they made public the pronouncements of the shaman, such as when to plant crops. Later Chinese rulers inherited the Shang kings' association with divine contact, scholarship, and writing.

Over the course of about a millennium after the Shang Dynasty, the Chinese writing system slowly metamorphosed from an ideographic to an iconographic system, whereby many characters had a symbolic rather than a directly representational meaning. During this period of development, the practice of combining characters to represent complex ideas came into practice. Beginning in 213 B.C.E., Li Si (d. 208 B.C.E.), chief minister of the Qin Dynasty (221–206 B.C.E.), undertook a massive project to standardize the various script systems that had developed throughout China over the preceding thousand years into one national system. Through this process, Li Si gave the empire a uniform writing system that made it accessible to Chinese who lacked the esoteric education required to read earlier script systems. These men could thus participate more easily in the Qin government's administration. Ironically, Li Si also ordered the burning of all books unrelated to medicine, divination, and agriculture.

Li Si's system consisted of iconography that combined a radical (that is, a word that indicates the essence of an idea) and a phonetic element to remind a user how the word is pronounced (and thus its meaning), sometimes adding pictographs to clarify meaning. In this way, characters became recognizable across multiple dialects. Today, 214 radicals are used in Chinese. Li Si produced about 3,300 characters and suggested ways to produce more characters, as new words became necessary. During the Tang Dynasty (618–907 C.E.), the translation of Buddhist texts into Chinese from Sanskrit (a sacred language originating with the Aryan peoples of the area around the Black Sea who had migrated to India after 1500 B.C.E.) enabled a great expansion of the Chinese

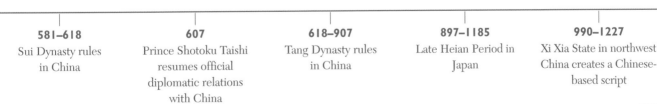

581–618	607	618–907	897–1185	990–1227
Sui Dynasty rules in China	Prince Shotoku Taishi resumes official diplomatic relations with China	Tang Dynasty rules in China	Late Heian Period in Japan	Xi Xia State in northwest China creates a Chinese-based script

language and a common literary style of writing. After the Tang, Chinese writing became less aristocratic and flowery. In 1716 C.E., Emperor Kangxi (r. 1661–1722 C.E.) of the Qing Dynasty (1644–1911 C.E.) had a dictionary produced with 40,000 total characters, although a literate Chinese person would use only about 4,000 characters.

Chinese Script Spreads across East Asia

For thousands of years, war, trade, and diplomacy brought Chinese, Koreans, Japanese, Vietnamese, and nomadic steppe-dwelling peoples together. Since at least the Shang Dynasty, and perhaps before, however, China had served as an example of advanced civilization for most of these peoples. Not only did China have the most advanced technology, social organization, and economy in East Asia, it was also a center for the philosophical and religious beliefs and practices for many peoples in East Asia.

Korea

Although Korean culture resembles that of China in many ways, at its core Korea possesses many cultural elements similar to a society that may have originated in Manchuria (in present-day northeast China) as long ago as 5000 B.C.E. Evidence suggests that unified local kingdoms existed in Korea as long ago as the early fourth century B.C.E. The Chinese under the emperor Wudi (r. 141–87 B.C.E.), leader of the Han Dynasty (206 B.C.E.–220 C.E.), set up Chinese colonies in Korea in about 109 B.C.E. that existed alongside native kingdoms but about which scholars know very little. The most important of these colonies, Lolang (now Pyongyang, North Korea's capital), endured until chaos overtook China after the fall of the Han Dynasty. Thereafter, the local kingdoms that evolved (Koguryo in the North, Paekche in the southwest, and Silla in the southeast) were strongly affected by the cultural influences of the Chinese colonies. These kingdoms endured until the late seventh century C.E., when Silla became dominant and developed a kingdom that encompassed the whole of the Korean peninsula; it would endure until 935 C.E. The individual kingdoms (and the Kingdom of Silla that unified Korea) consciously adopted Chinese culture and writing. Korea also benefited from the moderate but important traffic that traversed the peninsula

between China and Japan. Koreans used Chinese as their national script until the fifteenth century C.E., when a modified system more representative of spoken Korean made its appearance.

Japan

For its part, Japanese civilization is a complex mixture of indigenous and imported influences. The Japanese adapted to Chinese culture and used Chinese script later than Korea because of its geographical distance from China and the relative underdevelopment of Japanese society at the time. Humans lived in Japan as early as 35,000 B.C.E., and the Japanese developed pottery in about 10,000 B.C.E. At this time, two ethnically distinct groups, proto-Japanese and the more Caucasian Ainu and Ezo peoples, lived side by side. Complex society evolved under the influence of the Koreans, who emigrated to Japan in increasing numbers during Japan's Yayoi Culture Period (250 B.C.E.–250 C.E.), but who already had a long history of trade and exchange with Japan. During this time, more advanced pottery, wet-rice agriculture, metallurgy, textile production, and Korean-style burials became widespread throughout Japan.

Chinese chronicles begin to address the existence of individual states in Japan beginning with the ancient *Wei Chih*, a Chinese world history of the third century. By the time of the Wei Dynasty (220–64 C.E.), Japanese emissaries traveled to China and vice versa. Since the Japanese exchanged letters with the Wei, at least some members of the court must have known how to write in Chinese. After a long gap in correspondence that historians attribute to the chaotic conditions in Japan, the Japanese began their most fruitful exchange with China and Korea, demonstrating their more advanced knowledge of writing. Sometime in the late fourth century C.E., the Japanese had unified and strengthened sufficiently to begin to attack and dominate parts of Korea. Likewise, the Koreans may have initiated military campaigns in Japan. As a result of these interactions, China, Korea, and Japan exchanged knowledge and skills, including the transmission of writing.

The introduction of Buddhism from Korea to Japan in the fifth century C.E., just after their period of conflict and the sinification (the process of making something more Chinese) of the Japanese administration, was very important to the advancement of a written culture in Japan. The Japanese of this period hungered for knowledge from their neighbors. The introduction of foreign cultural traditions received official impetus in 607 C.E., when Crown Prince Shotoku Taishi (574–622 C.E.) of the Yamato court of Japan reinstated the dispatch of Japanese ambassadors to China. These ambassadors not only reestablished diplomatic relations with China's Sui (581–618 C.E.) and Tang dynasties, the ambassadors also brought large numbers of Japanese to China to study at its great centers of learning; many skilled Chinese and Koreans returned to Japan with the ambassadors. In particular, Shotoku considered administrative reform and the introduction of Buddhism as effective methods for centralizing his leadership and destroying traditional allegiances to clans (*uji*) and the indigenous Shinto religion. Shotoku began a long process of centralization in Japanese politics. He was aided by the Chinese system of writing, which allowed the effective communication of ideas, ideal for establishing bureaucratic control. Likewise, Buddhist texts arriving in Japan were written in Chinese, and the rapid growth of Buddhism, especially during the reign of Prince Shotoku, demanded a vast increase in lettered priests drawn from the Japanese masses.

As the Tang Dynasty fell into disarray in the ninth century C.E., and as contact between China and its neighbors declined, the Japanese began to pull away from China as a source of cultural inspiration. This process occurred in part because of Japan's lack of access to Chinese scholarship and models, but also because by this time, the Japanese had modified Chinese models to suit their own needs. At first, starting in about 750 C.E., when the Japanese began to write in ways that differed from standard Chinese, Japanese writers tended to Japanize Chinese, inserting pronunciation cues and modified characters. As a result, readers had to know Chinese and Japanese quite well to be able to read. Alongside this tendency to Japanize Chinese was the development of phonetic representation of Japanese using simplified Chinese characters, called *kana*, which had two versions. *Katakana* represented selected parts of characters cursively, while *hiragana* abbreviated whole characters in cursive form. An early

Cross-Cultural Exchange

↔ The Chinese language becomes understood and read across East Asia

↔ East Asia reads Chinese classics and gains access to Chinese cultural ideas

↔ East Asia develops national script systems based on Chinese models

↔ East Asia produces a lively national literature, especially in Japan and Korea

↔ Japanese, Koreans, and Vietnamese receive translated foreign materials (such as on Buddhism) through Chinese

manifestation of this system appeared in the eighth-century collection of poems known as *Manyo-shu* (Collection of Myriad Leaves). Those who did not know Chinese or those who wished to write in a vernacular style used straight kana, but depending on their level of education often added those Chinese characters they knew for concepts borrowed from Chinese. Some well-educated scholars continued to write in a heavily Japanized version of Chinese. This profusion of systems led to one of the most complex writing systems, in which context and the use of characters to show meaning became very important.

Vietnam

During the first millennium C.E., Chinese script did not have as significant an impact on Vietnamese society and culture as it did in Japan or Korea, despite Vietnam ironically having had the longest and most direct contact with the Chinese. Between 111 B.C.E. and 939 C.E., the Chinese occupied northern Vietnam (the area in present-day Vietnam north of the city of Ha Tinh). An indigenous script system may have existed at the time the Chinese occupied Vietnam, but all evidence of it has been lost. Throughout the period of occupation, Chinese culture influenced mainly elite Vietnamese who collaborated with the Chinese. During the third century C.E., a man by the name of Shi Xie, a member of an elite Chinese-Vietnamese family, contributed to the use of the Chinese writing system in Vietnam when he translated Chinese classics into Vietnamese using Chinese characters. The elites, educated in the Chinese classics, influenced their fellow Vietnamese, but sinification occurred slowly in Vietnam, becoming pervasive only after about the year 1200 C.E.

Because of Vietnam's long connection with the Chinese, the relatively late development of a national state, and the utility of Chinese for Vietnam's elites, the Vietnamese did not develop their own version of the Chinese writing system until quite late, when the Vietnamese sought to assert a stronger national self-definition while remaining loosely within the Chinese cultural and commercial sphere. Chu Nom (southern writing) was embraced by scholars in Vietnam after 1300 C.E. and linked Vietnamese phonetics to Chinese symbols to create a distinctly Vietnamese writing system.

Nomadic Groups

During a process of civilization, sinification, and state building, the nomadic peoples on China's borders also consciously adopted or created Chinese-influenced scripts. This adaptation of Chinese script occurred during or after the Tang Dynasty when nomadic peoples of China's northern borders attempted to develop settled societies with imperial administrations that imitated the government of the Chinese. The Khitan, a seminomadic people of northern China, became important leaders in that area after the fall of the Tang Dynasty in 907 C.E. Their leaders consciously imitated Chinese cultural and political patterns and adapted Chinese writing to their language. In 1038 C.E., the leader of the Tangut people, who lived to the west of the Khitan in the state of Xi Xia (990–1227 C.E.) in present-day Chinese Inner Mongolia and Mongolia, had a very complex script developed to express his people's language. The Jurchen, a people of southern Manchuria who briefly dominated northern China between 1115 and 1234 C.E., adopted the script system of the Khitan but also created an alphabetic script system. The alphabetic system, based on the Aramaic system (an alphabet-based language of the Middle East that reached central Asia when many central Asian peoples converted to Nestorian Christianity, whose liturgy is in Aramaic), facilitated communication with trading communities of the Middle East. The Uighur, a people of central Asia especially influential in Tang China, also had two scripts for their language, one based on Chinese characters and the other on Aramaic. Thus, the Jurchen and the Uighur used two different scripts to facilitate communication with the two civilizations with which they dealt.

Creating Bridges through Writing

The exchange of ideas was and remains the greatest consequence of the spread and adaptation of Chinese to the other peoples of East Asia. Even if they could not understand each other's spoken languages, encounters between the Chinese and their neighbors could take place in written form among the educated classes of Korea, Japan, and Vietnam who understood the meaning of Chinese characters. In this way, innovations in philosophy, political science, medicine, technology, and literature traveled with some fluidity between the peoples of East Asia and linked them to one another in terms of culture, even if they often were at odds politically. In the case of the nomadic peoples of northern and western China, the development of national scripts did not give these peoples the same kind of cultural fluidity as it did East Asia's other peoples because the character sets were modifications rather than adaptations of Chinese and the percentage of well-educated people who could spread this knowledge remained low. It did give these peoples, however, the cultural cachet they needed in China to begin to engage in cross-cultural conversations based on written knowledge.

The core texts of Chinese civilization all enjoyed wide readership throughout East Asia as Chinese script became the foundation of written civilization in Korea, Japan, and Vietnam: Confucius's (551–479 B.C.E.) *Analects* (compiled c. 400 B.C.E.); Mencius's (371–289 B.C.E.) commentary on Confucius, the "Five Classics" (*Classic of Songs, Classic of Documents, Classic of Changes,* the *Spring and Autumn Annals,* and the *Record of Rituals,* all compiled after Confucius's life); Sun Tzu's (c. fourth century B.C.E.) great study of strategy *Art of War;* the novel *The Water Margin,* which was possibly co-written around 1370 C.E. by Luo Guanzhong (c. 1330–1400 C.E.) and unknown authors. The ideas presented in these works and hundreds of other texts provided the peoples of East Asia with an advanced understanding of all aspects of human experience, albeit heavily shaped by Chinese experience, that they could in turn adapt to their own needs and national characteristics. Although on the surface the system of characters appeared rigid in its form, in fact it proved sufficiently flexible to represent languages that had very little in common with Chinese phonetically or syntactically. The Chinese model formed a foundation on which the other peoples of East Asia could build their own civilizations.

The influence of China's written script contributed to the successful development of a written culture in Japan. The versatility of the many forms of written Japanese that developed in the latter half of the first millennium allowed for a flourishing of literature and poetry. For example, *Manyo-shu* deals with themes and images of indigenous Japanese culture prior to its exposure to Buddhism or Confucianism. Likewise, the eighth-century *Kojiki* (Records of Ancient Matters) and *Nihon shoki* (Chronicles of Japan) provide the earliest presentation of Japan's history by Japanese. These early books served as the touchstone for Japan's national identity and were passed down to later generations in their written form. During the late Heian Period (897–1185 C.E.), Japan broke off contact with China because of the high cost of sending missions and the chaos in China following the collapse of the Tang Dynasty. During this time, the written Japanese language evolved beyond its Chinese models. Court women especially, who tended to know Chinese less well than their male partners and husbands, produced interesting and insightful narratives and works of fiction. Lady Sei Shonagon's *Pillow Book* and Lady Murasaki's *The Tale of Genji* are but two examples, and the latter may qualify as the world's first novel.

The link of Korea, Vietnam, Japan, and some of the nomadic peoples of northern China (including Mongolia and Manchuria) to China via the use and adaptation of Chinese script created a great cultural sphere perhaps equaled only by the spread of classical Arabic from the seventh to the tenth centuries C.E. in the Middle East, North Africa, Southwest Asia, and central Asia. Late into the nineteenth century C.E., Chinese served as the medium through which a great deal of knowledge traveled across national boundaries. For example, Phan Boi Chau (1867–1940 C.E.), a famous Vietnamese nationalist active during the period of the French occupation of Vietnam (1859–1954 C.E.), learned about Western philosophy by reading translations of European philosophers in Chinese translation. The adoption of the Chinese language, however, also implied the adoption of Chinese culture and its limitations.

The use of Chinese characters by the peoples of East Asia confirmed the Chinese perspective in which China was the center of world civilization, with a culture's level of barbarity determined according to its distance from China. Since Korea, Vietnam, and Japan used Chinese culture as a foundation on which to build their own national cultures and states, and since traditional Chinese culture emphasized conservatism, these societies were not prepared for the onslaught of new ideas and European domination in the nineteenth century. Only Japan resisted direct foreign control, and all of East Asia had to reject parts of the Chinese model in favor of new systems. The Vietnamese even abandoned regular use of their Chinese script system in the early 1920s for a modern, romanized writing system that used Latin letters (*quoc ngu*, meaning "national script") of European origin, although many Vietnamese still read at least some Chinese. Into the twenty-first century, Chinese competes with English as a medium of cultural exchange in East Asia.

See Also

VOLUME ONE: The Silk Roads; Barbarians in China
VOLUME TWO: Buddhism in China

Bibliography

Forrest, R. A. D. *The Chinese Language.* London: Faber & Faber, 1973.

Kim-Renaud, Young-Key, ed. *The Korean Alphabet: Its History and Structure.* Honolulu: University of Hawaii Press, 1997.

Korean National Commission for UNESCO. *The Korean Language.* Arch Cape, Ore.: Pace International Research, 1983.

Seeley, Christopher. *A History of Writing in Japan.* Honolulu: University of Hawaii Press, 2000.

Takeuchi, Lone. *The Structure and History of Japanese: From Yamatokotoba to Nihongo.* Edited by R. H. Robins, Geoffrey Horrocks, and David Denison. New York: Longman, 1999.

Thompson, C. Michele. "Scripts, Signs, and Swords: The Viêt Peoples and the Origins of Nôm." *Sino-Platonic Papers,* no. 101 (2000).

Tsien, Tsuen-Hsuin. *Written on Bamboo and Silk: The Beginnings of Chinese Books and Inscriptions.* Chicago: University of Chicago Press, 1962.

—*David W. Del Testa*

Primary Document

The Diamond Sutra

The world's earliest dated printed book is the Diamond Sutra. *This woodblock printed version of the book includes individual sheets of printed text and a frontispiece depicting the Buddha preaching to an aged disciple. It was discovered in 1907 in a cave near Dunhuang, in northwest China, along with many thousands of manuscripts. The inscription at the end of the book reads, "Reverently made for universal free distribution by Wang Jie on behalf of his parents on the fifteenth of the fourth moon of the ninth year of Xiantong," which corresponds to May 11, 868.*

Source: © Werner Forman/Art Resource, NY.

China's Contact with Southeast Asia

200 B.C.E.–1433 C.E.

Between 399 and 414 C.E., a Chinese monk named Faxian (c. 337–422 C.E.) traveled from China to India and Sri Lanka and wrote a famous account of his travel entitled *Record of Buddhist Kingdoms* (published after about 410 C.E.). Buddhism was just beginning to become a popular religion in China at this time, and Faxian traveled to India in order to visit sites important to the life of Siddhartha Gautama (c. 563–483 B.C.E.), known as the Buddha, and to bring back Buddhist texts. To reach India, he followed the Silk Roads that ran from China through central Asia to northern India. He then spent 12 years in India and Sri Lanka before returning to China by sea via Indonesia. During the trip home, Faxian found the Bay of Bengal and South China Sea busy with large boats full of people and cargo. No doubt, these ships transported pilgrims traveling to and from the great Buddhist study centers in Sri Lanka and Indonesia and contained cargoes of the cloves, nutmeg, cinnamon, and silk that formed the backbone of maritime trade at this time. In his book, Faxian provided, among other valuable descriptions, one of the first written records of the Chinese encounter with Southeast Asia.

Although scholars still debate what distinguishes Southeast Asia from the rest of Asia, most would agree that Southeast Asia consists of the regions east of India, south of China, and north of Australia and that its peoples have been heavily influenced by Malay and Indian cultures. Today, Southeast Asia consists of Myanmar (formerly Burma), Thailand, Laos, Cambodia, Malaysia, Indonesia, Borneo, Brunei, and Vietnam. Before the aggressive Yuan Dynasty (1279–1368 C.E.) of the Mongols galvanized resistance movements across Asia, this region was loosely divided into decentralized principalities with weak national identities. Despite the changing nature of its political organization, it has always served as a site of cross-cultural contact and a source of precious commodities, especially for the Chinese.

Beginning in about 200 B.C.E., the influence between China and Southeast Asia remained subtle during the first thousand years of their contact. By the time the Chinese began frequent contact with Southeast Asia after 300 C.E., its peoples had already developed an advanced civilization as a result of their interaction with

Pottery figure of a Vietnamese dancer from China's Tang Dynasty. (© Victoria & Albert Museum, London/ Art Resource, NY)

c. 400s B.C.E.	403–221	221–206	206 B.C.E.–220 C.E.	1st century–500s
Kingdom of Yüe formed in southern China	Warring States Period, during which China divides into many competing states	Qin Dynasty rules in China	Han Dynasty rules in China	Funan state flourishes in Cambodia, Vietnam, and Thailand

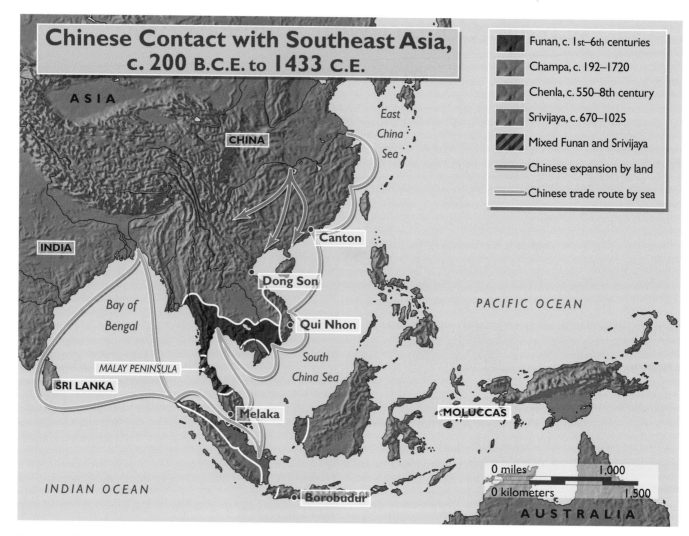

Chinese Contact with Southeast Asia, c. 200 B.C.E. to 1433 C.E.

Legend:
- Funan, c. 1st–6th centuries
- Champa, c. 192–1720
- Chenla, c. 550–8th century
- Srivijaya, c. 670–1025
- Mixed Funan and Srivijaya
- Chinese expansion by land
- Chinese trade route by sea

Between about 200 B.C.E. and 1433 C.E., Southeast Asia served as an important site of cross-cultural exchange for China. The Chinese expanded into Southeast Asia by land and by sea, establishing trade networks and diplomatic contacts in the region that would contribute to the exchange of religious and cultural ideas like Buddhism, technological innovations, and aromatic products such as spices.

Sources: Some data compiled from Gungwu Wang, ed., *Community and Nation: Essays on Southeast Asia and the Chinese,* Asian Studies Association of Australia, Southeast Asian Publications Series (Singapore: Heinemann, 1981), 6:50; Jerry H. Bentley and Herbert F. Ziegler, *Traditions and Encounters: A Global Perspective on the Past,* 2nd ed. (Boston: McGraw-Hill, 2003), 433; and John K. Fairbank, Edwin Reischauer, and Albert M. Craig, *East Asia: Tradition and Transformation,* rev. ed. (Boston: Houghton Mifflin, 1989), 194.

the cultures and societies of India and their own innovations. From approximately 150 B.C.E. to 900 C.E., India's political organization, Hindu art styles, and Buddhist religion had heavily influenced the peoples and nations of Southeast Asia. Upon China's first contact with Southeast Asia, the region came to hold an important place in the imagination of the Chinese as a source of the exotic and for fanciful writings and legends. As the states

220–589	399–414	618–907	670–1025
Three Kingdoms/Six Dynasties Period in China	Faxian voyages to India, Sri Lanka, and Java	Tang Dynasty rules in China	Kingdom of Srivijaya rules in Sumatra, Java, and Malaysia

of Southeast Asia became more fully developed and powerful, however, China's relationship with them changed, and they became both geopolitical rivals and commercial partners. Similar to the role of the Silk Roads in Eurasia, Southeast Asia served as an important point of contact between China and the peoples of the rest of the world. It served as a place where the Chinese acquired foreign influences, either through their own commercial, diplomatic, or cultural efforts or through the many kinds of merchants who reached Southeast Asia's and China's shores.

Early Contact between China and Southeast Asia

China

Until late in the first millennium C.E., southern China remained, relative to northern China, less densely populated and developed. The Yüe people of the Kingdom of Yüe (formed around the fifth century B.C.E.) located in southern China had a society and culture different from the Chinese in the north (known as the Han Chinese). During the reign of the Han Dynasty (206 B.C.E.–220 C.E.), Emperor Wudi (r. 141–87 B.C.E.) brought the Yüe Kingdom, Yunnan (in southwestern China), and northern Vietnam under Chinese control. Over time, the south's agricultural wealth and better access to lucrative maritime trade stimulated its population growth, and political disruptions in the north encouraged the southward migration of the Han Chinese. The Han Chinese adapted to the intensive rice agriculture and maritime and riverine orientation of southern China, which was warmer, more humid, and more geographically varied than the north. (By the time of the Song Dynasty in 960–1279 C.E., southern China was more populous than the north.)

For the Han Chinese, the south held particularly wild and exotic connotations. Even though the Han Dynasty had brought southern China firmly under its control, this region remained a place of mystery and legend. Similar to how Africa provided fodder for all kinds

of fanciful stories for European novelists of the nineteenth century (such as Edgar Rice Burroughs's Tarzan series), south China provided an excellent setting for fanciful literature during the Tang (618–907 C.E.) and Song dynasties. This fascination was built on the foreignness of trade goods; of desirable, exotic female slaves; and of beliefs in legendary creatures, such as trolls and imps. As southern China became increasingly sinicized (that is, acculturated to Chinese customs) between the first and tenth centuries C.E., however, the lands and peoples of Southeast Asia began to fulfill the role as a place of mystery and legend.

The worldview of historical China had an impact on its early relationship with Southeast Asia. Before about 2000 B.C.E., the Chinese had very little contact with ancient civilizations such as Mesopotamia (present-day Iraq), Egypt, and Harappa (present-day Pakistan and western India). They had considered themselves the only true civilization, the so-called Middle Kingdom, surrounded by "barbarians." The advanced nature of their culture and government only reinforced this notion. The Chinese state, when unified after 220 B.C.E., had the world's largest economy, and its government successfully manipulated its resources (the building of the Great Wall during the Qin Dynasty between 221 and 206 B.C.E. providing but one example). The farther a people were from the Yellow River in northern China, the center of ethnic Chinese culture, the less civilized the Chinese considered the peoples to be. Based on hierarchical obligations to elders, the Confucian moral system, which had come to dominate China during the Warring States Period (403–221 B.C.E.), reinforced this perception of non-Chinese as inferior, including such immediate and ethnically related neighbors as the Yüe. All foreign nations wanting a relationship with the Chinese had to participate in the tribute system, which had operated as a tool of foreign relations since the Han Dynasty. Foreigners brought gifts for the Chinese emperor, acknowledged his supremacy, and in return received the right to trade and learn about China.

| 960–1279 | 1279–1368 | 1283 | 1284 |
| Song Dynasty rules in China | Yuan (Mongol) Dynasty rules in China | Mongols invade Burma | Mongols invade Vietnam |

By the second century B.C.E., Chinese merchants and navies gained the technological capability to travel south to what is present-day central Vietnam. It was at this point that the Chinese began their exploration into Southeast Asia. Much of the contact that developed between China and Southeast Asia revolved around trade. The Southeast Asian principalities in central Vietnam, Cambodia, and Indonesia participated in the tribute system from early on because of Chinese demand for spices and the possibility of acquiring silk for reexport, at a large profit, to India and the Mediterranean Basin. Through contact with China, Southeast Asian kingdoms gained a steady income from the spice trade and the protection, even if illusory, of the Chinese emperors. Until the middle of the first millennium C.E., the Chinese had a monopoly on the production and trade of silk, a fabric highly esteemed everywhere in Europe, Asia, and Africa. Therefore, in order to obtain silk, visitors (including those from Southeast Asia) accepted the hierarchical order established by China that placed foreigners at a lower position than that of the Chinese.

Southeast Asia

Although archeological evidence remains quite scarce, it appears that many of the societies of Southeast Asia before 500 B.C.E. resembled the Dong Son culture of northern Vietnam that originated independently from other civilizations in Vietnam in about 1000 B.C.E. Dong Son culture was divided into small, independent, and widely dispersed animistic or shamanistic chiefdoms, apparently often matriarchal in nature. By the time the Chinese made contact with them around 150 B.C.E., they had already come under the strong influence of India's culture, society, and political structures. Southeast Asia's peoples had created bureaucratic states, although without the centralizing tendency of polities in India. They also were engaged in small-scale trade among themselves. For example, the tin needed to make the bronze artifacts of Dong Son culture in northern Vietnam seems to have come by sea from Malaysia by at least 500 B.C.E.

During much of the period of initial contact between China and Southeast Asia, a series of states controlled various parts of Southeast Asia. At this time, openness to outsiders characterized most of them, with rulers adopting foreign religions and cultures into syncretic (fusion of different belief systems) practices that suited their needs. The Chinese first had contact with Funan, a trade-oriented kingdom on the coast of present-day Vietnam, Cambodia, and Thailand that flourished from the first to sixth centuries C.E. The Kingdom of Funan reaped enormous profits controlling trade that connected Indonesia and India with China.

Spices and Sutras: Chinese Trade with Southeast Asia

The encounter between the Chinese and the people of Southeast Asia developed gradually as the Chinese pushed further southward in their quest for trade and diplomatic contacts and as visitors (merchants and diplomats, among others) began to travel by sea to China. The first contacts the Chinese had with the people of Southeast Asia occurred during the Han Dynasty, when tribute missions arrived occasionally from India, bringing news of the kingdoms and trade of Southeast Asia, and from the kingdoms of the coast of what is today central Vietnam. More frequently, contacts occurred during the chaotic Three Kingdoms/Six Dynasties Period (220–589 C.E.), when merchants from the southern Chinese kingdom of Wu (222–80 C.E.) traded with the merchants of Funan.

Chinese contact with Southeast Asia followed two routes, overland and by sea. Overland, the Chinese traveled as traders to the countries of Southeast Asia along China's southern border, including the regions of present-day Burma, Thailand, and Vietnam. By sea, the Chinese visited the Indonesian archipelago and the Malay Peninsula as well as all of the important ports of Southeast Asia, including Melaka in Malaysia and Qui Nhon in Vietnam. For all their curiosity and desire for foreign contact, however, the Chinese rarely settled in Southeast Asia. The Chinese acquired a great deal of

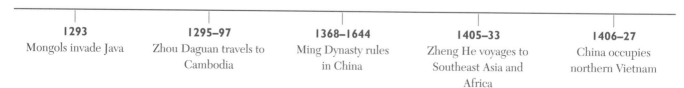

| 1293 | 1295–97 | 1368–1644 | 1405–33 | 1406–27 |
| Mongols invade Java | Zhou Daguan travels to Cambodia | Ming Dynasty rules in China | Zheng He voyages to Southeast Asia and Africa | China occupies northern Vietnam |

the exotic imports they desired by visiting the early trade depots of central Vietnam, such as at Qui Nhon, or by having the trade goods brought to them in Canton. Foreign traders could acquire Chinese products at these ports as well. The traffic of Chinese into Southeast Asia grew from a trickle beginning around 100 B.C.E. to a large flow by the time of the Ming Dynasty (1368–1644 C.E.).

The importance of religion to the Tang Dynasty provided the first great impetus for the Chinese to travel in great numbers to Southeast Asia beyond northern Vietnam. After the arrival of Buddhism in China during the first century C.E., the religion gradually became more popular, enjoying a real flowering during the Tang Dynasty. Desiring more contact with the centers of Buddhism and better copies of religious texts important to Buddhists, Chinese monks began to travel directly to the centers of Buddhism in Java (and from there, if they desired, to the even more important South Asian centers in Sri Lanka and India).

During the first half of the eighth century, the internal rebellions and external military defeats experienced by the Tang government disrupted official contact between the Tang and foreign nations and effectively closed off trade by land from China to central and western Asia. The Tang Dynasty was unable to maintain as vigorous diplomatic relations as it had in the early part of its rule. From 686 to 731, for example, the Tang received 15 tributary missions just from Chenla, a precursor of the Kingdom of Cambodia; between 758 and 878, only a few tributary missions came from any Southeast Asian country. Seaborne trade actually increased at this time, however, but instead of Chinese merchants going abroad, Muslim Arab merchants carrying Southeast Asian products came to China, especially to Canton, to trade. Late in this period, Chuanzhou, in Fujian province on China's eastern coast, came to rival Canton for foreign trade.

During the Song Dynasty, a period of renewed interest in Southeast Asia began. More ethnocentric than their dynastic predecessors, the Song sought to strengthen China against the foreign aggression and internal troubles that had marked the Tang rule by encouraging a strong domestic economy. The Song believed that domestically produced goods would create an important source of revenue on the international

Cross-Cultural Exchange

↔ Southeast Asia serves as an important site for the exchange of food products, such as spices to China and citrus from China, and technological innovations, such as the magnetic compass from China

↔ Southeast Asia serves China as an important site for learning about Buddhism

↔ Southeast Asia provides an imaginary world that the Chinese of the Tang Dynasty use as a backdrop for their fantasy writings

market. With an increase in China's population, the Song Dynasty had the commercial resources and domestic security necessary to again venture abroad. At this time, the most important Southeast Asian state was the Kingdom of Srivijaya (encompassing parts of present-day Sumatra, Java, and Malaysia), which dominated insular Southeast Asian commerce and politics between 670 and 1025. Without large cities, a fixed capital, a standing army, or firm boundaries, Srivijaya's rulers welcomed all traders openly while displaying a strong government. Whereas during the eleventh century C.E., when Chinese merchant houses had funded 10-year voyages of commercial agents to Southeast Asia in return for 100 percent interest on the initial loan, the governments of the Song Dynasty officially encouraged overseas Chinese trade through government loans with lower interest rates. The state advanced capital to reliable traders in exchange for 70 percent of the total profit and received healthy tax revenue from foreign trade as a result.

The Yuan Dynasty (1279–1368) of the Mongols disrupted the steadily increasing Chinese-controlled trade in Southeast Asia. Beginning with Kublai Khan (r. 1260–94), the Mongols began a vigorous expansionist policy that eventually brought much of Eurasia under their control. Their efforts to conquer Southeast Asia, however, proved unsuccessful. An invasion of Vietnam in 1284 literally foundered as a result of the strong resistance of the Vietnamese. An even bolder invasion of Java in 1293 met with equal disaster. Only a temporary conquest of Burma in 1283 had some fleeting success.

On the surface, the actions of the Yuan Dynasty seemed to completely change the dynamic of the relationship between China and Southeast Asia. As a result of Mongol aggression against Southeast Asia, distrustful sentiments and political aims replaced the openness that had characterized the relationship between China and Southeast Asia during the Song Dynasty. Despite their brutality, however, the Mongols also had an unending curiosity and tolerance of foreign ideas, so long as one did not question their political domination. Their relationship to Southeast Asia was no different. Zhou Daguan (d. 1324) was a Chinese diplomat employed by the Mongols who traveled to Cambodia between 1295 and 1297 and wrote a Chinese report on Southeast Asia in 1297. Zhou's *Recollections of the Customs of Cambodia* reflects the mixed fascination and ethnocentrism of Chinese reports on Southeast Asia, although *Recollections* has a distinctly political tone.

Impact of Religious and Cultural Exchange between China and Southeast Asia

The trade networks that developed between China and Southeast Asia initiated cross-cultural change. Most important for China was the spread of religious ideas. Although China had learned about Buddhism from its nomadic neighbors in central Asia, the Chinese created their own version of Buddhism in part through contact with Southeast Asia. Most Chinese monks could not travel all the way to India (the center of Buddhist learning), but travel to and study at the Buddhist centers at Palembang on Sumatra or at Borobudur on Java was feasible. China stood on the edge of a larger, Indian-influenced Buddhist sphere that became increasingly centered in Southeast Asia as Buddhism faded in popularity in India in the eighth century and its adherents were officially persecuted in China in the mid–ninth century. Indeed, besides Sri Lanka in South Asia and Japan in East Asia, the Southeast Asian nations of Thailand, Cambodia, Laos, and Vietnam remain the world's most important Buddhist nations.

Southeast Asia served as a point of exchange for all kinds of nonreligious ideas as well, especially during the Tang and Song dynasties. Through contact with Southeast Asia and its many inhabitants—both native and foreign—China received entertainers and philosophers, and religious figures served as teachers. China learned a great deal about astronomy through contact with Indians living in Southeast Asia. In return, the Muslim empires of the Middle East especially valued Chinese knowledge about alchemy (that is, early scientific experiments with the material world that had a spiritual component). Chinese contact with Southeast Asia also became a valuable conduit for the exchange of technology around the world. At the Southeast Asian trade centers, Arab merchants learned about an important Chinese invention, the magnetic compass, and began employing it on their vessels during the twelfth century.

The Chinese especially valued the aromatic products they could import from Southeast Asia. In premodern times, cloves came only from the Moluccas islands in the Indonesian archipelago. They served as breath sweeteners, flavoring, as scents for perfumes and incense, and as medicines. In addition to Moluccan cloves and nutmeg, Java sent pepper, while Champa (192–1720), a kingdom of central Vietnam, sent cinnamon. As a result, during the Tang Dynasty, Chinese cookery underwent a revolution, becoming spicier and more complex through the use of pepper and other spices. "Chinese five-spice," a popular flavoring in Asian foods today, has its origin at this time. Likewise, the Chinese brought their food products to markets in Southeast Asia for trade, introducing pomegranates, walnuts, lemons, and oranges to the rest of the world.

At the start of its rule in the fourteenth century, the Ming Dynasty appeared as if it would combine the ethnocentrism and concern with commerce of the Song with the foreign curiosity of the Tang and the aggressiveness of the Han. The foremost example of this was the state sponsorship of the commercial and exploratory voyages of Zheng He (c. 1371–1435), who, between 1405 and 1433, traveled on successive voyages from China to Southeast Asia and the Indian Ocean (as far as the east coast of Africa). These expeditions coincided with China's abortive attempt to reoccupy Vietnam between 1406 and 1427, which failed because the Vietnamese resisted too strongly for the Chinese to maintain effective control.

Ironically, the stories of Zheng He's voyages that circulated in China after the conclusion of his trips to

Southeast Asia and the lands bordering the shores of the Indian Ocean encouraged a great deal of emigration of Chinese to Southeast Asia even though the Ming emperors effectively outlawed such travel. The isolationist tendencies of the Ming coincided with the rise of new national states throughout Southeast Asia. Some scholars believe these new states developed because of Southeast Asia's declining contact with India as it became increasingly influenced by Hinduism, competition from Muslims, or the tendency of the various Mongol invasions to incite forms of resistance that leant themselves to a new national identity. For instance, Burma, Vietnam, Java, and Melaka all transformed into early modern nation-states, in which monarchs no longer conceived of themselves as the pinnacles of a hierarchy of leading families but as the leaders of the nation. Although these new nations of Southeast Asia still maintained their deference to China for purposes of trade, they no longer had to define their political identity in harmony with the political, cultural, or religious beliefs of China.

See Also

VOLUME ONE: India's Cultural Expansion to Southeast Asia; The Silk Roads; Barbarians in China
VOLUME TWO: Buddhism in China; Chinese and Islamic Empires in Central Asia; The Mongols and the Civilizations of Eurasia; Marco Polo in Asia

Bibliography

Adshead, Samuel Adrian M. *China in World History*. 3rd ed. New York: St. Martin's Press, 2000.

FitzGerald, C. P. *The Southern Expansion of the Chinese People: "Southern Fields and Southern Ocean."* Canberra: Australian National University Press, 1972.

Gungwu, Wang. *The Nanhai Trade: The Early History of Chinese Trade in the South China Sea*. Singapore: Time Academic Press, 1998.

Gungwu, Wang, ed. *Community and Nation: Essays on Southeast Asia and the Chinese*. Vol. 6, Asian Studies Association of Australia, Southeast Asian Publications Series. Singapore: Heinemann, 1981.

Marr, David G., and A. C. Milner, eds. *Southeast Asia in the 9th to 14th Centuries*. Singapore: Institute of Southeast Asian Studies; Canberra, Australia: Research School of Pacific Studies, Australian National University, 1986.

Ptak, Roderich. *China's Seaborne Trade with South and Southeast Asia, 1220–1750*. Variorum Collected Studies Series. Brookfield, Vt.: Ashgate, 1999.

Reid, Anthony. *Southeast Asia in the Age of Commerce, 1450–1680*. Vol. 2. *Expansion and Crisis*. New Haven, Conn.: Yale University Press, 1993.

Schafer, Edward H. *The Vermilion Bird: T'ang Images of the South*. Berkeley: University of California, 1967.

—David W. Del Testa

Primary Document
Faxian's *Record of Buddhist Kingdoms*

Chinese monks of the first millennium C.E. have often provided unique insights into cultures and societies of which scholars would otherwise have no record. In regard to China's contact with Southeast Asia, Faxian's Record of Buddhist Kingdoms, written between 399 and 412, is of paramount importance. Here, Faxian's writing reveals the simultaneous fascination the Chinese had with the exotic environment they experienced in Southeast Asia, along with the familiarity of the Buddhism embraced by the Chinese and many Southeast Asians. This foreign yet friendly tension appears in many examples of literature.

Faxian abode in this country two years. . . . Having obtained these Sanskrit works, he took passage in a large merchantman, on board of which there were more than 200 men, and to which was attached by a rope a smaller vessel, as a provision against damage or injury to the large one from the perils of the navigation. With a favorable wind, they proceeded eastwards for three days, and then they encountered a great wind. The vessel sprang a leak and the water came in. The merchants wished to go to the smaller vessel; but the men on board it, fearing that too many would come, cut the connecting rope. The merchants were greatly alarmed, feeling their risk of instant death. Afraid that the vessel would fill, they took their bulky goods and threw them into the water. Faxian also took his pitcher and washing-basin, with some other articles, and cast them into the sea; but fearing that the merchants would cast overboard his books and images, he could only think with all his heart of Guanshiyin, and commit his life to [the protection of] the Buddhist congregation of the land of Han, [saying in effect], "I have travelled far in search of our Law. Let me, by your dread and supernatural [power], return from my wan-derings, and reach my resting place!"

In this way the tempest continued day and night, till on the thirteenth day the ship was carried to the side of an island, where, on the ebbing of the tide, the place of the leak was discovered, and it was stopped, on which the voyage was resumed. On the sea [hereabouts] there are many pirates, to meet with whom is speedy death. The great ocean spreads out, a boundless expanse. There is no knowing east or west; only by observing the sun, moon, and stars was it possible to go forward. If the weather were dark and rainy, [the ship] went as she was carried by the wind, without any definite course. In the darkness of the night, only the great waves were to be seen, breaking on one another, and emitting a brightness like that of fire, with huge turtles and other mon-sters of the deep [all about]. The merchants were full of ter-ror, not knowing where they were going. The sea was deep and bottomless, and there was no place where they could drop anchor and stop. But when the sky became clear, they could tell east and west, and [the ship] again went forward in the right direction. If she had come on any hidden rock, there would have been no way of escape.

After proceeding in this way for rather more than ninety days, they arrived at a country called Java-dvipa, where vari-ous forms of error and Brahminism are flourishing, while Buddhism in it is not worth speaking of. After staying there for five months, [Faxian] again embarked in another large merchantman, which also had on board more than 200 men. They carried provisions for fifty days, and commenced the voyage on the sixteenth day of the fourth month.

Faxian kept his retreat on board the ship. They took a course to the north-east, intending to reach Guangzhou. After more than a month, when the night-drum sounded the second watch, they encountered a black wind and tempestu-ous rain, which threw the merchants and passengers into consternation. Faxian again with all his heart directed his thoughts to Guanshiyin and the monkish communities of the land of Han; and, through their awesome and mysterious protection, was preserved to day-break. After day-break, the Brahmins deliberated together and said, "It is having this Sramana on board that has occasioned our misfortune and brought us this great and bitter suffering. Let us land the bhikshu and place him on some island-shore. We must not for the sake of one man allow ourselves to be exposed to such imminent peril." A patron of Faxian, however, said to them, 'If you land the bhikshu, you must at the same time land me; and if you do not, then you must kill me. If you land this Sramana, when I get to the land of Han, I will go to the emperor, and inform against you. The emperor also reveres and believes the Law of Buddha, and honors the bhikshus." The merchants hereupon were perplexed, and did not dare immediately to land Faxian.

At this time the sky continued very dark and gloomy, and the sailing-masters looked at one another and made mistakes. More than seventy days passed [from their leaving Java], and the provisions and water were nearly exhausted. They used the salt-water of the sea for cooking, and care-fully divided the [fresh] water, each man getting two pints. Soon the whole was nearly gone, and the merchants took counsel and said, "At the ordinary rate of sailing we ought to have reached Guangzhou, and now the time is passed by many days— must we not have held a wrong course?" Immediately they directed the ship to the north-west, look-ing out for land; and after sailing day and night for twelve days, they reached the shore on the south of mount Lao, . . . and immediately got good water and vegetables. They had passed through many perils and hardships, and had been in a state of anxious apprehension for many days together; and now suddenly arriving at this shore, . . . they knew indeed that it was the land of Han.

Source: Excerpted from Alfred J. Andrea and James H. Overfield, *The Human Record: Sources of Global History,* 4th ed. (Boston: Houghton Mifflin, 2001), 1:170–171.

The Roman Empire and the Mediterranean World

46 B.C.E.–330 C.E.

In 46 B.C.E., Julius Caesar (100–44 B.C.E.) organized a triumphal procession in Rome to commemorate his recent conquest of Egypt. For the crowds standing in the streets, the sight was spectacular. Caesar himself, crowned with a laurel of victory, stood on a chariot drawn by four powerful white stallions. In front of him marched columns of senators, centurions, and musicians. A group of war prisoners was also forced into the line, at the head of which trudged the shackled Egyptian princess Arsinoe. After this procession, the crowds were treated, at state expense, to a magnificent variety of amusements. Tables were laden with eels and wine, such exotic animals from Africa as a giraffe (which had never been seen by European eyes) were displayed, and sailors gathered on an artificial lake near the Tiber River to fight a mock Roman-Egyptian naval battle. As a climax, gladiators gathered in the enormous Circus Maximus to battle one another to the death.

This colorful event marked a turning point in the history of the ancient Mediterranean world, due in part to the role played by the queen of Egypt, Cleopatra (69–30 B.C.E.). The sister of Arsinoe and a member of Egypt's Ptolemy Dynasty, Cleopatra had abandoned her family loyalty immediately before Caesar's conquest. Seducing the general during a sumptuous tour of the Nile River, she soon bore him a son and named the potential heir Ptolemy (47–30 B.C.E.; commonly called Caesarion). She now appeared with the boy in Rome during the triumph in order to propose an alliance that would preserve a measure of Egypt's political autonomy. Even so, she must have regarded Caesar with some misgiving as she watched him drive her sister forward in chains under a banner proclaiming *"veni, vidi, vici"* (I came, I saw, I conquered).

Cleopatra's plan for an alliance with Rome actually began to bear fruit when, in the immediate aftermath of the triumph, Caesar erected an honorary statue of her in the temple of the Roman goddess Venus. In 44 B.C.E., however, Caesar was assassinated, and his successor, Octavian, who later ruled by the name of Augustus (r. 31 B.C.E.–14 C.E.), repudiated the alliance. Destroying Cleopatra's fleet at Actium in 31 B.C.E., Octavian chased her and her new ally, Marc Antony (c. 82–30 B.C.E.), back to Alexandria, where the hapless couple committed suicide. Octavian annexed Egypt as an imperial province, massacred Caesarion, and brought the Ptolemaic dynasty to an end. Thus, as a result of the triumph of 46 B.C.E. and the events that followed it, Rome began to dominate the East. Ironically, the Hellenistic civilization of Egypt and other lands simultaneously began to transform the West.

A fresco, from about 50 B.C.E., depicting a woman's initiation into the cult of Dionysus. (© Massimo Listri/Corbis)

c. 3100 B.C.E.	c. 750	509	333	323–283
Pharaohs begin to rule Egypt	Foundation of Rome	Roman constitution bans monarchy	Alexander the Great forms Greek Empire after Battle of Issus	Reign of Ptolemy I of Egypt

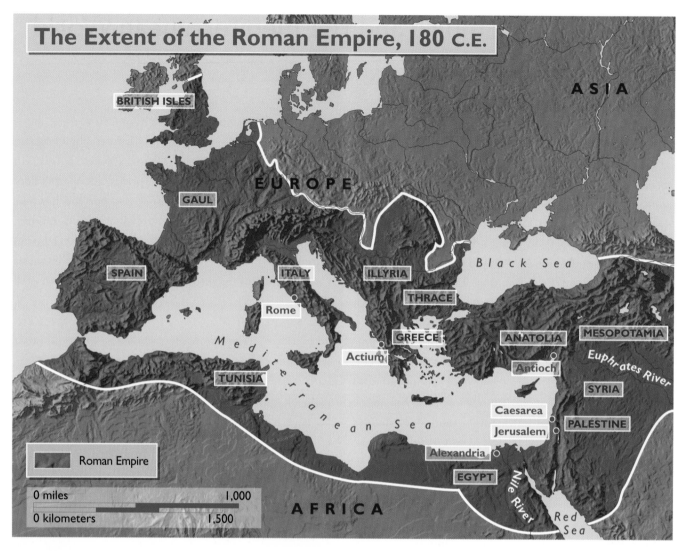

The Extent of the Roman Empire, 180 C.E.

In 180 C.E., the Roman Empire reached its greatest extent under the rule of Emperor Marcus Aurelius. The establishment of Roman imperial rule across the empire led to many political, religious, and cultural exchanges such as the introduction of Roman administrative structures and law in the eastern Mediterranean, and the Roman Empire's adoption of Hellenistic political institutions and religious ideas.

Source: Some data compiled from Gerald A. Danzer, *Atlas of World History* (London: Laurence King, 2000), 38.

The History of Politics and Religion in the Mediterranean during the First Millennium B.C.E.

Rome had been founded in about 750 B.C.E. After more than two centuries of deplorable rule by monarchical tyrants, the Roman senate established a republican constitution in 509 B.C.E. that banned the monarchy.

Thereafter, Rome grew steadily, subduing first the Italian peninsula and later expanding westward into Gaul (present-day France) and eastward into Greece. Despite such territorial growth, however, the Roman Republic (509–27 B.C.E.) retained the constitutional ban on kings. Citizens voted for various bodies, such as the council of plebeians, and conservative aristocrats in the

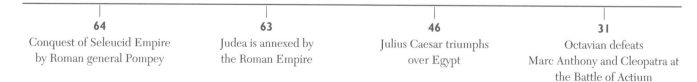

64	63	46	31
Conquest of Seleucid Empire by Roman general Pompey	Judea is annexed by the Roman Empire	Julius Caesar triumphs over Egypt	Octavian defeats Marc Anthony and Cleopatra at the Battle of Actium

senate exercised control over executive statesmen called consuls. Nevertheless, as military expansion brought generals into public prominence, the republican constitution was repeatedly imperiled. Caesar's dictatorship represented its final demise, but after his assassination in 44 B.C.E., it was not immediately clear to Octavian what the new order should be.

Egypt possessed an even longer heritage than Rome, having come into existence during the third millennium B.C.E. Initially ruled by monarchs called pharaohs, the state had been incorporated into the colossal Greek Empire of Alexander the Great (356–323 B.C.E.; king of Macedonia, 336–323 B.C.E.) after the Battle of Issus in 333 B.C.E. As a result of Alexander's efforts to promote a Greek-like, or Hellenistic, culture, his empire gave rise to the Hellenistic civilization that dominated the Mediterranean for centuries. Alexander built a great new capital on the Nile and named it Alexandria, in honor of himself. After he died in 323 B.C.E., Egypt fell under the rule of a general named Ptolemy. Following the example of Alexander's successors in Greece and Mesopotamia, Ptolemy I (r. 323–283 B.C.E.) established a monarchy in Egypt that remained stable until the time of Cleopatra. Ptolemaic kings and queens exercised unrestricted power over their subjects, in contrast to the constitutional order of republican Rome. The Egyptian monarchy's authority was enhanced by its regular claims to embody traditional Egyptian deities. Thus, when Cleopatra insisted on being worshipped as both queen and goddess in Rome, she was following an ancient tradition.

Ptolemy II (r. 284–246 B.C.E.) was especially ambitious and went so far as to officially deify his parents and his sister (whom he married). He also introduced a tax to support the construction of state-supported temples for the new royal deities. Later Ptolemaic rulers assumed epithets such as "Benefactor" and "Manifested One" in order to assert their claims to divinity. However, simultaneously with the rise of ruler worship, and no doubt in reaction against it, religions appeared in Egypt that focused special attention on the common individual. Here and elsewhere in the Hellenistic world, cults of personal savior-gods began to displace the public cults of ruler-gods. From Egypt a cult of Isis arose, and in Syria cults of Baal and Astarte spread. Added to these was the very different monotheistic religion of the Jews, who during the Ptolemaic period began to settle in large numbers in Alexandria.

Cultural Exchanges during Roman Rule

The effects of Rome's conquest of Egypt were in many ways ironic. While military subjugation brought Egypt a restructured governmental administration and greater taxation, changes brought to the Egyptians themselves were relatively few. Most of the population continued to live in the countryside as it had done under the Ptolemies.

Roman rule altered other Hellenistic lands more noticeably than it did Egypt. After the Seleucid Empire in Mesopotamia and Syria had been conquered by Caesar's rival general Pompey (106–48 B.C.E.) in 64 B.C.E., its territory became dotted with Roman colonial settlements, such as Duro-Europa on the Euphrates River and Caesarea on the coast of Palestine. These provincial capitals served as centers of Roman administration, enforcing Roman law among the native populations and introducing Roman gods to them. Even among the most exclusive provincial peoples, the impact of Roman occupation could be profound. The Palestinian land of Judea is a particularly good example. Incorporated into the empire in 63 B.C.E., this heartland of the Jews was soon placed under a Roman puppet, King Herod the Great (73–4 B.C.E.). The Jews had a long history of opposition to foreign rule and were regarded by the Romans as hopelessly unassimilable. Nevertheless, under Herod, their Temple in Jerusalem was entirely rebuilt, incorporating Roman architectural motifs into its design. The influence of Rome was thus manifested at the very center of Jewish life.

The most remarkable changes to result from Rome's contact with Egypt and other Hellenistic lands affected the conqueror. First in importance was the rise of a monarchical political culture in Rome. During the triumphal procession of 46 B.C.E., Caesar had placed a

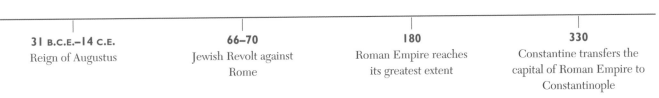

| 31 B.C.E.–14 C.E. | 66–70 | 180 | 330 |
| Reign of Augustus | Jewish Revolt against Rome | Roman Empire reaches its greatest extent | Constantine transfers the capital of Roman Empire to Constantinople |

slave behind him on his chariot whose function was to shout repeatedly, "Remember that you are only a man!" This action, so paradoxical amid the spectacle of dictatorial power, was contrived to pay homage to the antimonarchical political culture of the republic. In 27 B.C.E., however, with the constitution in shambles and Roman power stretching to Africa and the Middle East, Caesar's successor, Octavian, decided to abandon this antimonarchical pretense and assume the title emperor. Thus he formalized the existence of the Roman Empire with a monarchical political system. His successors went even further, subverting the senate and naming their own successors to the imperial title. The powers of the Roman emperor were expanded to such a degree that they resembled the divine Ptolemaic kings of Egypt and other Hellenistic monarchs. The effects of this transformation were often turbulent. First-century emperors, such as Caligula (r. 37–41 C.E.) and Nero (r. 54–68 C.E.) abused their power terribly through violence and caprice. Architectural artifacts from this period reflect the influence of Egypt in this change. In the bas-relief of a temple located at Latopolis in Egypt, for instance, the Roman emperor Titus (r. 79–81 C.E.) is depicted as an Egyptian pharaoh making sacrifices to Egyptian gods.

Rome's exchange with foreign lands after the conquest of Egypt also influenced its religious traditions. The symbolism of the slave's declaration that Caesar was "only a man" had been designed not only to assure senators that the Roman dictator would not pursue too much power, but also that he would not adopt the Hellenistic practice of deifying himself either. Again, Caesar's immediate successor took a different course. Octavian complemented his new title of emperor with that of Augustus, or "revered one." This turn to the Egyptian custom of royal epithets was only the beginning, for later emperors likewise followed the Egyptian model of deifying their predecessors. Soon after Augustus's death in 14 C.E., for instance, he was actually proclaimed a god by his successor, Tiberius (r. 14–37 C.E.). During the course of the first century, then, the place of religion within Roman political culture came to resemble that of the vanquished Ptolemies.

Yet the Roman imperial cult never assumed the grand proportions of its Hellenistic model. The Romans were by character a conservative people, and extravagant claims to divinity were an exception. The Roman Empire built temples, and its citizens made sacrifices, but the cult of the emperors never inspired more than civic devotion. For personal contact with deities, Romans increasingly turned to mystery cults, and these too were imported from Egypt and the Hellenistic East. As the imperial cult matured during the first century C.E., Rome witnessed an explosion of interest in such religions. This was facilitated in part by the return of Roman soldiers after their encounters with distant imperial provinces. The influx sometimes destabilized Rome's social order. The cult of Dionysus especially, with its orgies and occasional ritualistic murders, shocked the conservative senators of Rome. In times of prolonged crisis, such as the troubled third century C.E., the government repeatedly lashed out against the foreign cults and insisted on conformity to what it began to regard as Rome's traditional cult of the emperors. The most severe treatment was reserved for the Christians, whose religion, growing out of Jewish monotheism and expanding within the empire at a rapid rate after the crucifixion of Jesus in about 30 C.E., unconditionally forbade participation in the imperial cult. As a result, Christians were subjected to fierce waves of persecution, and thousands perished as martyrs.

Contribution of Roman Rule: The Pax Romana

The consequences of Rome's conquest of Egypt and other Hellenistic lands were obviously considerable. As Roman imperial rule was established throughout the Mediterranean world—reaching its greatest extent in 180 C.E. under the rule of Emperor Marcus Aurelius (r. 161–80 C.E.)—political, religious, and cultural exchanges took place between various peoples. For the provincials, many of whom possessed centuries if not millennia of history, the influence of Rome was often limited. In Rome, however, due to the new political and religious challenges, contact with the East brought very marked changes. For nearly three centuries the Mediterranean peoples benefited from the Pax Romana (Roman peace), which was inaugurated during the reign of Augustus. Some remained resentful, of course. In 66 C.E., the Jews finally revolted, and in 70 C.E. the Roman army, led by the future emperor Titus, laid waste to Jerusalem and utterly destroyed Herod's recently completed Temple. Yet the cultural exchange fostered by Roman rule survived even in the midst of Jewish hostility. Two examples demonstrate this. In the first case, a Jewish general named Josephus abandoned the revolt, moved to Rome, and, after adding the Roman name Flavius to his own, wrote famous histories of the Jews in the Roman language of Latin. In the second case, a Jewish convert to Christianity named Saul used the flexible conditions of the Pax Romana to travel unimpeded throughout the eastern Mediterranean preaching the gospel (good news) to polytheists. He too adopted a Roman name, Paul, and it is by this name that he became known to posterity after his martyrdom in the imperial capital in Rome in about 66 C.E.

With its military spectacles, exotic animals, and the living trophy of Queen Cleopatra, Julius Caesar's Egyptian triumph of 46 B.C.E. had been a display of Rome's domination over the East. Yet in a certain way it was the East that finally triumphed over Rome. In 330 C.E., Caesar's distant successor, Emperor Constantine (r. 306–37 C.E.), having converted to the religion of Christianity in 312 C.E., moved the imperial capital to the East, away from Rome and its pagan temples, to the new city of Constantinople. From there, the Byzantine Empire (395–1453 C.E.) would rule for almost eleven hundred years.

See Also

VOLUME ONE: The Phoenician Trading Empire and the Spread of the Alphabet; The Greek Bronze Age: Minoan and Mycenaean Influence and Exchange; Jerusalem and the Rise of the World's Monotheistic Civilizations; The Greek Empire: The Creation of the Hellenistic World; Barbarians in the Roman Empire

Cross-Cultural Exchange
- ↔ Hellenistic monarchical political institutions adopted by Rome
- ↔ Egyptian cults of the ruler adopted by Rome
- ↔ Hellenistic personal religions disseminated throughout Roman Empire
- ↔ Roman law introduced in the eastern Mediterranean
- ↔ Roman imperial administrative structures transferred to eastern Mediterranean
- ↔ Exotic animals transported to Europe from Asia and Africa

Bibliography

Ball, Warwick. *Rome in the East: The Transformation of an Empire.* London: Routledge, 2001.

Balsdon, J. P. V. D. *Romans and Aliens.* Chapel Hill: University of North Carolina Press, 1979.

Chauveau, Michel. *Egypt in the Age of Cleopatra.* Translated by David Lorton. Ithaca: Cornell University Press, 2000.

Jiménez, Ramon L. *Caesar against Rome: The Great Roman Civil War.* Westport, Conn.: Praeger, 2000.

Lewis, Naphtali. *Life in Egypt under Roman Rule.* Atlanta: Scholars Press, 1999.

Millar, Fergus. *The Roman Near East, 31 BC–AD 337.* Cambridge: Harvard University Press, 1993.

Wardman, Alan. *Religion and Statecraft among the Romans.* Baltimore: Johns Hopkins University Press, 1982.

Williams, Derek. *The Reach of Rome: A History of the Roman Imperial Frontier, 1st–5th Centuries AD.* New York: St Martin's Press, 1997.

—*John Strickland*

Primary Document
Dio's Account of Julius Caesar's Egyptian Triumph
Roman administrator and historian Cassius Dio Cocceianus (c.150–235 C.E.) describes Julius Caesar's Egyptian triumph and the celebrations that followed.

[Caesar] conducted the whole festival in a brilliant manner, as was fitting in honour of victories so many and so decisive. He celebrated triumphs for the Gauls, for Egypt, for Pharnaces, and for Juba, in four sections, on four separate days. Most of it, of course, delighted the spectators, but the sight of Arsinoë of Egypt, whom he led among the captives, and the host of lictors and the symbols of triumph taken from the citizens who had fallen in Africa displeased them exceedingly. The lictors, on account of their numbers, appeared to them a most offensive multitude, since

never before had they beheld so many at one time; and the sight of Arsinoë, a woman and once considered a queen, in chains,—a spectacle which had never yet been seen, at least in Rome,—aroused very great pity, and with this as an excuse they lamented their private misfortunes. She, to be sure, was released out of consideration for her brothers; but others, including Vercingetorix, were put to death.

The people, accordingly, were disagreeably affected by these sights that I have mentioned, and yet they considered them of very slight importance in view of the multitude of captives and the magnitude of Caesar's accomplishments. This led them to admire him extremely, as did likewise the good nature with which he bore the army's outspoken comments. For the soldiers jeered at those of their own number who had been appointed by him to the senate and at all the other failings of which he was accused, and in particular jested about his love for Cleopatra. . . .

After the triumph he entertained the populace splendidly, giving them grain beyond the regular amount and olive oil. Also to the multitude which received doles of corn he assigned the three hundred sesterces [silver or bronze coins] which he had already promised and a hundred more, but to the soldiers twenty thousand in one sum. Yet he was not uniformly munificent, but in most respects was very strict; for instance, since the multitude receiving doles of corn had increased enormously, not by lawful methods but in such ways as are common in times of strife, he caused the matter to be investigated and struck out half of their names at one time before the distribution.

The first days of the triumph he passed as was customary, but on the last day, after they had finished dinner, he entered his own forum wearing slippers and garlanded with all kinds of flowers; thence he proceeded homeward with practically the entire populace escorting him, while many elephants carried torches. For he had himself constructed the forum called after him, and it is distinctly more beautiful than the Roman Forum; yet it had increased the reputation of the other so that that was called the Great Forum. So after completing this new forum and the temple to Venus, as the founder of his family, he dedicated them at this very time, and in their honour instituted many contests of all

kinds. He built a kind of hunting-theatre of wood, which was called an amphitheatre from the fact that it had seats all around without any stage. In honour of this and of his daughter he exhibited combats of wild beasts and gladiators; but anyone who cared to record their number would find his task a burden without being able, in all probability, to present the truth; for all such matters are regularly exaggerated in a spirit of boastfulness. I shall accordingly pass over this and other like events that took place later, except, of course, where it may seem to me quite essential to mention some particular point, but I will give an account of the so-called camelopard, because it was then introduced into Rome by Caesar for the first time and exhibited to all. This animal is like a camel in all respects except that its legs are not all of the same length, the hind legs being the shorter. Beginning from the rump it grows gradually higher, which gives it the appearance of mounting some elevation; and towering high aloft, it supports the rest of its body on its front legs and lifts its neck in turn to an unusual height. Its skin is spotted like a leopard, and for this reason it bears the joint name of both animals. Such is the appearance of this beast. As for the men, he not only pitted them one against another singly in the Forum, as was customary, but he also made them fight together in companies in the Circus, horsemen against horsemen, men on foot against others on foot, and sometimes both kinds together in equal numbers. There was even a fight between men seated on elephants, forty in number. Finally he produced a naval battle, not on the sea nor on a lake, but on land; for he hollowed out a certain tract on the Campus Martius and after flooding it introduced ships into it.

Source: Excerpted from *Dio's Roman History*, translated by Earnest Cary on the basis of the version of Herbert Baldwin Foster (London: Heinemann; Cambridge: Harvard University Press, 1970–1987), 4:245–253.

Barbarians in the Roman Empire

C. 300–700 C.E.

In the late fifth century C.E., Odoacer (r. 476–93 C.E.; also called Odovacar), a general in the Roman army of Germanic birth, virtually ruled a much-reduced Roman Empire in the West, an empire that by this time controlled not much more than the Italian peninsula. Nominally, emperors continued to reign, but they served as mere figureheads stripped of any real power. In 476, Odoacer decided to depose the last emperor in Italy, a youth by the name of Romulus Augustulus (r. 475–76), the son of a Roman general. Odoacer ordered the Roman senate to send the imperial regalia to Constantinople (present-day Istanbul), the capital of the still-intact eastern Roman Empire, stating that there was no longer any need for an emperor in the West. Odoacer professed to recognize the authority of the eastern empire, and was given the title of patrician, an official title that gave him the authority to act in the name of the Roman Empire. In reality, he ruled Italy as a king, free from imperial control.

The deposition of Romulus Augustulus by a Germanic leader marks the transition from Roman to Germanic rule in the West. The disintegration of the western Roman Empire in the early medieval period into smaller Germanic kingdoms occurred partly as a result of the absorption of Germanic forces in the Roman army, the chief method of Germanic integration into Roman society. This process eventually created a new European civilization, shaped by the Roman and Germanic cultures and their interaction.

Background of the Germanic Peoples and the Roman Empire

The fall of the western Roman Empire came more than a thousand years after the founding of Rome in the eighth century B.C.E. Beginning in the fourth century B.C.E., the Romans expanded their empire from the Italian peninsula to eventually include vast territories, such as Britain,

the European continent to the Rhine and Danube rivers, and the lands surrounding the Mediterranean Sea. In this era of expansion, the Romans came into contact with the Germanic peoples, whom they called "barbarians" because they were considered uncivilized foreigners who did not speak either Greek or Latin.

Unlike the Romans, the Germanic peoples did not have a single ruler. They organized themselves around extended families, kinship groups, or clans. These clans made up tribes, all claiming a common mythological ancestor and common laws and customs. These tribes often organized themselves into confederations dominated by one particularly powerful tribe. A warrior elite controlled the government. The king (more like a tribal

An illustration of the baptism of Frankish ruler Clovis from about the fifteenth century. (© Archivo Iconografico, S.A./Corbis)

c. 750 B.C.E.	9 C.E.	284–305	c. 300
Rome is founded	German forces defeat Roman legions	Reign of Emperor Diocletian	Alamans invade Gaul

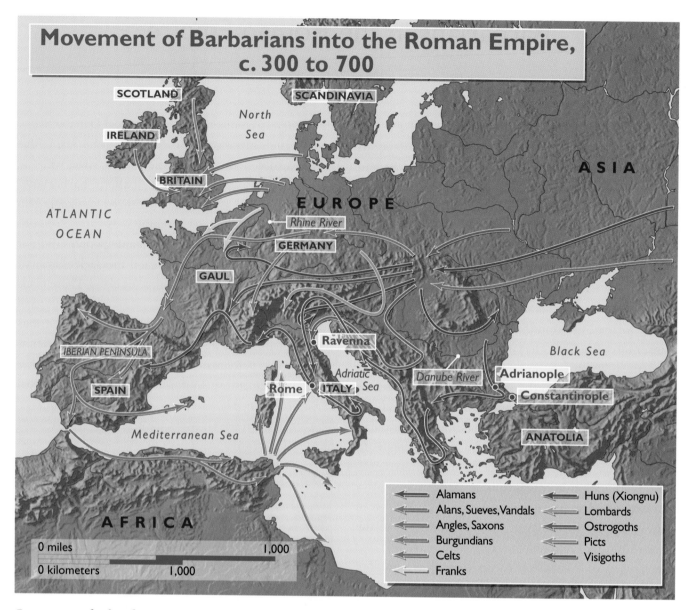

Movement of Barbarians into the Roman Empire, c. 300 to 700

Beginning in the fourth century, Germanic peoples (referred to as "barbarians" by the Romans) began to move into Roman territory and establish a large presence in the empire. These Germanic invaders slowly took control of the Roman Empire, establishing independent political entities ruled by German kings. The Germanic rulers adopted such Roman features as political systems, law, social structures, and Roman Catholic Christianity.
Source: Some data compiled from Gerald A. Danzer, *Atlas of World History* (London: Laurence King, 2000), 39.

chieftain) was the individual who succeeded most often in battle; other warriors bound themselves to him by an oath. The king was considered the intermediary between the gods and the people. Thus, Germanic tribes practiced a form of personal rule, with little

bureaucracy, that relied on the personal loyalty of the warriors to the king. These warriors were known as the *comitatus* (the king's companions). This political structure was highly unstable, however, and dynasties were often short and violent; primogeniture (the custom by

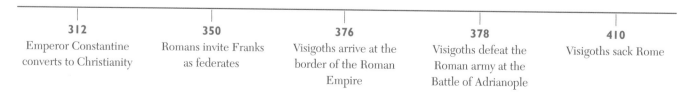

| 312 | 350 | 376 | 378 | 410 |
Emperor Constantine converts to Christianity | Romans invite Franks as federates | Visigoths arrive at the border of the Roman Empire | Visigoths defeat the Roman army at the Battle of Adrianople | Visigoths sack Rome

which the eldest son inherits the domain of the father) was not practiced, and potential successors often fought pitched battles for power.

These Germanic peoples halted Roman expansion beyond the Rhine and Danube rivers when their forces annihilated three legions of the Roman army in 9 c.e. The line of fortifications subsequently constructed by the Romans along the Rhine-Danube frontier in the first century c.e. proved to be quite permeable. Trade took place across the border, and Roman artifacts and coins have been excavated at sites located as far away as eastern Europe and Scandinavia. The Germanic peoples were also adopting Roman farming methods, which involved the creation of large landed estates often worked by slave labor producing crops to sell on the open market. More importantly, many Germans hired themselves out as mercenaries for the Roman army, defending the very border that was supposed to keep them out.

In the third century c.e., Rome experienced a prolonged social, political, and economic crisis, resolved temporarily when the emperor Diocletian (r. 284–305) instituted wide-ranging reforms to stabilize the empire. He established a military dictatorship that exalted the grandeur of the imperial title, enhancing its semidivine status. He reorganized the provinces into districts and greatly expanded the military and the bureaucracy. Recognizing that the empire had become too vast for one monarch to rule from a single capital, Diocletian appointed a co-emperor (which he called *augustus*) and two lieutenants (which he called *caesars*). This system, a tetrarchy (rule by four), divided the empire into two equal halves, East and West, with one augustus and one caesar for each half. These reforms did not ultimately save the empire in the West. By the end of the fifth century, the Roman Empire's political and economic problems provided the necessary conditions that allowed the Germanic peoples on the border to invade the western Roman Empire and create a number of successor states, some of which have evolved into the European nation-states of the present day.

The Barbarian Invasions and the Establishment of Germanic Kingdoms in the West

The interaction between the Germanic peoples and the Roman Empire paved the way not only for the fall of the Roman Empire in the West, but also for the transformation of Germanic society into a new European civilization. Although they had initiated a series of invasions and migrations into Roman territory starting in the fourth century, the Germans were not inherently nomadic peoples. Rather, they usually resided in small villages and engaged in animal husbandry and subsistence farming.

The Germanic peoples left their ancestral homes in response to specific historical circumstances. In the late fourth century, the Huns, a nomadic central Asian people (also known as the Xiongnu), began to put pressure on their Germanic neighbors to the west, the Ostrogoths and Visigoths, who had dominated the Black Sea region but were now forced by the Huns to move westward toward Roman territory. In 376, large numbers of Visigoths arrived as refugees at the Danube River, the northern border of the Roman Empire. They negotiated an agreement with the Romans whereby they could reside in the empire in exchange for military service. In 378, the Visigoths rebelled against harsh treatment by the Romans and defeated a Roman army in the Battle of Adrianople in Anatolia (present-day Turkey). This victory by the Visigoths was a turning point for the Germanic peoples and for the Roman Empire because it established a permanent large-scale barbarian presence in Roman territory.

The fourth century also saw incessant civil wars between contenders for the imperial throne that significantly weakened the Roman Empire's defenses along the Rhine River. Roman frontier troops (known as *limitanei*) were often involved in this internecine fighting, and so were unavailable to protect the borders. Often the contenders would cultivate the support of the very Germanic peoples they once fought against in order to make up for the loss of veteran soldiers as the civil wars continued to the end of the century. The decision to rely increasingly

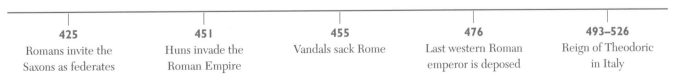

425	451	455	476	493–526
Romans invite the Saxons as federates	Huns invade the Roman Empire	Vandals sack Rome	Last western Roman emperor is deposed	Reign of Theodoric in Italy

on Germanic troops hastened their integration into the Roman military and administrative hierarchy.

The inclusion of barbarian troops in the Roman army did not ultimately prevent invasions by other Germanic peoples. For example, starting in about 300, the Germanic Alamans invaded eastern Gaul (present-day France). In response, the Romans appointed the Franks, another Germanic people, as federates, who served Rome but remained under the command of their own chieftains; sometimes the Frankish warriors received grants of land in return for their services. With the help of the Franks, the Romans drove the Alamans back east, after which the Franks took the opportunity to occupy part of Gaul, with no opposition by the Romans.

In 408, the Visigoths, angered at continued ill treatment by the Roman government, invaded the Italian peninsula and in 410 sacked the city of Rome. Although the capital of the western empire had by then been moved to the more easily defended Ravenna (located northeast of Rome on the Adriatic coast), the attack on Rome struck a blow to the morale of patriotic Romans. At approximately the same time, other Germanic peoples, such as the Vandals, Sueves, and Alans, crossed into Gaul, eventually driving the Visigoths into southern Gaul and the Roman province of Spain. The Vandals continued into northern Africa, also part of the Roman Empire, to take control of fertile lands that produced grain. To protect the Italian peninsula, Roman troops withdrew from the outlying areas of the western empire throughout the first half of the fifth century, from Britain, Spain, North Africa, and finally from Gaul.

In 451, the Huns, now organized into a confederacy under a single leader, Attila (r. 434–53), began their drive westward as far as Gaul, threatening Italy. The following year Attila invaded northern Italy, but was persuaded by Pope Leo I (r. 440–61) and his delegation to withdraw. After this event, the western emperor lost much of his authority. A succession of generals assumed the real power behind the throne. In 455, Vandals sailed from their new home in northern Africa and sacked Rome, revealing the continued vulnerability of the Italian peninsula to invasion. An attempt to secure the sea routes in the Mediterranean

against Vandal attack also resulted in failure. By 476, when the last western Roman emperor was deposed, what was left of the Roman Empire in the West controlled nothing more than Italy and parts of southern France.

By the late fifth century all of the western empire had been "delegated" to Germanic kings by the rulers of the eastern empire. However, these kingdoms effectively ruled as independent political entities. While some Germanic states, such as the Burgundian (located in present-day southeastern France), were eventually absorbed into other, more powerful Germanic states, several survived to forge a new civilization in the West. Despite common Roman and Christian influences, each region developed in its own distinctive way. Italy witnessed rule by successive Germanic peoples and a resurgent eastern empire. In 493, Odoacer was defeated and killed by the Ostrogoths. They took control of Italy under the leadership of Theodoric (493–526), who became a leading power in western Europe. The Ostrogoths were defeated by an eastern empire newly resurgent under Emperor Justinian (r. 527–65), who launched a campaign to reunite the two halves of the Roman Empire in 533. Justinian's forces succeeded in recapturing parts of North Africa, Spain, and Italy, but faced new Germanic invaders who limited their reconquest. These were the Lombards, who originated in northern Germany and entered northern Italy in 568, led by King Alboin (r. 565–73).

In Gaul, the Franks were unified in the late fifth century under the leadership of Clovis (r. 481–511), a member of the Merovingian Dynasty (476–c. 750). In 507, Clovis defeated the Visigoths, driving them out of southern France and into Spain, ensuring Frankish rule in nearly all of Gaul. After the Romans had abandoned the defense of Britain in 410, the island was open to invasion from Scotland and Ireland. In 425, Roman-British aristocrats had invited the Germanic Saxon warriors (who were later joined by the Angles) to serve as federates by helping to defend Roman Britain from the Scottish Picts and the Irish Celts. By 550, the eastern two-thirds of Britain had come under control of the Anglo-Saxons. The central government disappeared as a number of small-scale, mutually hostile kingdoms were

507	**533**	**568**	**c. 587**
Clovis defeats the Visigoths and drives them out of Gaul	Justinian launches an invasion of the West	Lombards invade northern Italy	Visigothic king Reccared converts to Roman Catholicism

established. By the late fifth century, the Germanic kings had virtually finished carving up the western portion of the empire, starting the process that would create a European civilization in the centuries to come.

Barbarian, Roman, and Christian Synthesis Creates a New Europe

The different Germanic peoples who had interacted with the Romans as federates, mercenaries, or enemies now grappled with the legacy of the Roman Empire. Although they faced the contempt many Romans expressed for barbarians in general, in many respects the Germanic peoples of the fifth century had become "Romanized," adopting many Roman political and cultural practices. Indeed, there is ample evidence of a great deal of continuity between the late imperial era and the advent of the Germanic successor states. Despite the fact that the West was now politically fragmented, administrative, legal, intellectual, and material cultural traditions that had taken shape in the later centuries of the Roman Empire continued to be practiced. The prolonged contact between Rome and the barbarians encouraged the Germanic peoples to abandon their previous forms of social and political organization based on chieftains and to adopt the more developed Roman state system. An important consequence of the interaction between Romans and barbarians was the promulgation of law codes by the Germanic kingdoms that were largely adapted from Roman provincial law. Starting in the sixth century, Germanic kings began to collect, write, and publish their laws, based on customs handed down by tradition. Roman law forms the basis of most law codes still used by European nations in the twenty-first century.

The political and institutional reforms of Diocletian emperors left an important legacy for the barbarian kingdoms that succeeded the empire in the late fifth century. They reinforced an image of the emperor as remote and closely connected to the divine. The tetrarchy also permanently divided the empire, and the two halves diverged socially, politically, and ultimately on religious matters as well. Finally, these reforms created a new military elite

Cross-Cultural Exchange
- ↔ Germanic rulers adopt the Roman political system, such as royal dynasties
- ↔ Germanic cultures adapt Roman law and social structure to their societies
- ↔ Roman Catholic Christianity, the state religion of Rome, spreads to the Germanic peoples
- ↔ Germanic peoples adopt Roman farming methods

class, into which Germanic mercenaries and others were able to integrate. The Germanic kings drew on the legacy of military service to the empire to legitimize their takeover of Roman lands. Most of the Germanic monarchies established royal dynasties (also a Roman influence) that adopted many of the imperial trappings and rituals of the late Roman Empire, including displays of wealth and claims of divine approval. Almost all Germanic kings adopted Roman titles, such as consul or patrician, and in these officially conferred titles resided the authority necessary to govern Roman populations that sometimes expressed contempt for their new overlords. For example, the Frankish king Clovis adopted the dress of Roman officials, wore a royal diadem (crown), and adopted traditional imperial practices, such as handing out coins to crowds of his subjects. Ostrogoth ruler Theodoric's respect for Roman culture ensured that Greek and Roman works of literature and philosophy were preserved and recopied, transmitting Greco-Roman culture into the Middle Ages. The Lombards were also able to make use of the Roman tax gathering and administrative systems, which had been maintained under Ostrogothic rule. Although most cities declined in both population and cultural vitality throughout much of western Europe during the early medieval period, in the former heartland of the Roman Empire, Lombard rule was centered in the relatively densely populated cities. The adoption of Roman practices ensured that life for the average inhabitant of the now-defunct empire did not change very much, assisting in the transition to Germanic rule.

The relationship between the Germanic rulers and the Roman Catholic Church also affected the success of the

Germanic kingdoms that emerged in the fifth century. Rome had become a Christian empire when the emperor Constantine (r. 306–37) converted to Christianity in 312. In succeeding centuries, the bishop of Rome claimed leadership of the Church, and began to call himself *pope* (derived from the Latin word for "father"). As the Germanic peoples came into contact with the Romans, they too converted to the new faith, hastening the integration of the barbarians into Roman culture. Virtually all wealthy Roman landowners in the provinces were Roman Catholic Christian and many of them had become bishops (high officials in the church who often took over the daily administration of the cities within their districts). These landowners retained their property and a measure of autonomy, but now they answered to the new Germanic kings rather than to the imperial authority. They also often served as administrators and eventually merged with the Germanic ruling elite, creating a new medieval aristocracy.

A large number of Germans, however, converted to a form of Christianity called Arianism, considered heretical by the Roman Catholic Church for believing that Jesus Christ and God the Father were different divine entities. The conflict between orthodox Catholics and Arians often hindered opportunities for the Germanic rulers to integrate the Roman population into their administrations. For instance, Clovis cultivated the support of the Gallo-Roman population by converting to Roman Catholicism and driving the Arian Visigoths out of southern Gaul in 507. In Spain, Visigothic rule was troubled because the first Visigothic kings were Arian Christians, which put them at odds with the orthodox Catholic Hispano-Roman population. It was only when King Reccared (r. 586–601) converted to Catholicism in about 587 that the Visigoths were able to consolidate their rule with the help of powerful and able Catholic bishops. These bishops supported a unified Spanish kingdom because they believed it enhanced the power of the Church to impose religious orthodoxy. The Visigoths' establishment of a stable ruling order in Spain would be cut short by the Muslim Arab conquest of the Iberian Peninsula in 711.

At the same time, some rulers accommodated their rule to reflect this religious diversity. Although an Arian Christian, Theodoric encouraged tolerance between his Arian Christian and orthodox Roman subjects, enhancing cooperation in repairing Italy's infrastructure, damaged after many years of invasion and civil war. The Lombard kings and people who succeeded the Ostrogoths decided to convert to Roman Catholic Christianity, which hastened the creation of a successful synthesis of Roman and Germanic cultures in Italy.

The conversion of the Anglo-Saxon kingdoms to Christianity began after Pope Gregory the Great (r. 590–604) sent missionaries to convert the Saxon king Ethelbert of Kent in 597. The eventual baptism of Ethelbert strengthened ties between the Roman Catholic Church and distant Britain, resulting in a very successful synthesis of Roman and Germanic cultures there. Anglo-Saxon rule in Britain proved very durable. The small-scale kingdoms were replaced by larger, more coherent kingdoms in Kent, Wessex, Mercia, and Northumbria, and by 1000, a single, relatively centralized state had succeeded these kingdoms. Not until 1066, when William the Conqueror (r. 1066–87) established a Norman ruling dynasty, did the Anglo-Saxons cease to rule in Britain.

With the establishment of individual kingdoms all adopting Christianity, the populations that once distinguished themselves as either Roman or barbarian had, by the eighth century, merged to form the new ethnic groups that define medieval and modern Europe. Latin, once the common language of the empire, broke down into several languages, among them French, Italian, and Spanish; Latin was used only by members of the clergy.

The fact that the two halves of the Roman Empire never reunited played a key role in defining a new civilization in the West. The Roman Empire in the East did not fall and continued to rule the eastern portion of the empire from its capital at Constantinople for centuries after 476. Historians call the eastern Roman Empire the Byzantine Empire (395–1453; named after Byzantium, the village on which Constantinople was founded in 330 C.E.) because it developed its own institutions in the centuries following the collapse of the western empire. Unlike in the West, where secular and religious institutions developed separately (although often in cooperation with one another), the Byzantine Empire fused church and state into one political institution. The emperor and patriarch (the supreme religious authority in Constantinople) represented the two pillars of divine rule, with the emperor the ultimate authority. This method of rule came into conflict with the bishops of Rome, who asserted authority over all Christians, including kings, and eventually claimed the title of pope. The patriarch of Constantinople resisted this claim, further distancing the two churches in the centuries to follow. In 1054, the Roman Catholic Church and what became known as the Orthodox Church would sever their connections. This split, known as the Great Schism, has never been mended.

The invasion of Byzantine lands by Muslim forces in the seventh century forced the empire to turn its attentions to the east to combat the new enemy, dooming Justinian's vision of a reunited empire and further distancing the West from the East.

The Byzantine Empire struggled on for another eight hundred years, to be overthrown with the conquest of Constantinople by Muslim Turkish (Ottoman) forces in 1453. By that time, Western European society had developed the social, political, and economic institutions it needed to expand its influence around the world in the modern era. The merging of Roman and Germanic cultures at the end of the fifth century, with little influence from the Roman East, coalesced in the course of the early Middle Ages, and eventually created a new Western European society.

See Also

VOLUME ONE: The Roman Empire and the Mediterranean World
VOLUME TWO: The Celts and the Civilizations of Western Europe; The Establishment and Spread of Islam; Islam in Spain; The Seljuk Turks and Islamic Civilization

Bibliography

Brown, Peter. *The World of Late Antiquity.* New York: W. W. Norton, 1989.
Collins, Roger. *Early Medieval Europe, 300–1000.* London: Macmillan, 1991.
Ferrill, Arthur. *The Fall of the Roman Empire: The Military Explanation.* London: Thames & Hudson, 1986.
Goffart, Walter. *Barbarians and Romans, A.D. 418–584: The Techniques of Accommodation.* Princeton: Princeton University Press, 1980.

—*Florence Lemoine*

Primary Document

Gregory of Tours Recounts the Conversion of Clovis to Christianity

Gregory of Tours (538–94) was a Gallo-Roman bishop and aristocratic landholder from central France. He represented the accommodation of the old Roman elite to Germanic rule. Gregory approved of King Clovis's rule (r. 481–511), despite the fact that his methods were often brutal and violent, because Clovis had converted to Roman Catholic Christianity. In this passage, Gregory describes Clovis's initial reluctance to convert and the event that convinced him to embrace Christianity.

The first child which Clotild bore for Clovis was a son. She wanted to have her baby baptized, and she kept on urging her husband to agree to this. "The gods whom you worship are no good," she would say. "They haven't even been able to help themselves, let alone others. They are carved out of stone or wood or some old piece of metal. The very names which you have given them were the names of men, not of gods. Take your Saturn, for example, who ran away from his own son to avoid being exiled from his kingdom, or so they say; and Jupiter, that obscene perpetrator of all sorts of mucky deeds, who couldn't keep his hands off other men, who had his fun with all his female relatives and couldn't even refrain from intercourse with his own sister . . .

What have Mars and Mercury ever done for anyone? They may have been endowed with magic arts, but they were certainly not worthy of being called divine. You ought instead to worship Him who created at a word and out of nothing heaven, and earth, the sea and all that therein is, who made the sun to shine, who lit the sky with stars, who peopled the water with fish, the earth with beasts, the sky with flying creatures, at whose nod the fields became fair with fruits, the trees with apples, the vines with grapes, by whose hand the race of man was made, by whose gift all creation is constrained to serve in deference and devotion the man He made." However often the Queen said this, the King came no nearer to belief. "All these things have been created and produced at the command of *our* gods," he would answer. "It is obvious that *your* God can do nothing, and, what is more, there is no proof that he is a God at all."

The Queen, who was true to her faith, brought her son to be baptized. She ordered the church to be decorated with hangings and curtains, in the hope that the King, who remained stubborn in the face of argument, might be brought to the faith by ceremony. The child was baptized;

he was given the name Ingomer; but no sooner had he received baptism than he died in his white robes. Clovis was extremely angry. He began immediately to reproach his Queen. "If he had been dedicated in the name of my gods," he said, "he would have lived without question; but now that he has been baptized in the name of your God he has not been able to live a single day!" "I give thanks to Almighty God," replied Clotild, "the Creator of all things, who has not found me completely unworthy, for He has deigned to welcome to His kingdom a child conceived in my womb. I am not at all cast down in my mind because of what has happened, for I know that my child, who was called away from this world in his white baptismal robes, will be nurtured in the sight of God."

Some time later Clotild bore a second son. He was baptized Chlodomer. He began to ail and Clovis said: "What else do you expect? It will happen to him as it happened to his brother: no sooner is he baptized in the name of your Christ than he will die!" Clotild prayed to the Lord and at His command the baby recovered.

Queen Clotild continued to pray that her husband might recognize the true God and give up his idol-worship. Nothing could persuade him to accept Christianity. Finally war broke out against the Alamanni and in this conflict he was forced by necessity to accept what he had refused of his own free will.

It so turned out that when the two armies met on the battlefield there was great slaughter and the troops of Clovis were rapidly being annihilated. He raised his eyes to heaven when he saw this, felt compunction in his heart and was moved to tears. "Jesus Christ," he said, "you who Clotild maintains to be the Son of the living God, you who deign to give help to those in travail and victory to those who trust in you, in faith I beg the glory of your help. If you will give me victory over my enemies, and if I may have evidence of that miraculous power which the people dedicated to your name say that they have experienced, then I will believe in you and I will be baptized in your name. I have called upon my own gods, but, as I see only too clearly, they have no intention of helping me. I therefore cannot believe that they possess any power, for they do not come to the assistance of those who trust in them. I now call upon you. I want to believe in you, but I must first be saved from my enemies." Even as he said this the Alamanni turned their backs and began to run away. As soon as they saw that their King was killed, they submitted to Clovis. "We beg you," they said, "to put an end to this slaughter. We are prepared to obey you." Clovis stopped the war. He made a speech in which he called for peace. Then he went home. He told the Queen how he had won a victory by calling on the name of Christ. This happened in the fifteenth year of his reign.

Source: Excerpted from Saint Gregory Bishop of Tours, *The History of the Franks,* translated by Lewis Thorpe (Baltimore: Penguin, 1974), 141–143.

Volume One: Timeline

35,000 B.C.E. *Homo sapiens sapiens* settle in central Asia

9000–7000 Earliest agriculture develops in Mesoamerica

6000 Evidence of human habitation on Crete, in the eastern Mediterranean Sea

3500–1800 Pre-Ceramic Period in trans-Andes western South America

3300 Writing systems emerge in Mesopotamia (present-day Iraq)

3000 Migrations of European steppe peoples to Anatolia (present-day Turkey) and the Tarim Basin in central Asia

2500 Beginning of Harappan civilization in the Indus Valley

2000 Farmers and herders migrate from East Africa to West Africa

1766–1122 Shang Dynasty in China; frequent use of early Chinese script

1700–1450 Height of Minoan civilization on Crete

1500 Migration of Indo-Europeans (Aryans) into the Indus Valley begins

1500–500 Vedic Age in South Asia

c. 1450 Mycenaean civilization takes control of Crete

1200–800 Dark Age of ancient Greek history

1000 Dong Son culture emerges in Southeast Asia

1000 Jerusalem is conquered by King David of Israel

1000 Emergence of early Phoenician alphabet

c. 950 Embassy of the Queen of Sheba to Jerusalem

900–200 Early Horizon Period and dominance of Chavín culture in pre-Columbian Peru

800–323 Greek Renaissance and the Classical Age

750 Indo-Europeans bring iron smelting to South Asia; Etruscans adopt the Euboean alphabet, a variation of the Greek alphabet

c. 750 Foundation of Rome

c. 586–466 Life of the Buddha Gautama Siddhartha

c. 550–330 Reign of the Persian dynasty of the Achaemenids

521–486 Reign of Darius I in the Persian Empire

500 Early Hinduism appears in South Asia

500 End of great migrations by Indo-European speakers

c. 500 First Indian traders travel to Southeast Asia

500–479 Persian Wars between Persia (present-day Iran) and the Greek states

403–221 Warring States Period, during which China divides into many competing states

330 Alexander the Great defeats the Persian Achaemenids, ending the dynasty

323–283 Reign of Ptolemy I of Egypt

c. 273–232 Indian ruler King Asoka of the Maurya Dynasty converts to and patronizes Buddhism

250 B.C.E.–250 C.E. Yayoi Culture Period in Japan

221–206 Qin Dynasty rules in China

206 B.C.E.–220 C.E. Han Dynasty rules in China

200 Beginning of Turko-Mongol migrations into Chinese, Persian, and Roman lands

138 Zhang Qian's travels to Bactria contributes to the opening of the Silk Roads, trade routes between Europe and Asia

111 B.C.E.–939 C.E. China occupies northern Vietnam

109 Chinese colonies are established in Korea

63 Jerusalem is annexed by the Romans

46 Julius Caesar triumphs over Egypt

31 B.C.E.–14 C.E. Reign of Augustus in the Roman Empire

1–500 C.E. Migration of Bantu speakers in Africa, who carry Nok culture to Senegal, southern Africa, and Angola

18–663   Kingdom of Paekche rules in Korea

30   Christ is crucified

1st century–500s   Kingdom of Funan flourishes in Cambodia, Vietnam, and Thailand

180   Roman Empire reaches its greatest extent under Emperor Marcus Aurelius

192–1720   Kingdom of Champa rules in Vietnam

220–589   Three Kingdoms/Six Dynasties Period in China

300   Olmec disappear as separate culture in Central America

312   Roman emperor Constantine converts to Christianity

330   Constantine transfers capital of the Roman Empire to Constantinople (present-day Istanbul in Turkey)

451   Huns invade the Roman Empire

476   Fall of the Roman Empire in the West

Volume One: Glossary

agriculture: The practice of cultivating the soil and rearing animals

alchemy: Early scientific experiments with the material world that had a spiritual component

animal husbandry: The controlled breeding and raising of domestic animals, such as dogs, sheep, cattle, and bees

animism: A belief that natural things possess spirits and can influence human events

arianism: The belief, considered heretical by the Roman Catholic Church, that Jesus Christ and God the Father are different divine entities

aristocracy: Members of a hereditary nobility; a privileged class that governs or has authority within a society

asceticism: The practice of self-denial as a spiritual discipline

barbarians: Individuals from a different society or culture, often with a strong military tradition, who are considered less civilized

bureaucracy: A nonelected administrative body

caste: A hereditary societal division in Hinduism based on social groupings that enforces limitations on one's profession, behavior, and diet and restricts intermarriage and contact with other castes

chiefdoms: Small areas ruled by a hereditary leader who maintains his position through the force of tradition, physical or moral strength, and the distribution of resources

city-state: A city and the territory immediately around it that form a self-governing state

clan: A group of people united by kinship, especially through a common ancestor

Confucianism: A set of beliefs based on the ideas of Confucius, a Chinese philosopher of the sixth and fifth centuries B.C.E. who espoused morality, virtue, hierarchy, and leadership by example

cosmology: A theory or belief that describes the origins and nature of the universe

cult: An exclusive or self-defining group of individuals who show devotion to a particular god or body of beliefs

cultural homogeneity: The state of having similar cultural influences in one area with little external influence

cuneiform: Wedge-shaped characters used as a type of alphabet by ancient Mesopotamians

Daoism: A religion developed in ancient China that promotes respect for nature, harmony and a simple way of life

deductive logic: A system of reasoning that derives universal principles from the study of specific evidence

desertification: The process by which a piece of land becomes a desert, from either misuse or climate change

dialect: A variation of a language created by geographical, regional, or social differences

doctrine: Principles accepted by a religious or political group; dogma

dynasty: A succession of people from the same line of descent who rule over a particular region

ethnocentrism: The belief that one's own group is superior to another group

glyphs: Symbols that convey information nonverbally

hegemony: A situation whereby one group has great influence or dominance over another group

hierarchy: The classification of groups or individuals according to ability or social and economic position

hieroglyphics: An ancient Egyptian system of writing using pictorial symbols to represent words and phrases

Hinduism: Popular name for the Vedic religion of India, Sanata Dharma (or "the Eternal Way"), which emphasizes ritual and social observances

indigenous: Having been born in, grown in, or occurring naturally in a particular geographic region

Indo-European: The family of languages spoken in most of Europe, areas of the world colonized by Europeans since

1500, Persia, the subcontinent of India, and certain areas in Asia; the people who speak Indo-European languages

kingdom: A politically organized community or territory with a monarchical government

Legalism: The political philosophy originating in ancient China that stresses harsh punishment for the most minor infractions and rich rewards for obedience

maritime: Pertaining to the navigation and commerce of the sea

matriarchy: A social system in which women control the family, group, or state

mercenary: A hired soldier

Messiah: In Judaism, the king of the Jews who will be sent by God; in Christianity, Jesus Christ

monarchy: A political system whereby absolute sovereignty lies with an individual who inherits power

monosyllabic: Refers to a type of language in which individual syllables are strung together to produce complex meanings

monotheism: The belief in one god

myth: A traditional story that explains a world view, cultural mores, or natural phenomenon

nirvana: A Buddhist concept referring to the ultimate state of release and transcendence (beyond the limits of the material universe)

nomad(s): A person or group of people who have no fixed residence and move from one place to another, often as a function of the way they produce or acquire food

paganism: The worship of many gods

pantheon: A set of officially recognized gods of a people or religion

pastoralism: An economic system that revolves around the breeding and raising of livestock

patriarchy: A social system in which the family is run by the male head and men have authority over women

phonograms: Pictograms or ideograms with modifying marks for sounds

pictograms: Pictorial representations of everyday objects, mainly commonly traded items

plebeian: Referring to the common people of the ancient Roman Empire

polity: A political unit

polysyllabic: Refers to a type of language in which syllables are brought together in the same word to form a complex word

polytheism: The belief in more than one god

primogeniture: The custom by which the eldest son inherits the domain of the father

satrapy: A province or region ruled by a satrap (governor)

scripture: A written work that is considered to be sacred

settled agriculture: The harvesting and producing of edible plants and crops to sustain a population

shaman: A priest whose followers believe he can heal and affect events through magic or contact with the afterlife

sinification: The process of making something more Chinese in character

steppe: Vast, grassy, treeless plain common in southeastern Europe and in central Asia

syncretism: An instance in which two or more traditions blend into a new practice

tetrarchy: Rule by four individuals

tonal: Refers to a type of language in which the same word might have different meanings depending on its pronunciation

topography: The physical characteristics of a piece of land or any surface

Torah: The five books of the Old Testament said to be given to Moses by God

transhumance: A type of pastoralism that involves the moving of large herds from summer grazing in mountain meadows to winter pasturage

tribute: A gift or tax given to a leader from his people or from foreigners

vassalage: A condition in which one people swears loyalty and pays tribute to another

ziggurat: A pyramidal tower built by the ancient Babylonians

Volume One: Bibliography

Adshead, Samuel Adrian M. *China in World History*. 3rd ed. New York: St. Martin's Press, 2000.

Allchin, Bridget, and Raymond Allchin. *The Rise of Civilization in India and Pakistan*. Cambridge: Cambridge University Press, 1982.

Armstrong, Karen. *Jerusalem: One City, Three Faiths*. New York: Alfred A. Knopf, 1996.

Asali, Kamil J., ed. *Jerusalem in History*. 1st American ed. Brooklyn, N.Y.: Olive Branch Press, 2000.

Aubet, María Eugenia. *The Phoenicians and the West: Politics, Colonies and Trade*. 2nd ed. Translated by Mary Turton. New York: Cambridge University Press, 2001.

Ball, Warwick. *Rome in the East: The Transformation of an Empire*. London: Routledge, 2001.

Balsdon, J. P. V. D. *Romans and Aliens*. Chapel Hill: University of North Carolina Press, 1979.

Barfield, Thomas J. *The Perilous Frontier: Nomadic Empires and China*. Cambridge: Basil Blackwell, 1989.

Benda, Harry J., ed. *The World of Southeast Asia: Selected Historical Readings*. New York: Harper & Row, 1967.

Bentley, Jerry H. *Old World Encounters: Cross-Cultural Contacts and Exchanges in Pre-Modern Times*. New York: Oxford University Press, 1993.

Boulnois, Luce. *The Silk Road*. New York: Dutton, 1966.

Briant, Pierre. *From Cyrus to Alexander: A History of the Persian Empire*. Translated by Peter T. Daniels. Winona Lake, Ind.: Eisenbrauns, 2002.

Brown, Peter. *The World of Late Antiquity*. New York: W. W. Norton, 1989.

Bryant, Edwin. *The Quest for the Origins of Vedic Culture: The Indo-Aryan Migration Debate*. New York: Oxford University Press, 2001.

Burger, Richard L. *Chavín and the Origins of Andean Civilization*. London: Thames & Hudson, 1995.

———. *The Prehistoric Occupation of Chavín de Huántar, Peru*. Berkeley: University of California Press, 1984.

Chauveau, Michel. *Egypt in the Age of Cleopatra*. Translated by David Lorton. Ithaca: Cornell University Press, 2000.

Chittick, H. Neville, and Robert I. Rotberg, eds. *East Africa and the Orient: Cultural Syntheses in Pre-Colonial Times*. New York: Africana Publishing, 1975.

Clapp, Nicholas. *Sheba: Through the Desert in Search of the Legendary Queen*. Boston: Houghton Mifflin, 2001.

Codès, George. *The Indianized States of Southeast Asia*. Translated by Susan Brown Cowing. 3rd ed. Honolulu: East-West Center, 1968.

———. *The Making of South-East Asia*. Translated by H. M. Wright. Berkeley: University of California Press, 1966.

Collins, Roger. *Early Medieval Europe, 300–1000*. London: Macmillan, 1991.

Culican, William. *The Medes and Persians*. London: Thames & Hudson, 1965.

Davidson, Basil. *The Lost Cities of Africa*. Rev. ed. Boston: Little, Brown, 1970.

Davies, Nigel. *The Toltec Heritage: From the Fall of the Tula to the Rise of Tenochtitlan*. Norman: University of Oklahoma Press, 1980.

Davis-Kimball, J., V. A. Bashilov, and L. T. Yablonsky, eds. *Nomads of the Eurasian Steppes in the Early Iron Age*. Berkeley: Zinat Press, 1995.

Dickinson, Oliver. *The Aegean Bronze Age*. Cambridge: Cambridge University Press, 1994.

Diringer, David. *A History of the Alphabet*. Old Woking, U.K.: Unwin Brothers, 1977.

Ellis, Walter M. *Ptolemy of Egypt*. London: Routledge, 1994.

Elvin, Mark. *The Pattern of the Chinese Past*. Stanford: Stanford University Press, 1973.

Fage, J. D., with William Tordoff. *A History of Africa*. 4th ed. London: Routledge, 2002.

Fairservis, Walter A. *The Roots of Ancient India*. 2nd ed. Chicago: University of Chicago Press, 1975.

Ferrill, Arthur. *The Fall of the Roman Empire: The Military Explanation*. London: Thames & Hudson, 1986.

Fitton, J. Lesley. *The Discovery of the Greek Bronze Age*. Cambridge: Harvard University Press, 1996.

FitzGerald, C. P. *The Southern Expansion of the Chinese People: "Southern Fields and Southern Ocean."* Canberra: Australian National University Press, 1972.

Foltz, Richard. *Religions of the Silk Road: Overland Trade and Cultural Exchange from Antiquity to the Fifteenth Century*. New York: St. Martin's Press, 1999.

Forrest, R. A. D. *The Chinese Language*. London: Faber & Faber, 1973.

Frazier, Kendrick. *People of Chaco: A Canyon and Its Culture*. New York: W. W. Norton, 1999.

Georges, Pericles. *Barbarian Asia and the Greek Experience: From the Archaic Period to the Age of Xenophon*. Baltimore: Johns Hopkins University Press, 1994.

Goffart, Walter. *Barbarians and Romans*, A.D. *418–584: The Techniques of Accommodation*. Princeton: Princeton University Press, 1980.

Green, Peter. *From Alexander to Actium: The Historical Evolution of the Hellenistic Age*. Berkeley: University of California Press, 1990.

Grimal, Pierre. *Hellenism and the Rise of Rome*. London: Weidenfeld & Nicolson, 1968.

Grousset, René. *The Empire of the Steppes: A History of Central Asia*. New Brunswick, N.J.: Rutgers University Press, 1970.

Harden, Donald. *The Phoenicians*. Middlesex, U.K.: Penguin Books, 1971.

Hood, M. S. F. *The Minoans*. London: Thames & Hudson, 1971.

Hooker, J. T. *Mycenaean Greece*. Boston: Routledge/Kegan Paul, 1976.

Jiménez, Ramon L. *Caesar against Rome: The Great Roman Civil War*. Westport, Conn.: Praeger, 2000.

Kano, Chiaki. *The Origins of the Chavín Culture*. Washington, D.C.: Dumbarton Oaks, 1979.

Kim-Renaud, Young-Key, ed. *The Korean Alphabet: Its History and Structure*. Honolulu: University of Hawaii Press, 1997.

Korean National Commission for UNESCO. *The Korean Language*. Arch Cape, Ore.: Pace International Research, 1983.

Kuhrt, Amélie, and Susan Sherwin-White, eds. *Hellenism in the East: The Interaction of Greek and Non-Greek Civilizations from Syria to Central Asia after Alexander*. Berkeley: University of California Press, 1987.

———. *From Samarkhand to Sardis: A New Approach to the Seleucid Empire*. Berkeley: University of California Press, 1993.

Lattimore, Owen. *Inner Asian Frontiers of China*. New York: American Geographical Society, 1940.

Lekson, Stephen H. *The Chaco Meridian: Centers of Political Power in the Ancient Southwest*. Walnut Creek, Calif.: AltaMira Press, 1999.

Levine, Lee I., ed. *Jerusalem: Its Sanctity and Centrality to Judaism, Christianity, and Islam*. New York: Continuum, 1999.

Lewis, Naphtali. *Life in Egypt under Roman Rule*. Atlanta: Scholars Press, 1999.

Liu, Hsin-ju. *The Silk Road: Overland Trade and Cultural Interactions in Eurasia*. Washington, D.C.: American Historical Association, 1998.

Loewe, Michael. *Everyday Life in Early Imperial China during the Han Period, 202* B.C.*–*A.D. *220*. New York: Putnam, 1968.

Logan, Robert K. *The Alphabet Effect: The Impact of the Phonetic Alphabet on the Development of Western Civilization*. New York: William Morrow, 1986.

Lorentz, John H. *Historical Dictionary of Iran*. Lanham, Md.: Scarecrow Press, 1995.

Mallory, J. P. *In Search of the Indo-Europeans: Language, Archeology and Myth*. New York: Thames & Hudson, 1989.

Mallory, J. P., and Victor H. Mair. *The Tarim Mummies: Ancient China and the Mystery of the Earliest Peoples from the West*. London: Thames & Hudson, 2000.

Marcus, Joyce, and Kent V. Flannery. *Zapotec Civilization*. New York: Thames & Hudson, 1996.

Markoe, Glenn E. *Phoenicians*. Berkeley: University of California Press, 2000.

Millar, Fergus. *The Roman Near East, 31 B.C.–A.D. 337*. Cambridge: Harvard University Press, 1993.

Mokhtar, G., ed. *Ancient Civilizations of Africa*. Berkeley: Heinemann/University of California Press, 1981.

Molitor, Martha. *The Hohokam-Toltec Connection: A Study in Culture Diffusion*. Occasional Publications in Anthropology, Archeology Series, vol. 10. Greeley: Museum of Anthropology, University of Northern Colorado, 1981.

Moscati, Sabatino. *The World of the Phoenicians*. 1968. Reprint, London: Phoenix Giant, 1999.

Moseley, Michael E. *The Incas and Their Ancestors: The Archaeology of Peru*. Rev. ed. New York: Thames & Hudson, 2001.

———. *The Maritime Foundations of Andean Civilization*. Menlo Park, Calif.: Cummings, 1975.

Osborne, Milton E. *Southeast Asia: An Introductory History*. Boston: Allen & Unwin, 1979.

Peters, F. E. *Jerusalem: The Holy City in the Eyes of Chroniclers, Visitors, Pilgrims, and Prophets from the Days of Abraham to the Beginnings of Modern Times*. Princeton: Princeton University Press, 1985.

Pfeiffer, Charles F. *Jerusalem through the Ages*. Grand Rapids, Mich.: Baker Book House, 1967.

Ptak, Roderich. *China's Seaborne Trade with South and Southeast Asia, 1220–1750*. Variorum Collected Studies Series. Brookfield, Vt.: Ashgate, 1999.

Ratnagar, Shereen. *Encounters: The Westerly Trade of the Harappa Civilization*. Delhi: Oxford University Press, 1981.

———. *Understanding Harappa: Civilization in the Greater Indus Valley*. New Delhi: Tulika, 2001.

Renfrew, Colin. *Archeology and Language: The Puzzle of Indo-European Origins*. Cambridge: Cambridge University Press, 1987.

Robinson, Andrew. *The Story of Writing*. New York: Thames & Hudson, 1995.

Roy, S. B. *Early Aryans of India, 3100–1400 B.C.* New Delhi: Navrang, 1989.

SarDesai, Damodar R. *Southeast Asia, Past and Present*. Boulder: Westview Press, 1997.

Scarborough, Vernon L., and David R. Wilcox, eds. *The Mesoamerican Ballgame*. Tucson: University of Arizona Press, 1991.

Seeley, Christopher. *A History of Writing in Japan*. Honolulu: University of Hawaii Press, 2000.

Soustelle, Jacques. *The Olmecs: The Oldest Civilization in Mexico*. Translated by Helen R. Lane. Garden City, N.Y.: Doubleday, 1984.

Takeuchi, Lone. *The Structure and History of Japanese: From Yamatokotoba to Nihongo*. Edited by R. H. Robins, Geoffrey Horrocks, and David Denison. New York: Longman, 1999.

Thompson, C. Michele. "Scripts, Signs, and Swords: The Viêt Peoples and the Origins of Nôm." *Sino-Platonic Papers*, no. 101 (2000).

Tsien, Tsuen-Hsuin. *Written on Bamboo and Silk: The Beginnings of Chinese Books and Inscriptions*. Chicago: University of Chicago Press, 1962.

Vansina, Jan. *Paths in the Rainforests: Toward a History of Political Tradition in Equatorial Africa*. Madison: University of Wisconsin Press, 1990.

Wang, Gungwu. *The Nanhai Trade: The Early History of Chinese Trade in the South China Sea*. Singapore: Time Academic Press, 1998.

Wang, Gungwu, ed. *Community and Nation: Essays on Southeast Asia and the Chinese*. Vol. 6. Asian Studies

Association of Australia, Southeast Asian Publications Series. Singapore: Heinemann, 1981.

Wardman, Alan. *Religion and Statecraft among the Romans.* Baltimore: Johns Hopkins University Press, 1982.

Whitfield, Susan. *Life along the Silk Road.* Berkeley: University of California Press, 1999.

Wiesehöfer, Josef. *Ancient Persia: From 550 B.C. to 650 A.D.* Translated by Azizeh Azodi. London/New York: I. B. Tauris, 1996.

Williams, Derek. *The Reach of Rome: A History of the Roman Imperial Frontier, 1st–5th Centuries A.D.* New York: St. Martin's Press, 1997.

Index

Page numbers in **boldface** type indicate full articles on subject. Page numbers in *italic* type indicate illustrations or maps.

34035 00283 9153